AUSTIN CLARKE: COLLECTED PLAYS

AUSTIN CLARKE

Collected Plays

THE DOLMEN PRESS

Printed and published at the Dolmen Press
23 Upper Mount Street, Dublin
in the Republic of Ireland
June 1963

*

Distributed outside Ireland by
the Oxford University Press

Acknowledgement is made to
An Chomhairle Ealaíon
(The Arts Council of Ireland)
for their assistance in making
the publication of this collection possible

CONTENTS

THE SON OF LEARNING

A COMEDY IN THREE ACTS

to

George Moore

CHARACTERS

King	Demon
Abbot	Monks
Scholar	Lay Brothers
Woman	Mendicants
	Military

Period: MIDDLE AGES

Place: ABBEY OF CORC

THE SON OF LEARNING

ACT I

*The Guest-house; a large hall with arched walls, central
door with steps, doors to left and right leading to cloisters.
In the gloom, candles on the deal table light only the
faces of the* BEGGARS, *some of whom wear ragged Irish
cloaks. The* RED BEGGAR *is lanky, tall, with foxy hair
and a patch over one eye. The* AMADAN, *or Natural, has
matted hair, in a glib, as behung as a bush over a holy
well. A* PILGRIM *crouches in the shadow by right door, with
staff and scrip. The* BEGGARS *are eating loudly and talking,
but the Latin chanting of the* MONKS *in the Chapel can
be heard outside as the play begins. The* BEGGARMEN *speak
in a childlike sing-song.*

OLD BLIND MAN

Ssh! Holy men are praying for the
King.

AMADAN

jumping up
Oh, oh, oh!
My little milk-tooth is spilled, is spilled. There is
A devil in the baker's heel.

ONE-LEGGED MAN

Had I
The heady buck-tooth that I weaned at Michaelmas
In Cashel Fair when I was daring man
And bucking horse, I'd bite.

ONE-ARMED MAN

A lucky bit.

BLIND MAN

Ssh! Holy men are praying for the King.

BLACK BEGGAR

Like buckets in
The well of knowledge, hierarchies go
Up and down.

3

ONE-ARMED MAN

. . . I did:

I seen you ducking in an empty barrel,
A cockshot for the boys.

ONE-LEGCED MAN

It was

A stand-up fight, a roaring battle, tooth
And toe-nail.

They squabble

BLIND MAN

dreamily

Their lovely prayers will cure the King.

RED BEGGAR

Oh, there was many a fine horsey fight
In the old days before the hunger came.

OTHERS

In Bantry and Kilkenny town
There's fine accommodation,
And feather beds are shaken down
For every occupation.
Oh, lashings of rich bragget,
Ripe buttermilk and beer,
With plenty for my faggot
And nothing for your dear.

OLD BLIND MAN

My curse upon you all,
I cannot say my beads.

RED BEGGAR

Those were the days

For cadging the red pence until the King
Took bad and ate the people out of pot
And pocket.

ONE-LEGCED MAN

I've seen publicans that had

An ale-bush at the fair grow lean again
As their own shutters.

AMADAN

running from PILGRIM

Oh, oh, oh!

OTHERS

to AMADAN

Grey droppings of a goose upon you. Quit

The man.

To PILGRIM

Was it a mortal sin
Behind a hedge put heaven in your mind
Or thinking?

ONE-LEGGED MAN

He is too pure and knowledgeable
To sup with rags and lazybones.

ONE-ARMED MAN

On bran

And backward cabbage.

BLIND MAN

The holy man is on

Retreat.

RED BEGGAR

Aye, crops are black
And party men say that it is a woman's
Fault. I had a wife, oh, a fine shifty woman,
But windy o' nights. They say . . .

He stops to pick a back tooth

OLD BLIND MAN

A lying pack

And great deceivers.

BLACK BEGGAR

What was the name

The priest wet her with?

ONE-LEGGED MAN

Ligach.

ONE-ARMED MAN

The daughter of Maeldune.

BLIND MAN

An idle rip.

ONE-LEGGED MAN

It was a little apple that she sent
The King.

AMADAN

Give me a napple.

A napple.

RED BEGGAR

'Twas him, I say.

ONE-LEGGED MAN

'Twas her.

RED BEGGAR

rapidly by rote
　　　Her wicked brother when
　　　She was to wed the King of Cashel put
　　　A pagan spell into the pip that he
　　　Had learned from poets.

BLIND MAN

　　　　　　　　God preserve us from them!

RED BEGGAR

The poor King ate the pippin and began to
Swell.

BLIND MAN

God help us all!
God help us!

RED BEGGAR

There was a maggot in

That apple.

AMADAN

A napple in that worm.

RED BEGGAR

　　　　　　　　It turned

Into a demon and that demon made
The poor King eat from fire to bed and back.

BLACK BEGGAR

Where is the demon?

AMADAN

　　　　　　　　In his belly, fool.

RED BEGGAR

Now that I have my second wind, begod,
I'll tell the tale or burst. Be quiet now.
Oh, men, the King grew ravenous, roaring,
Rampaging as a yellow lion. No food
Could race his hunger. On the marriage day
He gobbled up the banquet while the bride
Was in the chapel.

OTHERS

together

　　　　　　　　He was guttling in

The kitchen.

　　　　　Scraping pan and crock.

　　　　　　　　　　　His head

Was in the pantry.

BLACK BEGGAR
It was,

For I was there.

RED BEGGAR
She said she did not care, that
She would marry him another day and
Cure him.

BLIND MAN
The hussy!

ONE-LEGGED MAN
The King is hiding

Inside.

ONE-ARMED MAN
She could not follow him

Here.

RED BEGGAR
No, no.
He came here for the blessed cure.
They say a wandering scholar said between
Two public-houses that the poor King took
Four roasted boars, eight heifers on the jack,
A draining barrel and a sack of apples
To whet his royal appetite before
Each grace and yet that hungry demon howled
In him for more.

OTHERS
It was Mac Conglinne
That made the rann.

He tied the knot upon
The tale.
They say he was
In Tirnanogue.

BLIND MAN
A vagabond,

A rogue.

RED BEGGAR
They say he was in Hell, boys.
He went down by the black mouth of the Red Lake
And cheated the devil himself at a burning game
Of cards.

OTHERS
The people say he knows

All tricks and magic.
                              OLD BLIND MAN
                                        A wicked unbeliever,
A great deceiver.
                              OTHERS
                              And he can dry a cow
With seven rhymes.
                              RED BEGGAR
                                        Oh, anybody could
Make poetry if he were lazy enough.
They make up this catch, each line in turn.
                    The king was growing thinner
                    For the demon ate his dinner
                    Of a thousand crubeens,
                    Pot of new beans,
                    Tripe and trotters,
                    Fish caught by otters,
                    Beef and sirloin,
                    Those we'd purloin.
                    A lake of milk, a sea of beer.
                              OLD BLIND MAN
          I'd swim in it and have no fear.
                              ALL
          We'd swim upon those tides of beer
          And pray no shore was ever near.
                                                (ad lib.)

A lupine howl is heard outside. They retreat in terror
                              AMADAN
          Oh, oh! The demon in the King.
                              OTHERS
                                                  Maybe
He heard us talking of the food.
                                        He roars
Because the King is fasting.
                              AMADAN
          I am glad
He is the right side of the King.
They creep back to table

                                        Oh, I
          Could do with a demon or two if I had been
          A king and well-to-do.

RED BEGGAR
Aye, but the demon gets
The food.

AMADAN
Aye, but the King has got the taste
In his mouth, not in his guts; and what's in food
But the tasting, the sweetness, the juiciness of meat,
The sloppiness of custard, the sourness of green apple,
With crunching, munching, scrunching? Aye, it's all
Between brother tongue and gum. What is after
The taste but belching, roaring winds and a heart
On fire?

BLIND MAN
What are you paring,
Boy?

AMADAN
My nail.

OTHERS
I smell.
Though I've but one eye,
I see
Cheese.
Cheese, the little grandson
Of milk.
Where did you steal it?

AMADAN
It was a tinker's wife
That gave it to me.

OTHERS
You have stolen it
And must go to confession.
They quarrel over the rind while the AMADAN whinges

RED BEGGAR
Now give me the loaf,
For once I was a carpenter.
*A BEGGAR throws the bread, which falls with a loud sound
as a young LAY BROTHER enters from left*

LAY BROTHER
Who threw that stone?

BEGGARS
Nobody,
Good Brother, nobody.

BROTHER

    Oh, *panis, panis,*
Bread, blessed bread! Ungrateful mendicants,
To waste good loaves out of our very oven,
When there is hunger in the fields, to turn
Your unblown noses up at this pure leaven,
Though the King, the very lord of the land,
Goes empty.

A lupine howl outside

    Get to bed now, Lazarites;
To bed now, for the King is coming from his cell,
Lest you offend his grace in sight, in hearing
Or in smell.

BEGGARS

   Brother,

     Good Brother!

BROTHER

      Go now,
Go!

All but the PILGRIM *go to the flocks, hardly to be seen
in the alcoves*
To PILGRIM

   Go!

BEGGARS

  There is no tick
For him.

BROTHER

to AMADAN

  Share with this man of sin.

AMADAN

terrified

    No, no!

BROTHER

Share now.

AMADAN

No, daddy, I saw . . .

BROTHER

to PILGRIM

    These strolling saints are
A plague. Better than you have been thankful
To pull a blanket.

*He takes out the candles and the moonlight shines through
the leaky roof.*

ONE-LEGGED MAN

jumping up

Oh, oh! the devil's in my doss.

ONE-ARMED MAN

waving hands

He has me in his clutches.

BLIND MAN

Can ye not bear this cross?

OTHERS

He's cured him of the crutches.

BLIND MAN

hobbling out scratching himself

A thousand devils bite me.

They're hopping now to spite me.

OTHERS

Back, back, the King!

Dumb show: from right door or from the auditorium, penitential procession of monks in cream habits, with lit tapers; the KING, a tall, bulky, sinister figure, cowled in black, his golden crown peeping out, led by the ABBOT. The KING glides as by an invisible compulsion towards the table, but is guided past by the ABBOT. The PILGRIM follows with supplicating gestures, but is waved back by the monks as they pass out through left door.

BLIND MAN

His eyes were fire.

OTHERS

Poor King!

He stared

Upon the board.

The demon in him

Growled.

The palmer caught his habit.

He was

Begging.

He was stealing

Out.

OLD BLIND MAN

Sssh! Say your prayers and go to sleep.

Crepitus ventris. Sudden silence, gradually broken by snoring. A loud knocking is heard at the central door.

BEGGARS

waking
                                        Bad luck to your
Black music!
                    Who is it that is pulling down the
House? Get up, Amadan!
                    AMADAN
                                    No, no. It is
The tinker's wife.
                    OTHERS
                        Why did I suck those eggs?
Why did I whip the poultry into my bag? . . .
And milk the nannie? . . .
                                    Skim the churn? . . .
                    RED BEGGAR
uneasily
                                        It it
My wife. I know her fist.
                    BLIND MAN
                                Sssh!
Let on to be asleep upon the roost.
Silence. The door is pushed open slowly and the SCHOLAR
*stands on the top step in the moonlight. His clothes,
thinned by skies, should suggest those of the wandering,
medieval students of Europe, the vagi scholares goliardi
seu bufones, as they were named by Church Councils, but
with a racial or bardic touch. He acts all the time,
obviously with an eye and ear for his immediate audience*
                    SCHOLAR
If there is anybody in this house
Of holiness, awake or in his sleep,
My blessing on him. Rain has risen now
From the cold stone of music; there's no star
But can be found in water . . .
Stumbling down the steps, vehemently
                                    My sudden curse
Upon the threshold, on the journeyman,
The hammer and the chisel. Goban Saor
Fuddle the mason and the carpenter
Of the crooked plane and may they never hear
The harp again.
                        I am half-famished, surely,

With the cold drizzle of the glen.
Searching around
>   Nothing.
Nothing, nothing at all. I cannot smell
The shadow of a bacon rind. To-night
No rat would drip out of the black waters
Of Lee to this bare house.
>   My bones
Are sore; I will lie down upon a bed
Until an angel come.
Goes over to flocks
>   The beds are full,
But empty sleepers you will feast in dreams
As I to-night.
*He sits on table and takes a cruit or small harp out of
a sack. The BEGGARS sit up.*
>   Song,
We have borrowed the five lands and kept ourselves
Alive, and we have been cold bedfellows,
For all our years are Lent, yet we must fast
To-night that beggars may think their broken heads
Are bound with gold.
Tuning with a jack
>   Would I were in a turn of Kerry,
Eating blackberries out of my left hand.
He chants
>   *Macgillicuddy of the Reeks,*
My praise upon the hilly woody land
Where ruddy brambles are dark with feasting wings,
There in the grass the wind runs as a filly;
Could I sing as freely, it is I
>   *Would praise Macgillicuddy of the Reeks.*
He walks about, muttering
But I could swear as I came to the light,
Growing in wet bushes that the Red Swineherd
Had lost a pig to-night, for, by the smell,
The little monks were marrying fat bacon
And curly cabbage.
*An old LAY BROTHER enters from the left with basket and
bit of candle*

BROTHER

Who is it that is there?

SCHOLAR

Frater dilectus,

Pax tecum.

BROTHER

Oh, it is a Son of Learning.
Our Father Abbot thought he heard a row.

SCHOLAR

A row?

BROTHER

A cow? No, no, a breach of rule.
He sent me here, he did, with simple food
And silence, for this is a day of fast.
" Go, Brother Ruadan," says he, " for it
May be a sinner that has drink in heel,
Or storyteller; sure the air of night
Drives in queer soles. The King is meditating,"
Says he, " and must not be disturbed."

SCHOLAR

The King?

BROTHER

Yes, yes.
The King is fasting for a week
To vomit the green fiend of gluttony.
But come now, Son of Learning, to the refectory,
And put yourself before the fire and wash
Your feet. Supper is loud upon the spit,
And you shall eat.

My sight is turning grey.
Give me your gospel books.
He comes upon the harp

Holy Saint Barra!

It is a poet!

SCHOLAR

Frater, I am a Son
Of Learning, and I have read in the book
Full of green dragons and of holy language
And red-gold cherubim. I can recite
The pious lives of Patric, Bridget, Maeve
And Nuadha of the Silver Hand.

BROTHER

No, no,

The Abbot had been bothered lately by
A school of poets. You must lie here
Until the bell of dawn.
                         SCHOLAR
                    I can amuse
The King with merry narration.
                         BROTHER
                              You must stay here.
This is your ration.
                         SCHOLAR
takes up hunk and mutters
                         The naked bread is blue
With cold.
                         BROTHER
                  Speak aloud, for I am soft of hearing.
                         SCHOLAR
This goodly bread is whiter than the flower
Of wheat. I think that it was ground
Within a golden quern.
Taking up cup of whey
    Poor cow, rest, rest in peace,
For you have been eaten many a day since this
Was milked.
To LAY BROTHER
                    The paschal richness of the grass
Is in this cup.
                    Good Brother, we will make
A song upon the fare.
                         BROTHER
                         O, I will call
The Abbot.
                         SCHOLAR
                    No, you'll stay, my Brother.
                         BROTHER

                                                          I

Must ring the Vesper.
                         SCHOLAR
                         You shall pray with me
    And shout the Glorias.
Extemporizing to strings
        Were I in Clare of the ships,
        Drinking with fishermen, I would not care,

Not I, not I, until the keg ran dry,
Or were I sailing on a windy morrow
By Tory, where the barefoot women work
And a man can take a bellyful of ease
Nor fear the rats of sorrow.
                                    Were I backward
At a lake, when reeds were slipping their young
      shadows
Like black eels, I would take no care, not I,
Not I.
          But in Corc of the big-tongued bells
Where I put my foot in the coldness of day,
I will not eat the holey bread or drink
The parish whey.

He suddenly realizes that the BROTHER *has stolen out*
during the song
                Now that he is gone,
I might as well gnaw at the speckled dough
Myself, for I have had no scrap to eat
Since dawn but the grey berries at the Well
Of Loneliness.

He turns to table in time to catch the PILGRIM, *who has*
stolen out to snatch the food, roughly
          Robber, light-handed pilferer,
Plunderer of eggs beneath the clucking hen,
Poacher of woods and rivers, you'd take
The poet's bite. Oh, here's good money for song!
But I will fight you. Off with your stolen coat,
Your belt, if you're a man.

Cloak and cowl fall away from a slender, beautiful young
WOMAN, *bright-haired and strange in the moonlight*
                          A woman!

BEGGARS *swarm out*

BEGGARS

She's mine.
          No, mine.
                    She's mine.

SCHOLAR

driving them back
          Back, fleas and rags. You'd rob me, poachers of wood
          And river, red-handed pilferers, bagmen,
          Would steal the phoenix on her fiery egg.

Back, or you shall pace by the cold seas
Of Tirnanogue this night.
He turns to her: in cajoling tones
                                        O Fairywoman,
What hill untroubled by the day
Or meddled dance has blessed this house? Are you
Etain, who washes in a basin of gold
With carven birds or that horsewoman, Niav,
Taking the fences of the sea? Are you
The wife of the musician, Craftine,
Who was unhappy when the holeheaded flute
Began to play and so is lost for ever
In the grass and cannot find her lover? Tell me,
For I have heard such music to-night, I fear
The waters work in my mind.
As he is about to sweep the cup and bread from the board,
she runs to stop him

WOMAN

Oh,

I am so hungry.

SCHOLAR

I will call food
For you, the pure white bread and honeycomb
That drips the summer, dishes of rung silver,
A skin of wine the wearied sons of Tuireann
Drank in the south.

WOMAN

                                        You dream;
And what shall I do now in a hostel for
Men.

SCHOLAR

I dream of the large ruddy fires
In a fairy house and of the beaching noise
In waves that dance as jugglers when they fling
White knives, that we are playing at the chess,
With Bishop, Knave and King upon the board,
For you are more beautiful than Deirde or
Than Maeve.

WOMAN

flattered

                            I think you praise a dream,
Or a woman that is dead.

SCHOLAR

Have I not
Followed your bright heel on the road as a farmer
The price he will get at the big fair, even
To this house?

WOMAN

I heard a little music
About the priory but when the bat-light stirred
The bushes, I was full of fear and I
Came in.

Weeps

SCHOLAR

I'll be an abbot
To-night and I've a trick or two of tongue
Will cure the King, for I have been acquainted
With that most famous juggler, Mannanaun,
Who runs from lordly fire to fire when he
Has wearied of the cold warrens of the wave
To mend the table for a farthing's worth
Of praise from men by pulling a supper, a hound
Or music from his pocket. He's the patron saint
Of merry rogues and fiddlers, trick o' the loop men,
Thimblemen and balladmen that gild
The fair and his devotions are the crowd,
For he looks on until the sun is red,
The tide turned and the drink and the horses are gone.

WOMAN

These are but words.

SCHOLAR

Have I not seen an angel,
Bright as the rainy bracken of a gap,
Last moon, because I had no supper? I will have
Excellent food brought down in tablecloths
From heaven.

WOMAN

Want
Of food has made him dream.

SCHOLAR

wildly

To-night I will
Entice the demon from the King that souls
May huddle in the hospice of Lough Derg.

I'll deal a merry pack of words will make
You Queen.

WOMAN

surprised

Queen!

SCHOLAR

       And sanctify this house,
That foreheads will be thumbed with holy ashes
Again, big drovers stumbling as their curses,
Carters and men that lean with the old wheel
Outside the forge all day, will come like boys
Capping their way to Mass.

          These beggarmen,
To double their spit, will have a barrel
Large as the turfstack of a parish priest
And full of . . .

RED BEGGAR

Beer!

They swarm out, crying " Where? Where?"

SCHOLAR

Come, all you rogues, make merry and rejoice,
Dance, rags and bones, for you shall feast to-night.
*BEGGARS dance and caper in a ring with linked hands
around the SCHOLAR and the GIRL, singing*

     Buttermilk and beistings
     Enough for seven feastings,
     Boiled green cabbage and white bacon,
     Everything that we can take on.
     Let the poet court her
     While we drink black porter.

(Ad lib.)

*ABBOT enters with monks; all run aside except the
SCHOLAR, who bows*

ABBOT

Fellow, what is

This hullabaloo?

SCHOLAR

     Most Reverend Lord Abbot, I am a Son
Of Learning. I have read the holy book
Filled with green dragons, pious characters
And red-gold cherubim. I heard your praise
In Cashel of the kings, I can recite

The pious lives of Patric, Bridget, Maeve
And Nuadha of the Silver Hand.

MONKS

He is a rogue!

SCHOLAR

Most Reverend Lord Abbot, I was filling
These simple ears with news of Barra, Saint
Of Corc.

LAY BROTHER

He made a satire on
The blessed food.

ABBOT

Beggars at the pattern
Will sing this evil word and scandalize
The parishes.

SCHOLAR

Holy Lord Abbot!

ABBOT

Silence,

Fellow! You shall not mock the holy Church,
Nor me, her servant. I am a magistrate,
A man of law.

SCHOLAR

My Lord, I came to cure
The King.

ABBOT

He speaks against the King!
Let him be dipped into the river pool
At day-ring.

SCHOLAR

I can make another satire
To raise a purple blister on your back
With little brethren.

ABBOT

He threatens me!
Harper, you shall be whipped with more than rhymes,
For I have great power in the land.

MONKS *discover the* WOMAN

A woman!

He has dared to bring his sin, his wench, his baggage,
His hedge companion here! Holy Saint Kevin,
Defend us!

SCHOLAR

She is more beautiful than Deirdre,
Or the woman of the kindling town.

ABBOT

He contradicts me!
Am I not a bishop? Have I not
A mitre, a golden crozier, a red carbuncle
On my finger? Have I not secular power?
Am I not a prince in my own right?

SCHOLAR

Good Monk,
Good Monk, before your crook was jewelled,
Columcille opened the heavy door of praise
For us. My mind has broken fast in schools
Beyond the Shannon where the saints live. I
Have read so bright a book that kings
Warred for the lettered dragons and the gold.
Harper I am, now, a rogue for merriment,
A ballad-maker, a juggler at the fair
Of gaping, a wandering scholar in the glens,
With rain and hunger stitching in my bones,
But I'll not praise your Lenten bread nor drink
The parish whey . .

ABBOT

The law
Of Church in land has made the mind of man,
That is the troubled body of the soul,
Obedient, but the holy order, work
And prayer, the mortar of this house, are mocked
To-night. It may be that the demon in
Our King has turned a bad mouth from the road
To be a rod. Bring all these simple guests
To sleep in the cells — there is corruption here —
And send the woman to a convent. Let
This man count up his sins upon the hour
And pray. There is a cross upon the Hill
Of Ravens where the bones of all malefactors
Are chained, for, when the breath has suffered,
    heaven
Has mercy. I will try this wicked man
Within my court to-morrow.

MONK *locks central door. The guests, menacing the*

SCHOLAR, *are hurried out. He turns to the* WOMAN, *who walks past in disdain.* AMADAN *comes to the crestfallen culprit*

AMADAN

Frater, pax

Tecum.

SCHOLAR *alone. He tries all the doors and sits down in an attitude of despair. After some time the " Dies Irae, Dies Illa" is heard faintly without as the curtain falls*

C U R T A I N

ACT II

SCENE: *The Refectory: central door with steps. Door on left to Pantry. Door on right. A high carven armchair in front of a Lectern on which there is an illuminated book, to centre. A blazing wood-fire on hearth to left. Bright candlesticks on long table. A lean* LAY BROTHER *is setting the table in indifferent fashion, humming a hymn in a taciturn tone. A very fat* LAY BROTHER *bounces in from Larder or Pantry with dishes piled to his third chin.*

FAT BROTHER

bustling

Hurry

Now! Hurry, Brother Dove! The holy candles
Have been put out. Here are more platters.

THIN BROTHER

I

Am at my share, but you are jumpier than
A pot-lid even at your *Paters.*

FAT BROTHER

expansively

                                              Had you
To sweat, to toil before the blaze, to toast,
To roast, to boil, to broil, to baste, to braze,
To stew, to simmer, to grill to the very spill
O' the spit . . .

                    THIN BROTHER

sharply

                    And have I not to peel, to scrape,
To mince, to grind, to pluck, to singe, to draw
The guts o' the fowl, to crumble, season, truss
And skewer?

                    FAT BROTHER
          To carve?

                    THIN BROTHER
                         To carry?

                    FAT BROTHER
                              Ladle?

                    THIN BROTHER

                                   Slice

And portion?

                    FAT BROTHER
          Pour?

                    THIN BROTHER
               And sing the Grace?

                    FAT BROTHER

                                   Hand me

That breadknife.
They work.
Conciliatory:

                    Brother Dove,
I have another recipe for soup.
     A pinch of . . .
Whispers

                    mug of . . .

Whispers

                              and a tablespoon

     Of . . .
Whispers

                    THIN BROTHER

     Hum.

                    FAT BROTHER
          Shake and slowly stir

And put to sleep upon a little hob
Until the thickening gold comes up again.
                    THIN BROTHER

laying table
For Brother Goldsmith . . .
            Joiner . . .
                    Sacristan . . .
Harp outside
There's that wirepuller again.
                    FAT BROTHER
                                    A handy man.
Oh, Brother, when I was in smaller shoes
I, too, could pick a tune or two between
My teeth.
                    THIN BROTHER
I'll say a prayer.
                    FAT BROTHER
                    How is the King?
                    THIN BROTHER
snapping
                                    Better.

                    FAT BROTHER
        The Father Carpenter was saying
That they have blessed him with a bucketful
Of water from the holy wells of Croom
And Templemore.
                    THIN BROTHER
                    Hum.
                    FAT BROTHER
                            He was saying they
Have brought the King up to the silver shrine,
And he has kissed the relics, one by one,
Of Jarleth, Canice and the sainted daughters
Of Einan, rung the little bell that came
To Declan.
                    THIN BROTHER
impatiently
            The board is laid.
                    FAT BROTHER
expansively
                            O Brother Dove,
I love to hear all day of miracles,

Small children cured of ringworm, milk in cow
Again, devotions at the blind man's well
And every parish cross; for knees are feet
When a great pope is walking through the land
With bell and cope. They say that Bridget pegged
Her saintly linen on a beam of sun
To dry . . .

    Poor Brethren, I hammered out
A bung, for, as you say, their swallows are
On fire with plain-chant, parching matins, nones
And lauds . . .

THIN BROTHER

interrupting
The holy can . . .

FAT BROTHER

eagerly
    Yes, holy canticles.

THIN BROTHER

interrupting
The holy candles have been capped.

FAT BROTHER

    You prate
Too much. Go, Brother Dove, and bring the pail
Of soup in.
A crash and commotion outside.
Crossing himself
    Brother, Brother, what is that now?

THIN BROTHER

Alas, it must be that the heady scholar
Has broken down the door.
The KING *rushes in followed by the supplicating* ABBOT
and MONKS *carrying the royal cowl and habit; he charges
to the table. He is tall and corpulent, clothed in red and
gold.*

KING

roaring
    I'll fast no more,
No more, for I am starven, starven! I
Am drenched with holy water, bruised and sore
With kneeling down, half-moidered with your prayers
And penitential psalms. Where is the supper?
Is it carven?

ABBOT

Calm, calm your troubled soul,
O noble King.

KING

I'll meditate no more.
As I was nodding in the nave, I heard
An angel plucking up his harp and dreamed
My mouth was appled in a mighty pie.

ABBOT

The frightened demon like a wild doorkeeper
Runs between ear and eye.

KING

I tell ye, hunger
Is roaring in my belly now.

ABBOT

Resume,
O King, spiritual exercises.

KING

I
Am starven. I could eat the . . . rafters. Bring me
The larder.

ABBOT

aside

We must deceive the demon
By venial guile.

To KING

Such Lenten food as ours
Is not befitting for so great a king
As Cathal More. Our diet is but . . .

Considering

Simples . . .
Garlic . . . green cresses from the river . . . when
In season . . . a little bread . . . water . . . a pick
Of meat on Feastdays.

KING

Bring, bring me in your supper,
All, all of it, even if it be the bones
And gravy of a goose or some poor stew
Reheated in the pot. I will eat all
Your suppers. You shall fast for me to-night.

ABBOT

aside

The Tempter speaks.
Harp outside

KING

Am I in Cashel again?
You have a harper hidden in the house.
Oh, I'll have music too.

ABBOT

High King, it is
A vagabond whose grey bed is the wood,
An idle clerk that mocks the Church. I have
Condemned him.

KING

Bring him in, for I will salt
My supper with his music.

ABBOT

Let us pray.

KING

Bring, bring the harper.
Two MONKS are reluctantly sent

Hasten now
And carry in the crockery.

ABBOT

O King,
Repent. We have implored you not to break
The holy edge of fast, for public prayer
Will cast the demon out. Oh, do not let
This man of sin . . .
SCHOLAR brought in

SCHOLAR

Most reverend
Archbishop, I am a Son of Learning. I
Have read a pious book . . .
Seeing the KING

O mighty King
Of Munster, grandson of the noble Fingan,
Lord of the Southern Half, I can retell
The deeds of your forefathers from the Flood
In fourteen hundred verses.

ABBOT

Vanitas.
The King is going to prayers.

SCHOLAR

to KING

> I can amuse
> You — for no doubt you are about to sup —
> With merry tales of how the Daghda ate
> Too much or how the wanton women made
> Cuchullin blush again.

KING *beams*

ABBOT

> Secular stories
> Are most unsuitable. The King is on
> Retreat.

SCHOLAR

> I have more edifying tales,
> How Maravaun called dinner down from Heaven
> To entertain King Guairë, how Saint Cieran
> Rebuked a wench

KING *glooms*

ABBOT

> No doubt you have a poem
> Upon the Deadly Sins.

SCHOLAR

> On Simony
> And how an abbot fell by pride.

ABBOT

anxiously

> Perhaps
> An edifying vision.

KING

gloomily

> Visions! I
> Have had enough of them.

SCHOLAR

> I made a lesson
> Upon the supper I have had.

KING

hopefully

> On victuals?
> Go on. I love the marrow of sweet words.

SCHOLAR

> Praise to the guesting house, the generous house
> Of Corc, the pail of ready washing there,

The big-tongued fire that dried my shriven feet.
Two brothers shook out linen for a meal
And it was whiter than the tablecloth
That Peter saw the angels letting down
From heaven. In a blaze of wax they served
The platters, dishes, saucers and tureens.
Appetite steamed in them.

KING

impatiently

And what was on
Each plate?

SCHOLAR

slowly

O Savour of all savours!
Brown roasted beef, basted upon the spit
With lavish honey and the large white salt
From drying-pans, choice mutton that was suckled
Upon green tits of grass, a crock of gravy
In which the fattened geese could swim again
And poultry in the egg, parsley and sauce,
Green cabbage boiling with a juicy ham
Crumbled with meal; whole puddings, speckled
    puddings,
Fat puddings with their little puddings, sweet litter
O' the pig, loud celery.

KING

excitedly

I crunch!
I crunch!

SCHOLAR

Salmon too fat for leaping
And freckled trout.

KING

wildly

More, more!

SCHOLAR

Mustard
And red-eyed pepper; from their shaken woods,
Ripe hazel-nuts to waken teeth, custard,
Big steamy dumplings.

KING

ecstatically

Dumplings!

SCHOLAR

Hashed

With red apples!

KING

eagerly

And had you milk, for I

Love milk!

SCHOLAR

All the white brewing of the cow.

KING

Her new milk?

SCHOLAR

Skim milk?

KING

Old milk?

SCHOLAR

Buttermilk.

KING

And fat milk?

SCHOLAR

Lean milk.

KING

Yellow bubbling milk?

SCHOLAR

Her curd milk.

KING

Whey milk?

SCHOLAR

Cream milk.

KING

Double milk?

SCHOLAR

Aye, calving milk that blobs and blubbers down
The gullet till the first gulp cries to the last:
" Stop, cur, for by my doggedness, I swear,
O speckled mongrel, that if you come down
I will come up, for there's no share for two
Such dogs as us in this dark puppery,"

KING

I'll buy that cow!

He claps SCHOLAR *on back*

ABBOT
Our holy rule is mocked
To-night.

KING
Gillie of song, where is this food?
SCHOLAR
I smell it here.

MONKS
He is a rogue. There is
A hunger in the fields.

KING
Bring in the spit.
My grinders ache.

ABBOT
It is a sin to break
The fast.

MONKS
He has put spells upon the King.
SCHOLAR
Master,
I am inspired to work a miracle,
If you but eat and drink your fill and do
My bidding.

KING
heartily
That I will.
Sits down

SCHOLAR
The Abbot said
There is a barrel of white-hooded ale
Here. Send for Brother Ale.
KING
roars
Bring in
The beer!

MONKS
He lies.
SCHOLAR
O King, lend me your torc
Of gold that I may hold authority
Above the monks of Corc.
The KING puts his golden collar around him joyfully

SCHOLAR

to MONKS, with airs of authority

Put on

The royal cowl and habit.

ABBOT

pleased

Learned Scholar,

We shall obey you.

ABBOT and MONKS do, despite royal protests

SCHOLAR

Come, bind the King.

The KING jumps up with indignant exclamations

MONKS

He raves,

He raves.

SCHOLAR

*snatching cords from the waists of ABBOT and BURSAR and
slipping the ABBOT's keys into his pocket*

Come, bind the King!

KING

pompously

I am

The King!

SCHOLAR

O Branch of power, I put a spell
In these poor cords that have not swaddled food
Since they were spun. You gave a kingly word
To do my say.

KING

apologetically

I have heard tell that blacksmiths,

Red women, poets and the like can work
Queer spells. Do it.

*They bind the KING in the high chair, directly in front
of Lectern*

SCHOLAR

Out, Brothers, to your fast;

Hurry, Lord Abbot, to your stool, for I
Must exorcise the demon.

*Confusion. MONKS cast lingering looks as the LAY
BROTHERS carry in steaming dishes. Having driven them
out, the SCHOLAR juggles with the stolen keys and, sitting
down, eats ravenously, talking between mouthfuls.*

KING

cheerfully

                    That looks to me
Good Kerry mutton. Carve the dinner, carve,
For I am starving! Come, unbind my arms.
Gillie of song, make haste!

SCHOLAR

                    Soon, soon. The spell
Is working in the wool.

KING

                    You gobble up
My share, my grief.

SCHOLAR

                    O King, the beef
Is beautiful, crisp, done as I desire.
My blessing on the spit, the charcoal fire,
The luscious grease.

KING

                    Release me, for my mouth
Is thawing.

SCHOLAR

                    But the meat is yet too hot
For your royal demon.

KING

                              I have diabetes.

SCHOLAR

That is heretical.

Eating

                              O simple bacon,
Milky and fatter than rich honeycomb,
The dumpling . . .

KING

        I will hear no more. You've drunk
Three pots of ale!

SCHOLAR

              Come, I will drown
Your demon in a holy well of wine.
The monks have claret in a cellar, cold
As the flagstone of Hell.

KING

calling

                    Wine, bring me wine!

BROTHERS bring wine. The SCHOLAR takes wine half-way
and drives them back, capering
                                    SCHOLAR
                                                Wine, red noisy wine,
        More beaded than the Abbot. Oh, it danced
        Out of its little skin.
Drinking
                                    And litany,
        O litany, it fills my throat with rhyme.
                                    KING
        For God's sake, Poet, stop! Give me a cup
        Of wine, nay, half a cup to wash the lime
        Out of my mouth, a drop, a little drop
        Out of the lees.
                                    SCHOLAR
capering
                                        O wine, red litany wine,
        To fit any head.
                                    KING
                                    Scholar, I will give you
        Green pasture lands, a herd of lowing heifers,
        A silent wife . . .
                                    SCHOLAR
                                        Better to me the noisy wine,
        The scolding wine.
                                    KING
                                        Then, I will have you flogged.
                                    SCHOLAR
mocking
        Oh, oh, I will be cudgelled in a wood
        Of blackthorns, beaten in a tanner's yard
        And pounded by the miller. Ready your mouth,
        For I will give you wine.
He holds the cup to the KING's mouth, then slowly with-
draws and drinks. The KING splutters with rage while he
recites:

                        Summer delights the scholar
                            With knowledge and reason:
                        Who is happy in hedgerow
                            Or meadow as he is?

Paying no dues to the parish,
He argues in logic
And has no care of cattle
But a satchel and stick.

The showery air grows softer,
He profits by his ploughland,
For the share of the schoolmen
Is a pen in hand.

When mid-day hides the reaping,
He sleeps by a river
Or comes to the stone plain
Where the saints live.

But in winter by the big fires,
The ignorant hear his fiddle
And he battles on the chessboard
As the land lords bid him.

My mind was in the cup. I know
A fairywoman that shall come to sup
With us. I am in heart, in love, with this
Most notable lady.
He turns a somersault

KING
A woman?
SCHOLAR
Yes.

KING
They have
A woman hidden in this house. Oh, how
I am deceived!
SCHOLAR
Now you will see her.
KING
There is
No food for her.
SCHOLAR
at central door
She shall complete the cure.

KING

Stop, stop! There is no food for her!
The KING, *alone, talking to himself*
If I had married Ligach,
The daughter of Maeldune, I would be full
Of bacon. She has droves in every wood.
But I will say my prayers:
Raising his eyes, in pious tones

O . . .

The DEMON *tempts him*

cabbage, boiled
With bacon, thy butter green as peasoup . . .
Bewildered

Thoughts
Have tripped my words and I must say an act
Of nutrition.
Bowing his head, in a contrite tone
Through . . .

The DEMON *tempts him*

my dumpling. Through
My dumpling. Through my most suety dumpling.
Despairing

I cannot tell
My puddings, count the mutton-juicy, thick
And yellow-fatted, gravy-dripping joints.
His lips smack themselves as in a fit. The candles burn
dimly and in the half-darkness his cowled figure suggests
demonic possession

THIN BROTHER
putting in his head from the Larder
They're gone. A draught has sickened the light.
FAT BROTHER
cautiously putting his head in

Oh, save
My soup.
THIN BROTHER
entering
I'll not. I have to scrub,
To rub, to tub, to drub, to rinse, to wring,
To mangle, steep and scour, to wet, to whet,
To whiten, blow on, polish.

FAT BROTHER

waving him backwards towards the table

Have I not
To make, to bake, to roll, to thicken, thin,
To flour, to sour, to grate, to wait, to pan
And handle in the oven?

A lupine growl

BOTH BROTHERS

terrified

The Demon!

The Demon!

They retreat into the Larder

CURTAIN

ACT III.

SCENE: The same as in Act II, a few minutes later. The Refectory is bright again. The cowled head of the KING is bowed and he appears to slumber. The BEGGARS can be heard approaching in the corridor outside. They enter by central door singing a catch.

RED BEGGAR

Upon Lough Ale we sailed at rise o' day.

OTHERS

And golden were the waves O.

RED BEGGAR

*But when we turned the boat into a cup
They ran so high, we did not get a sup,
For none of us could blow the froth away.*

OTHERS

Oh, none of us could blow the froth away.

RED BEGGAR

standing with his back to the fire
        It's a fine life to beg the miles, to quit
        A scolding wife and shake a single shirt
        In holy houses.

BLACK BEGGAR

uneasily
                        Will the lucky Son
        Of Learning come back?

OLD MAN

                            A wicked unbeliever?
        A great deceiver.

RED BEGGAR
                        Oh, he has conjugated
        In Clare and women love a wordy man.
        I heard them say Mac Conglinne himself,
        Discoursing with Queen Maeve behind a bush,
        Would coax her, like the she-moon, on her back.
        But, theologians, what has two-legged man
        To pair with woman's tongue? Consider that
        Poor wagging piece of flesh: all day it runs
        That has no shin; being brought to bed, it is
        But livelier: it is the fiery branch
        Of wickedness . . .

*While he is talking, the others have crowded around the
table and have begun to quarrel violently over the food.
The* RED BEGGARMAN *drives them back angrily, imitating
the* SCHOLAR'S *tone*
        Stop, rogues and ragmen, broachers of wooded wine,
        Would steal the meaning from the Testament,
        The hairy cross upon a donkey's back.
        I am the first man here.

Pleased with his prowess, he fills and lifts a jug of ale
                        Well, here's luck, boys!

AMADAN

peering around the Lectern and seeing the KING'S *cowl*
        Oh!
        The Abbot's in the chair.

RED BEGGAR

hastily putting down the untouched jug
                            Holy Mother!
        He'll excommunicate us all!

They rush towards the central door as the SCHOLAR *enters*

SCHOLAR

Run, all you mouths, make merry in the larder,
And if head turns, the cure is drinking harder.

*As they disappear into the Larder by the left door, the
two* LAY BROTHERS *bounce across the stage and out by the
opposite door. The* WOMAN *appears on the central doorstep,
shading her eyes and the* SCHOLAR *stands before her.*

SCHOLAR

Proudly

Lady,
Though you have laughed at me, I rule this house,
And you shall dine, for I have turned your wishes
Into meat, into wine, into plentiful dishes.

WOMAN

surprised

But where is Father Abbot?

SCHOLAR

At his beads —
A worthy habit.

WOMAN

And where is the King?

SCHOLAR

Asleep, for he has eaten far too much.

KING

Ligach, Ligach!

WOMAN

running to him

Cathal, I have come
For you, now.

KING

Ligach, I have had no supper.

WOMAN

Lift me upon your lap again.

amazed

The monks
Have tied you up!

KING

nodding at SCHOLAR

He ate my beef. He did.

WOMAN

sharply

Unbind the King!

SCHOLAR

mysteriously
>There's magic in that wool
>That I have learned on hills where mighty Fionn
>Still sucks his thumb for wisdom when the hounds
>Are flatter than the hare.

WOMAN
>   Untie him!

SCHOLAR
>   Touch
>But a loop and from that royal mouth a demon
>Will leap in fire.

WOMAN

trying the cords
>The knot is blacker now.

She runs for a breadknife

SCHOLAR

mockingly
>Lady, he does not love you now. His eyes
>Eat up the table.

WOMAN

in a huff
>   Little Cathal, I
>Have hurried by house and bush with pilgrims that
>Took ship and women sided on their nags;
>Last night, when music went round at a merry
>Fair, packmen tumbled from a fiery tent
>And plucked my holy frock to bless them . . . I
>Was full of fear . . . I ran into the dark
>And came to water thinning in the light
>And called until the ferryman came out
>On sleepy oars and for your sake I hid
>With evil men. And, Cathal, do you love
>Me?

KING
>I am starving, starving!

WOMAN
>   But you look
>So well!

KING

crossly
>I'm not. I'm thinner than a shadow
>Hung out to dry.

WOMAN

But Cathal . . .

KING

I am starving!
I have not had a drink since I came here.

WOMAN

Is it all, is it all you have to say
To me?

KING

Beg him, implore him, if you love me,
To pass that barrel.

WOMAN

in rising temper

Black hedges pluck me
Again and strong arms saddle me upon
A horse before I kneel now. Am I not
The daughter of great acres? Gamble and wink
With the rude soldiers on a cloak until
The candle swim, acquaint the stablemen
The potboys and the cooks of Cashel, for
I am deceived again, again.

SCHOLAR

mocking

A health!
A health to a loving pair!

KING

I am deceived,
She does not care.

WOMAN

You do not care.

KING

I am
Deceived and I may die.

WOMAN

scornfully

And have you not
Abandoned me? Did you not leave me at
The altar foot? Oh, now let matchmakers
Put hedge to field and pair the board and blanket,
For I must house my face in shame and girls —
Before they have pinched the last decade of
Their penance — laugh at me and sun becomes
My enemy. Oh, you are fat!

KING

Fat?

WOMAN

And oh,

I hate you, for there is a baldy spot
Lighting your crown!

KING

indignantly

I never heard that like

Before!

WOMAN

sidling up to the SCHOLAR
This young man is my fancy now.

SCHOLAR

drinking

And this is mine.

WOMAN

in pretended distress to SCHOLAR
Oh, what will I do?
I will unlock my hair. I'll weep so. For
I think you do not love me any longer.
But an hour, less than a tallow, and your words
Are dark.

SCHOLAR

Poor thought must lag when fancy doubles
Back. You were proud.

WOMAN

I was afraid.

SCHOLAR

I know,

I know. You follow summer.

WOMAN

wringing her hands

Oh, he won't

Believe me and I will not dine. He does
Not care for me and I am nothing but
A rhyme that pleases best when it is new.

SCHOLAR

You hid in a house of men and are you not
The daughter of Maeldune?

WOMAN

Believe me now,

Believe me, for you are swift, merry and own
A mouth of honey. Are you not the dealer
Of magic in this house to-night? Am I
Spun of such common wool that I could love
An empty king when you pulled music in
The middling wood?

SCHOLAR
                        I fill a hidden ear
That has no drum.

WOMAN

mysteriously

                        Look in my eyes and tell
What seems is not, if by another logic
Reason can know itself.

SCHOLAR

he gazes silently; following a new fancy
                        O Fairywoman,
I see all clearly now. You are not Ligach,
The daughter of Maeldune? You put a cloud
Upon my mind, a spell upon the King,
That he should hear and see a mortal woman,
But you are lofty, apple-skinned and dance
In the dark grass?

WOMAN

mysteriously

                        My name grows in the woods.

SCHOLAR

wheedling

Are you Queen Aoibhill,
Who makes a yearly circuit for the silk
Of cattle, taxing the farmers by the Shannon
That she may have good wine?

WOMAN

                        I hold
My court where years have been.

SCHOLAR

                        I know, I know.
For I have heard an earful of good stories
About you when the fire was low.

WOMAN

alluringly

                        Cure, cure

The King and we will hurry to those glens
Of softness where the dews are heavier
Than blackberries and hid too well in grass,
Come on the stony hills, though days have broken
The last grey crop: and leaving the dim blue steps
Of Burren while the little airs of twilight
Take footing, rest in a big house beside
The waves.

SCHOLAR

enthusiastically
       I know a bay where blacksmiths are binding
The cartwheel twice upon the stone with fire
And cold. There as the tide the blowing sails
Have dropped and hands that rowed with blessed
   Brendan
Unload the chasubles from boats; nobles
Hurry with women, whose red lips are cut
By the salt dark, into a lighted house
To talk, to dance: and when fire thickens the roof,
White clergy bless their mirth in Latin, for
Their grace is such — a couple every night
Is married. and with candles, music, they
Prepare those innocent delights.

WOMAN

coaxing
                  Oh, cure
The King and we will hurry west to know
Those companies that never sinned and whisper
Together as we go.

SCHOLAR

shocked
                   We must be married
First.

WOMAN

indignantly
     Am I immodest in the look
Or tongue?

SCHOLAR
      Lady, you are more beautiful
Than the bright-sided women that caress
A hermit in his dreams and turn his bed
Of rock to down: but what is sin to man.

Even in the thinking, matrimony
Makes virtue and his duty.
                    WOMAN
flattered

                              And am I
So fair?
                    SCHOLAR
            So fair we must be wed. A bishop
Will join us when the wax is glittering
In Cormac's Chapel. Our indulgence shall
Be lawful.
                    WOMAN
            Oh, I have begun to dream
Of my own marriage day, now.
                    SCHOLAR
                              There would be
No sin if troubled lovers could be married
As quickly as confessed; for, to be good
Is to have pleasure freely. There is laughter
And dancing half the night, coming and going,
After a marriage, a crowd at food and cards,
A merry crowd at drink: when man and bride
Stop whispering at the last fiery lap
O' the candle, and knowing the ring is blessed
By prayer, are sporting shyly in the dark
Like . . . twopence in a beggar's pocket.
                    WOMAN

                                                I
Will dream no more, because your learned words
Surmount the altar step, where woman must
Remain.
                    KING
waking
            I starve! I starve!
                    WOMAN
to SCHOLAR

                              Let us be happy
And eat together.
They sit down at table

                    KING
                    No, no! You shall not dare!
That is my supper.

SCHOLAR
Here is white bread,

O Fairywoman.

WOMAN
Full of season, here,
Black honey that I love.

KING
Oh, this is treason!

It is my food.

SCHOLAR

to WOMAN
Dumpling?

KING
I'll marry for
A mouthful. I will give a hundred acres
For half that loaf.

The WOMAN *hesitates but the* SCHOLAR *leads her away*

SCHOLAR
Come, Queen, away from him,
And pledge me in a cup.

WOMAN

smiling at KING
And we shall mock
The King who ate too much.

The SCHOLAR *empties the cup*

SCHOLAR

slightly swaying
You have deceived me!

WOMAN

uneasily
No, no!

SCHOLAR
Are you not Cliodhna,
Who was a woman and is now a wave?

WOMAN

relieved
Men that have carved my head upon the prow
May tell.

SCHOLAR

sternly
If any tide can call you up,
Dance, dance before I turn.

To humour him, she moves slowly to the harp as in an
antique dance. The BEGGARS come in with bones and mugs
BEGGARS

A strapping girl!

A lovely pair!
They are so young

And her so fair.
She dances before the KING
KING

Huh! Fairywoman! I will never make you
My queen. Jig, for I know another one
That will not let me starve.
WOMAN

stopping
I know her, too.

It is that Lasarina. And she has
Red hair. She cannot dance so.
She whirls faster
KING

Rossie! Shameless

Woman!
She runs laughingly to the SCHOLAR and kisses him
SCHOLAR

staggering back
But where am I?

Is this the house of Con? After a night
Of wind, there is work for the wheelwright.
WOMAN

disturbed
You are

In Corc. You love me.
SCHOLAR

slightly fuddled
But I am a cleric

Then. I have been in minor orders. I
Remember. Blessings on the fisherman
Who smuggled in the wine! You have deceived
Me!
WOMAN

No, no!
SCHOLAR

Where is my little sister, the harp?

WOMAN

despairing

He will forget to cure the King.

SCHOLAR

Beggars,

Strip me a deck of cards.
He reels forward, rapt, to the front. WOMAN sidles to the
KING and during the song slips on to his regal lap

SCHOLAR

Had I the diamonds in plenty, I would stake
My pocket on kings that walked out with Queen
Maeve
Or wager the acre that no man digs in Connaught,
And after the drinking, I would cross my soul, there,
At the bare stations of the Red Lake.

WOMAN

to KING

I love your baldy spot!

SCHOLAR

They gave me hearts as my share of the dealing,
But the head that I love is not red and it is not black,
And I thought of the three that went over the water
And the earth they had when they brought Deirdre
back:
For who break their money on a card that is foolish
May find the woman in the pack.

RED BEGGAR

A little ewe between two rams!

SCHOLAR

Patric came, without harm, out of Hell . . .
A beggar nailed the black ace on the board.
I flung the game to the floor. I rose from their cursing,
And paler than a sword, I saw, before me,
The face for which a kingdom fell.

As the song closes, the WOMAN comes to him

WOMAN

Fancy is sharp upon the busy stone
Of wishing, but your merry say can change
To wine, food, fire and pleasure. I would now
Sweet mouth was turned to bitter tongue again,
The purple stole put by, the napkin shut,
For you can never cure the King.

SCHOLAR

indignantly

I can.

But who has heard the pot boil over when
The fuel was green? A passion is his demon
And his imagination must release him,
For prayer and fasting are desire again.
He fed on richer thought and he is full.
But since true argument attends the eye
And hearing, I must do a trick or three
The conjurers despise.

To BEGGARS

Give me a ladle, boys.

BEGGARS

accusing OLD BLIND MAN

He tuk it.

OLD MAN

indignantly

God forgive them! I
Am deaf and dumb!

The BEGGARS *search him and produce forks and spoons from his pockets while he protests.*
The AMADAN *with a howl runs forward clasping his stomach*

BEGGARS

He ate too much.

AMADAN

Diabolus in ventre meo est!

SCHOLAR

politely

Potes ructare?

AMADAN

Non possum.

The SCHOLAR *makes conjuring passes and as the* AMADAN *opens his mouth in astonishment, he draws slowly from it a ridiculously large ladle. They laugh. The* AMADAN *hides in terror.*

SCHOLAR

filling the ladle with food

Lady, your hand must fill the King.

WOMAN

approaching the KING *with the ladle, in playful nervousness*

Cathal,
Open your mouth and shut your eyes and see
What I shall give you.
The KING immediately does so.

RED BEGGAR

making for the Larder

Boys, the demon will
Jump out.
*The SCHOLAR steadies himself with a long drink and blows
out all the candles slowly except one, so that the Refectory
is in ruddy firelight. As the WOMAN holds the ladle to
the KING's mouth, the SCHOLAR, whispering and laughing
behind her, draws her back slowly by the waist.*

DEMON

in a terrible ventriloquent voice inside the KING

That was a foolish trick, Mac Conglinne.
I heard you whispering. You know that I
Am starving in the King.
WOMAN screams, drops ladle and flies

MAC CONGLINNE

A juggler's trick!
Imagination in the vat has brought
Up sound and bubble.
*He fills the ladle again and holds it cautiously under the
KING's nose.*

MAC CONGLINNE

Demon,
Here is a larger bite dripping with honey
And juice to dream on.

DEMON

*ventriloquently, as MAC CONGLINNE slowly withdraws the
big spoon*

My hunger
Is terrible and I will wait no longer.
I will come up before it is too late,
And you have emptied every cup and plate.

MAC CONGLINNE

gabbling in broken Latin

Vade retro, vade retro, sathane . . . in nom . . .
ejicient.
Obmutesce . . . exi, daemonia . . . ab eo . . . et . . .
cetera . . . exi . . . ab , . .

He leaps backward, knocking over the last candle. Black out. A rumbling of thunder outside. A blaze on hearth. Wild burst of harp music outside, diminishing with distance. Lights approach slowly in corridor outside and the WOMAN *is seen against the central door in an attitude of despair.*

WOMAN

Oh, oh, oh! The King
Is dead and I shall never be a Queen.

MILITARY *rush in with battle-axes,* MONKS *with lights,* BEGGARS *from Larder. The high chair and dishes are overthrown. Confusion.*

SOLDIERS

shaking off the rain

By Hell!
The storm was bucketed. We ran for shelter.

MONKS

Oh, oh! The Demon!
Run for the holy water!

We saw the Demon!
He sat upon the bell tower.

His eyes
Were flaming red.

He clanged his wings.

He flew
Away.

SOLDIERS

By Hell! The clap of rain
Came up again. We never saw the Demon.

BEGGARS

He had big horns.

And crooked
Hoofs.

A tail.

A fiery fork.

He knew
The Scholar's name.

RED BEGGAR

Why wouldn't he?
I knew it was Mac Conglinne himself.

SOLDIERS

By Hell! Where is the King?

OTHERS

                                        Alas! The King
       Is carried off!
The KING *rises majestically from behind the Lectern in*
his royal clothes. They draw back

WOMAN

running to him
                          Cathal!

KING

              My Ligach! I am cured. I have been ill, Dear.
       I have been in a dream, a terrible dream.
       Forgive the wicked words that I have said.
Withdrawing

                                            But I

       Remember . . . that clerk . . .

LIGACH

                          No, no! I was but desperate
       With love for you and I was wild and foolish
       Because you were so ill. And oh, let us
       Be married now.
They embrace. ABBOT *enters with rest of community.*
LIGACH *withdraws.*

KING

       Most Reverend Lord Abbot, I am cured,
       Cured by your prayers and holy offices,
       And I shall give this pious monastery
       Green pasturelands and golden candlesticks

ABBOT

              O noble King!

KING

       A hundred cows, a cart of frankincense.

MONKS

              O generous King!

ABBOT

                          Saint Barra
       Be praised! Our solemn prayers are heard and fast
       Has cured the King. Let hymns be chanted. Light
       Thanksgiving wax. Ahem. I had forgotten,
       The Demon hurries with that unbeliever.
       Let us remember him in private prayer!
       It may be that those fiery claws will drop
       The Poet into Purgatory.

LAY BROTHERS

coming from table

                                             Alas!
He did not leave a bone upon the board:
He ate them all.

ABBOT

seeing LIGACH

                              What is this . . . this woman
Doing here?

KING

                    It is Ligach, the daughter
Of Maeldune.

ABBOT

bowing

                    Most noble lady!

KING

                                             Good Abbot, you
Shall marry us with book and candle, for
The night is growing late.

ABBOT

                                        We shall
Obey our King.

BEGGARS

                    A noble Queen!
A lovely pair!
                    He is so grand
And her so fair.

*KING and LIGACH hold hands before the ABBOT. A procession
is formed. KING suddenly feels his neck.*

KING

                    Where is my collar?
My golden collar? It was worth a kingdom.

ABBOT

Great King, you gave it to that Scholar!

KING

resigned

                                                         It
Is melted now.

*The procession of chanting MONKS, MILITARY and MEN-
DICANTS passes out through central door. The RED BEGGAR-
MAN and the AMADAN linger behind*

RED BEGGAR

stretching himself comfortably at the fire
     Put on a tree.
                         AMADAN
     Red Muireadach, that tree has not been planted.
                         RED BEGGAR
     They say in Bantry that you are no fool.
                         AMADAN
     My grandfather was never late for school.
                         RED BEGGAR
     By my own wits I fill my mortal sack.
                         AMADAN
     But I, more wisely, live upon the lack.
                         RED BEGGAR
     I recommend this house for noble welcome.
Young LAY BROTHER *enters*
                    LAY BROTHER

sternly
     Beggars, have you not heard the blessed bell? Come!
     The candles have been lit and you are last.
Both get up reluctantly and come forward
                         RED BEGGAR
     When beggarmen can feast—
                         AMADAN

                                    their betters fast.
                         RED BEGGAR
     When youth is fire —
                         AMADAN
                    old men can warm their shins.
                         RED BEGGAR
     There's but one party wins —
                         AMADAN
                                    respect and power.
                         RED BEGGAR
     Be slow in thought —
                         BOTH

together
                                    for who can tell the ball
     That brings the best of jugglers to his fall?

                    C U R T A I N

THE FLAME

to

Seamus O'Sullivan

CHARACTERS

Nun

Novice

Abbess and Sisters of the Community

THE FLAME

SCENE: Interior — the "House of Fire" at Kildare.

As the curtain rises, the stage is in complete darkness and nothing can be seen but the gold flame of St. Brigid, remote and calm. A sound of unending prayer, a murmuring of many voices, metrical and monotonous, is heard below. The murmurings become a single murmur as the light gradually rises and the stage becomes clear. The scene is conventionalized but by builded glooms and sectional light, the massiveness of the early cyclopean architecture is suggested: this house of an older century remains unchanged though a new fashion prevails in ecclesiastical art, as indicated by the Celtic-Romanesque manner of the play. There is a low entrance, on right, well forward, with broad lintel and inclined jambs; a similar entrance, left side, set well back. The walls are plain; in centre, at back, wide steps lead up to the oratory or shrine, which is in the form of a deep and lofty recess; the lamp of the saint is sunken but the flame is represented by a screen or transparency of pure golden light. A settle is on right: a vessel of oil on step.

An aged NUN, *robed in white and heavily hooded, so that her face remains concealed during the scene, is kneeling on steps at right. A young* NOVICE, *in bluish grey and lightly veiled, is kneeling opposite her: the* NOVICE's *dress should be slightly secularized to indicate her state of mind. The aged* NUN *is motionless, with joined hands: and the monotonous murmur of her prayer is still heard. The* NOVICE *is glancing around nervously, restlessly, her hands working. Twice she is about to speak, twice she fails. Suddenly from outside, there is a harsh, vibrant stroke of a bell, as though an hour were marked, and the* NOVICE *starts to her feet.*

NOVICE

Sister,
I cannot pray to-night.
NUN *points to shrine*

with averting hands
                              No. No. I cannot
      Pray.
She runs aside in shadow
                                   NUN
slowly rising
      What is it, child?
      Why have you left the flame again?
                                 NOVICE
at distance
      I cannot pray, I cannot pray.
                                   NUN
coming down
                                   Temptation
      Can strike between the fingers and the font.
To herself as she peers around
      Had not the carvers seen, while storm broke
      On rubble and cut stone, a fiery serpent
      Tongue-tied beneath the tall unfinished Cross
      Of Flann?
Alarmed
                  Attracta, Attracta!
                                 NOVICE
nervously, coming into light
                                                    I

      Am here.
                                   NUN
                  Where? Where?
Groping
                              Come closer, for my sight
      Has but this flame to lean upon.
                                   Come closer
      Now.
                                 NOVICE
obstinately
      I am here.
                                   NUN
catching her arm
                  What mortal cold
      Has shaken you?
                              Why have you left the flame
            Again?

NOVICE

trembling
> I could not pray.
> I could not pray.

NUN

> The soul is found in crook
Of knee and neck.

NOVICE

> I bowed three times.

I could not pray.

NUN

meaningly
> Attracta, you have veiled
A secret. Tell it to me now.
She whispers to NOVICE

NOVICE

shrinking back

> No, no.

I told that in confession.
> Listen!
Looking fearfully to door on left
Sh-sh. Listen!
She runs to left entrance

NUN

> What do you hear?

NOVICE

puzzled and uneasy, coming back

> Nothing, and yet
I know that Mother Abbess walks alone
At night.
Mysteriously
> Once she stood by the Chapel door,
Pale as the shadows that fled across the Curragh,
For thaw outran the wind and the last snow
Was spirited away — nor did she stir
An icy foot, though I saw veil and fold
Escaping.

NUN

reprovingly
> She is holier than us.
But idle thought is an unknotted thread
Forgetful of the needle.

Bless your face
And do not speak.
                              NOVICE
                         But O it is the silence,
The silence that I fear and when you talk to
Me — why is it that I feel good again
If it is wrong to speak?
NUN shakes her head and moves to steps silently
                              NOVICE
pleading
                                        Stay but a little,
Stay with me; I am full of fear
To-night.
NUN beckons silently from shrine
                         Help me a little, help
Me; when I bow my head to pray, I seem
Much smaller than I am — in this great, lonely
Light.

                               NUN
pointing to shrine
                         Attracta, Attracta,
If you have told all in confession, kneel
Before the flame again.
                              Remember long ago
Saint Brigid, wrapped in her dark mantle, drew
The holy spark from heaven on a night
When she had fasted and the builders lay
Asleep beneath their ladders.
                              NOVICE
                                        But I am
Afraid.
                               NUN
                         Has not that flame been raised
To try the patience of our Order? Think
Of them who stayed the beam for centuries
With precious oil, as we do now, and kneel
If you have told all in confession.
The NUN kneels on step murmuring
                              NOVICE
with averting hands
                                                            Ah!

I fear the ancient flame.
Wildly to herself
                                   What can

I do?
Calling
                    Sister.
Desperately
                    I have told a lie.
                         NUN
coming forward, shocked
        A lie!
                         NOVICE
retracting
            It was a dream—
                         NUN
    A dream?
                         NOVICE
            —that troubled me.
                         NUN
                                When, when?
                         NOVICE
                                    Last night.
                         NUN
sitting down on settle and drawing the NOVICE *to her, eagerly*
        Now tell me, tell me. Have you dreamed
        Of that tormented spirit who must stem
        A boat of ice against the fiery falls
        Of Purgatory? Have you seen the beast
        That children fear? Brindled with green or blue,
        He banks his mighty head; but when they lie —
        Crinkling his hide and turning inside out
        So angrily that he is pawed and spotted
        With purple, ribbed in black and red, he sinks
        Into the night again, for he was stabled
        Beneath the Flood.
                         NOVICE
                        No, Sister; no, dear Sister.
        I dreamed that I was walking in the garden
        Along a pathway summer had made less
        And the great oaks had gathered all their leaves
        So close, I wondered how the ivy found
        A branch.
                    Then, halfway in the wood, I saw
        A fair-knee'd youth that had been trumpet-blown

Among those leaves and would escape them
On golden elbows but he was betrayed
And buckled by the anger of his hair —
Great hair that glittered like the tightened strings
When the long nails of the harp-player live
In the dark clef and the pale.

NUN

reassuringly

You dreamed
Of Absalom, the son of David, for
I told you but last week how he was vain
Of every tress that had been pegged with gold,
And then I said: " A novice, when her head
Is shaven, is not troubled as those women
Who knuckle their own foreheads nightly, spit
And rag their hair into so many knobs,
They search the pillow for poor sleep, catching
The day with curls."

While the NUN *is speaking, the* NOVICE *has been glancing
around uneasily. She interrupts*

NOVICE

But I dreamed more.

NUN

Tell me.

NOVICE

On the stone benches by the hedgerow
The nuns were sitting quietly together,
So quietly I thought that they were praying
Because the evening was so fair.

I looked up
And O the sun was but this holy flame.

pointing to shrine

No lamp seemed there — but when the metal-workers
Have chaliced a great jewel, is the shape
Not conquered by the light?

NUN

That was a good dream.
What do you fear?

NOVICE

O then my foot struck chill
Too deep for spade and as I fled, lustres
Of freezing rain were in the air . . . I saw

Behind the black grid of the sky, that flame
Grow dim.

NUN

O horrible!

NOVICE

I ran
To call the nuns, for they sat in the churchyard
So quietly I thought that they were praying
For that young man who died among the trees.
I cried "Attracta, poor Attracta is
Afraid." But as I plucked at them between
The tombs, they shook with my own shivers and all,
All, suddenly, fell to dust.

NUN

O horrible!

NOVICE

I did not sleep again.

NUN

Great Brigid, pray
For her to-night —

NOVICE

wildly

I do not want to grow
So old.

NUN

— And save her from temptation.

NOVICE

Never
To look across Kildare in sun and know
The far flocks move along the mountain slope
Before soft cries that drive them until grass
Is hushed with cloud.
Sound of rising wind outside

NUN

Winter has camped upon
The Curragh now. The sea is waked far inland
And the bright estuaries of the day
Are flooded. Chill can strike from every door.
Pray, pray, when fever strips the young.

NOVICE

childishly

I'll run from every ill

So happily along the old grey flags
The clergy will not hear at all and, if
They do, must think that I am running on
Bare toes.

NUN

Pray quickly, for that is
The dancing evil. Think of Lassara.

NOVICE crouches on step, the NUN bending over her

NOVICE

in terror

Ah, ah! The dancing nun! Do not tell me
Of her or I will dream again.

NUN

in a frenzy of aged asceticism
Ugh! She had little shoes
That danced her to a sin. " Confession-box! "
She cried, and clapped a red-hot coal within
Her heels. She cobbled them, she chilblain'd them,
And as she jigged the cinder, sang: " Burn, burn
To bone and make me pure again, that I
May hobble into heaven."

NOVICE

Ah, you frighten,
You pinch me!

NUN

What do you know of the shame
That virgins fly from?

NOVICE

But I tremble, pant!

NUN

Impurity of thought and act.

NOVICE

weeping

Fear is
A mad bird i' my throat.

NUN

prostrating herself before shrine
Saint Brigid, I
Am old. These lids that time has picked and glassed
With glues are overtaken by the hands
They once despised. The silver lattice has
Been closed; the blessed figures I have seen

Are smaller than the minims in the Mass-book
Now.

NOVICE

timidly touching the NUN'*s robe*
Sister

NUN

When I nod at night, the flame
Seems but a spark.

NOVICE

contritely

Rest, rest.

I have been bad, but I will get the oil
And serve the lamp.
She leads the NUN *to the settle, lifts the beaker carefully
and approaches the shrine*

NUN

pleased

My prayer is heard.
NOVICE

hesitating on step, her hand shaking
No, no, I cannot.
Tearfully

See, I cannot.

She replaces the vessel and runs to NUN

NUN

kindly

You

Are tempted and I know that you have veiled
A secret.
Drawing NOVICE *to her*
Tell me all.

NOVICE
I will. I will.

Because it is not wrong.
Confiding in a low eager voice, as she undoes her veil
I know it is not wrong,
For it has grown so shiny in the moonlight
Yet it is not like the moon; and not a soul
Can tell how I have treasured, tempered with
My happy tears and measured it upon
My fingers in the night until it weighed
So quickly, the bright balance of my hands

Could hold no more.
She rises and flings back her veil; a cymbal clash is
heard and her head is seen armoured with new half-grown
hair in abundant curls and rings that reflect metallically
the light from the shrine. Unveiled, she acts her thoughts,
her gestures become rhythmic; singing tones are heard in
her voice

NOVICE
Look. Look. Am I
Not beautiful now?
NUN
disturbed
Who is shining there?
What voice is that I hear?
NOVICE
rapt
Curl beyond curl,
They climb in falling and I shake them out
To ripple and ring, because I have no comb
To burnish what my fingers will uncrown
At night. But see how they are turned and curved
As capitals upon a page of gold
And dragon-red from which the choristers
Are reading. O I could be happy in
A house where armies have been kept, had I
A topheavy pin of fine bronze, a comb
To stay me, to hold me from ripple and ring.
NUN
coming forward, horror-stricken
Ah! Ah!
Attracta. It is evil, evil. When
The King of Heaven leaves his tent with cheek
Of flame and bright-topped hand, to count
His captives; pale in their far camp the saints
Await . . .
NOVICE
moving back from her grasp frantically
No. No.
It is not wrong, not wrong, though I have dreamed
Of Absalom who galloped under leaves
Nor shall I fear the branches when my own
Are longer than those tresses that unhorsed

   Him.
*There is a sudden harsh clangour of iron handbells in the
passage outside: represented by rapid beating of a gong.
The NOVICE runs aside veiling her head*

                    BOTH

      Mother Abbess!
*The clangour becomes maddening; for we hear, as well
as see through the distorted imagination of the NOVICE.
The sounds cease abruptly and the ABBESS appears, at doorway, right. She enters, swiftly, silently, followed by
SISTERS, from left and right doorways. All are habited in
white and heavily hooded: and their faces are hidden
during the scene, for they wear the face-veil, which is
attached to the bandeau on the forehead and is of fine net.
The actions and steps of the SISTERS are drilled. Two by
two, they come forward and bow before the shrine: at the
side of which the ABBESS stands. They take their places
along the side walls, left and right. The ABBESS comes
forward, alone, bows before the shrine and remains in
silent prayer. At last she turns and comes to front. The
stage is now brighter.*

                    ABBESS

to aged NUN, sternly

                 Sister,
   Why have you left the flame? Is this your place?

                    NUN

   The Novice was afraid.

                    ABBESS

                   Why did you not

   Remain?

                    NUN

            She could not pray.

                    ABBESS

                        Was not bowed gaze,
   The calm of counted hours, enough?

                    NUN

humbly

                        If I have failed, forgive me.

                    ABBESS

to NOVICE

                        Attracta,
   Why have you wearied Sister who is bowed
   In years as a dim candle by a cowl?

Did I not send you here to kneel, to mind
The precious oil? Have you been troublesome
Of tongue again?
                              Why are you fidgeting
And fingering your veil? Come here.
The NOVICE *hesitates*
                Obey me.
She pounces and pulls back the NOVICE's *veil. There is a*
cymbal clash, as the bright metallic halo of her head is
disclosed. The SISTERS *point rigid right hands towards the*
NOVICE, *with a low " Ah, Ah!" of horror*
                Saints above!
Checking herself and the SISTERS
                                What holy show
Is this? Has vanity made vow, mocked rule?
Is wanton curl and clip our fashion? Veil —
The secret lodging?
A silent pause
To aged NUN
                              Did you know this?
                    NUN
                                The girl is ignorant . . .
                    ABBESS
                Did you know this?
                    NUN
                              Aye.   Aye.
I groped, I guessed — but slowly.
                    ABBESS
                                            Why
Did you not tell me now?
                    NUN
                              The girl is young . . . She . . .
                    ABBESS
interrupting
        Are women not unchurched
By scandal of bare head? Has not Saint Paul
Written that demons strike their fiery tents
And hasten to such hair?
Sharply to aged NUN
                                    Sister, I
Will speak with you again . . .

NOVICE

interrupting, excitedly

                              No. No.

      It was my fault, my fault.
                      ABBESS

                              How dare you,
      Have you unlearned obedience and respect?
To others, aside
        These curls must now be cut.
She beckons a SISTER, instructs and sends her out. She
She beckons two other SISTERS to come and stand on each
side of her. During the questioning of the NOVICE, the
ABBESS consults them. She speaks in a conversational tone
                              Attracta, stand
      Here. Do not be afraid, but tell me what
      Has troubled you at night.
                              Have you
      Been at confession?
NOVICE nods

                      Speak.
                      NOVICE
                          Mother, I
      Have.
                      ABBESS
            You promised me you would
      Be good.
                      NOVICE
            Yes, Mother.
                      ABBESS
                      Have you tried?
                      NOVICE
                              I have.
                      ABBESS
      But when dark comes, your mind is bright, and
            you
      Forget this house?
                      NOVICE
                      Yes, Mother.
                      ABBESS
softly

                              I think
      You were afraid to tell me.
                      NOVICE

                              I have been

Afraid.

ABBESS

consulting SISTER *on right*
You told a sister you had visions?

NOVICE

startled, hesitating   I did.

ABBESS
And that these visions made you glad.

NOVICE
                                    Yes, Mother.

ABBESS

consulting SISTER *on left*
And I think . . . you sing yourself
To sleep . . . but very softly.

NOVICE

hesitating   Yes.

ABBESS
You know these dreams are good?

NOVICE

earnestly   I know,

I know, that they are good.

ABBESS

consulting SISTER *quietly*
                            Sister forgot
To cut your hair upon Saint Declan's eve.
You did not tell her?
The NOVICE *remains silent*
consulting SISTER
                            Did you not say
The month before . . . that you were ill?
The NOVICE *remains silent*
Soothingly
                            But do not be afraid.

You could not pray
To-night?

NOVICE
        No, Mother.

ABBESS
        But you tried?

NOVICE

Yes, Mother.

ABBESS

When you close your eyes
You seem in light.

NOVICE

eagerly

I do. I do.

ABBESS

And then
The vision comes again?

NOVICE

happily

Yes, Yes.

ABBESS

Now close
Your eyes, Attracta, think and tell us what
You see and hear.
*The NOVICE pauses and begins to speak at first in a low
tranced voice — then excitedly and male murmuring as
of distant crowds is heard without*

NOVICE

Faintly as in the dreams
Of Fionnuala on the wave, before
She was baptized, a stir of music comes
At dark.
                    O then I see a house where heads are
Bare; ruddied with impatient light, tall men
Come in, storm at their heels, for they have sailed
All day from the black soundings of the north
Beyond the gleam of sand — and laughing, they
Unharness the fierce tackle of the voyage
To shout and make up stories of themselves
And stir so noisily around the blaze
Of coal, I think that keels are grounding on
The very doorstep.

ABBESS

And what are they like —
These men you see?

NOVICE

dreamily

They are not like the red Apostles in

The book. They are not like those saints who cross
The ocean with bright tonsure.

ABBESS

to others

Sound and stir
Of Ireland, glitter of assemblies, fill
Her mind.

NOVICE

Each man is stronger than the big oar
Three monks must bend to pull: and women run
With welcoming hands — they are dressed in green
Or blue and they have drawn their long hair back
To show a pale sweet crown: they twiddle rings,
They laugh, they look, for every man's their glass,
And they are talking all the time as though
It were wrong.

ABBESS

And you would like to be
With them?

NOVICE

Yes. Yes. Nor would I care at all
If any woman spoke too loud or laughed
As though an arm were round her, had I sat
Awhile, favoured on the great bench beside
The fire.

The murmur and music fade away

ABBESS

And so you let those curls grow,
Attracta?

NOVICE

Yes, Mother.

ABBESS

Come now and listen

Patiently

The saints in their bright colleges
Are tempted when they pray. There is an eye
That keeps a mock in every mind, though sound
And sight be out. You have seen vanity
Whose food at first is delicate, whose beds
Are soft. But vanity grows violent
With flattery and quarrel, hating them
Whose hands are only raised to bless.

The SISTER who has been sent out, returns with a knife,
the ABBESS motions her to keep back
To NOVICE

Kneel down,

    Offer these fallen locks before the flame
    And rise in peace.
The ABBESS takes the knife and approaches
Come,

    Attracta.

NOVICE

with a startled glance of realization
No. No. I will not

Running to a SISTER

Sister, you were kind

    And spoke to me at lesson time. Please help me
    Now.
The SISTER remains motionless
Running to a second SISTER
Sister, the evening that I fell,

    You lifted me with little words. O help
    Me, now.
The second SISTER remains motionless
Running to a third SISTER
Sister, you never spoke,

    For you were always quiet, but you smiled
    At me one day and O at night I dreamed
    Of you.
She waits with outstretched hands. The SISTER starts but
remains silent
To ABBESS, tearfully
Reverend Mother, pity me,

    No soul can tell how I have treasured them
    And moon has tempered. Happy I at day
    Though head had ached in veil, to think that
     brow
    Went brighter.
Dashing back her tears
I confess, all, all . . . I'd wake

    Early — I thought — when they were longer, see
    Light battling, loose them — so — with wielded head
    To shine along my shoulder and bared arm.

ABBESS

Girl, rid yourself

Of vanity. Kneel down.
NOVICE
her voice harsh with self-will
No. No. I won't.
A murmur of horror from the Community
ABBESS
coming forward with knife

Obey me.

NOVICE
*moving back with a half-scream, guarding her hair —
and in a strange voice:*
>   Back, back, Mother Abbess. Do
> Not touch them. Do not look at me with those
> Unlidded eyes . . . All night the cold flags try
> To hide your footsteps . . . Where the thorn is sharper
> You kneel . . . But in the snow and rain you sigh
> Like those who have been in their graves. Back, back
> And do not touch them.

SISTERS
She is possessed! She is
Possessed!
ABBESS
>   Hold, hold her.
> I must cut down that spirit in her hair
> Lest it grow mighty; for demoniacs
> Break chain, rushing like the ear-blinded droves,
> To their destruction.

*SISTERS come forward, timidly hold the NOVICE. As the
ABBESS approaches, she struggles and screams, but her cries
are lessened by the loud ringing of handbells. Or the action
here may be silent and conventionalized. At the same time
the flame begins to sink to an angry red glow and the
stage fills with shadows.*

ABBESS
in alarm

The flame is sinking. Pray,
Pray.
*In consternation the SISTERS retreat to the walls, hide their
hands in their sleeves and bow, murmuring in prayer. The
NOVICE remains, alone in the middle of the stage*
NOVICE
strangely

See how they join great sleeves
And mourn within their hoods, for they have found
The son of David now. They cut him down
Among the convent oaks, they severed each
Thin strand his hanging body had uncurled
And left the bright grain quivering. See how
They join great sleeves and mourn in heavy hood.
The flame is dimmer

ABBESS

Evil spirits hide
The flame from us.
Pray, Pray aloud.
*The SISTERS raise their joined hands, lift their heads and
the murmuring rises, quicker and on a higher note. The
tranced girl remains in an attitude of listening, she smiles
and gestures*

NOVICE

I hear them coming,
For it is darkfall now. Men leave the deck
And laughing women have unbridled their
Own tresses . . .
But they stop, they bow,
And some of them are carrying the pall
Of that young man who died upon a tree.
And listen, listen, they are praying . . . They
Repent. Black and white clergy have put on
The purple stole and candles will be lighted
In sad procession.

ABBESS

loudly

Ring the evil back.
*The harsh exorcising bells are struck again. The clangour
ceases abruptly: as in silence all watch the NOVICE who
comes slowly to front, and, going on her knees, speaks in
a clear, simple voice, her face uplifted*

NOVICE

Holy Brigid, save
Me from the flame, for I am full of fear
Because there is a great pain in my head
That makes my body small. Hide me with pity,
Hide me in your blue mantle that was spread
By miracle until it covered half

The plain and I will find a fold there, warm
As bed in winter and too far for dream.
O hide, hide poor Attracta in your mantle
Now.

*During her prayer the flame disappears and for a few
moments lovely hues of blue seem to interweave themselves in the air with a rustling sound, as though the holy
mantle were descending, enfolding and enwrapping her
until there is complete darkness. The measured grieving
of the Community can be heard. Tapers are brought in
hurriedly, and now, as the stage becomes half-lit, the pale
faces of the crowding SISTERS are seen, human, agitated.
Their gestures are gentle, graceful, for we see them as
they really are.*

*The SISTERS withdraw to their places, again, at side walls
and, lying at the foot of the shrine, can be seen the veiled
form of the NOVICE, strangely still*

Several SISTERS hasten forward to steps

SISTERS

at steps

               Her brow is calm and cold. She breathes.
So quietly —
           We cannot hear.
                        Her sleep
Is stronger than our hands.

The ABBESS bends over the comatose girl

ABBESS

moved

               There is no evil left; and she will wake
Again.

*She veils the girl's face again: SISTERS lift and bear her
out, by doorway, left, while others pray*

SISTERS

on right

    Mother, we fear the darkness —

SISTERS

                    What have we heard,
What have we seen.

SISTERS

on right

           Mother, we fear the darkness.

SISTERS

on left

Where is the flame we served?

What punishment
Have we deserved?

SISTERS

on right

Mother, we fear the darkness.

The aged NUN *comes forward with uplifted hand*

NUN

I am the oldest. Let me speak.
Had not that blessed flame been raised
To try the patience of our Order, night
And day?

ALL

Yes: night and day.

NUN

I can remember how

At darkfall — and it must be sixty years
Ago — we trembled in this house . . . But they
Are dead . . . all dead . . . who prayed with me
   that night . . .

Her mind wandering

And sometimes, lately, when your hoods are lifted
I think those Sisters have come back again.

A pause

What was I saying to you? . . .
. . . We trembled for a great storm rang
And trampled in the convent. Every door
Was living. Evil spirits beat themselves
Against the shrine. They rose . . . it sank. We
   prayed . . .
It shone. And all that night with frantic robes
We fought among those climbing winds to keep
The lamp in oil.

ABBESS

Remember us.

We do not understand.

SISTERS

Remember us.

We do not understand.

NUN

Those spirits came to-night

In guile, tempting the young with vanity,
Plying the old with sleep.
Breaking down

                              ... And we forgot
The duty of the flame.

                    A SISTER
lifting the vessel carefully, from step
                    It is the truth,
Here is the oil. The lamp has not been filled.
A general murmur of consternation

                    ALL
                    The lamp has not been filled.

                    A SISTER
from the shrine
A miracle!

                    ALL
          A miracle!

                    SISTERS
from shrine
                    Deep in the lamp
The spark that Brigid drew from Heaven
Lives, lives!

                    ALL
joyfully echoing
          Lives, lives!
The ABBESS *comes to shrine*

                    . ABBESS
          A miracle!
The holy spark is bright.
Renewed murmurs of joy
Admonishing

                    Do not rejoice
So soon.
          Have we not doubted?

                    SISTERS
                    We have doubted!

                    ABBESS
Did we not fear?

                    SISTERS
          We feared.

                    ABBESS
Our faith was weak.

SISTERS

Our faith was weak.

All bow as the ABBESS takes the vessel and ascends to shrine: she returns, places the empty vessel on steps. Very slow action

ABBESS

Let us pray.

The SISTERS all come forward and kneel across stage, facing the shrine. The ABBESS kneels on steps. As they pray, the flame slowly rises, the tapers are extinguished one by one, and the rest of the stage darkens. The sound of unending prayer, murmuring of many voices is heard and only the gold flame can be seen, remote and calm

CURTAIN

SISTER EUCHARIA

A PLAY IN THREE SCENES

to

Gordon Bottomley

in admiration of his lyric plays.

CHARACTERS

Sister Gabriel   Reverend Mother

Sister Stanislaus   Father Sheridan

Sister Agnes   Sister Eucharia

Sister Jerome   First Speaker

Lay Sister   Second Speaker

Sister Angelica   Sisters of the Community

Souls of Sisters in Purgatory

SISTER   EUCHARIA

SCENE   I.

PLACE: A Convent Interior.

TIME: The Present.

*As the curtain rises the stage is in semi-darkness but
through the lofty central doorway, at back, light is shining
from the corridor which leads on left to the Chapel. The
scene is represented by curtains and this central doorway
is approached by a few steps. There are entrances right
and left of front stage. After a few moments a nun enters
from right, front stage. She crosses stage swiftly, silently
and goes up steps. She remains at side of doorway looking
along the corridor towards chapel in a listening attitude.
As she does so, other nuns come in quietly, left and right
front. They range themselves on each side of the stage.
Stage-light gradually increases as they do so until it is
normal. The stage is seen to be quite bare except for two
high hall chairs, one on each side of the central steps.
All the nuns are in white or cream habits. They all lean
forward listening but they are obviously restless and un-
able to remain still. They form a chorus but as the chorus
is within and, therefore, part of the action, they are not
grouped too formally. In the intense silence we are aware
of a general nervous tension and in the scene which
follows, the sisters speak at first on a clear yet subdued
note of excitement, as if with each syllable they broke
the rule of silence.*

SISTER

before coming down steps
Sister Eucharia is praying
Still.

CHORUS OF SISTERS

left and right — alternately
Praying

Praying
                    All night
All day
          She is praying still.
Yes, praying, praying still.

SISTER GABRIEL

coming forward

                              O God look down
On us! What can we do? What can we do
This night? She will not leave the chapel, when
We touch her hand and whisper it is time
To go.

CHORUS

left and right

          She will not stir.
                              She will not leave
When we have touched her sleeve
                              And whispered: ' It
Is time to go.'
                    Day after day
It is the same.

SISTER GABRIEL

          Day after day — the same.

CHORUS

She trembles at the sound of every bell
As though she served at Mass —
                              and was afraid
Of the responses we know by heart.

SISTER GABRIEL

At half-past-four, at half-past-four,
As I was standing in the corridor,
I heard her cry out from the altar rail
In an agony beyond all human help
And yet the day she was professed, a year
Ago, I saw, I saw her face
Before the Bishop hid it from the world
Forever . . .

CHORUS

          Tell us. Tell us.
                              What did you see?
What did you see in her face?

SISTER GABRIEL

slowly

              I saw
The living grace of God . . .
                   I might have been
A soul in pain as she is now, a soul
In darkness . . . her eyes were closed and I
Could see the nervous blush on her cheek
For she had been unveiled again in thought
By her own modesty. But O she was
Truly a bride of Heaven and her brow
Was shining like . . .

CHORUS

    Yes. Yes.

SISTER GABRIEL

           How can
I put that happiness into a word? . . .
I only know that when I looked at her,
The gain and glory of a new indulgence
Came to me in a blinding flash, as if
I were a soul in Purgatory.

distressed

             Poor,
Poor Sister Eucharia, what shall we do?
What shall we do to-night?
While she is speaking, Sister Agnes and Sister Stanislaus
enter. Both are obviously senior nuns.

SISTER STANISLAUS

               Come, sister, calm
Yourself.

SISTER AGNES

Yes, sister, we must all be calm,
Sharing the shadow of this unknown cross.

SISTER GABRIEL

Why am I always blamed for this
And that? You are not calm yourselves . . . and how
Can anyone be calm when every moment
Is like a thought that we have missed in prayer,
Annoying as a cold upon the lip,
Something or other that a tidy soul

Has put away with such great pains, nobody
Can ever find it.
                    SISTER AGNES
                    You forget yourself
Now, Sister Gabriel.
                    SISTER STANISLAUS
precisely
                                Yes, sister, we
Must give a good example to each other,
Be patient, for we promised Reverend Mother
That we would give this hour of recreation
To our own beads and private meditation.
                    SISTER GABRIEL
Reverend Mother should be here.
                    SISTER AGNES
                                    You know
That she is lying down.
                    SISTER STANISLAUS
                                    Her rheumatism
Is bad again to-day.
                    SISTER AGNES
                    And her poor heart
As troubled as her mind.
                    SISTER GABRIEL
                                And are we well
I beg to ask you, waiting here on pins
And needles, thinking of a silent bell,
pointing to central doorway
While *she* is falling into a new fast
Each hour or drags her anguish to the step
Calling for the last sacrament. I say
That she should be anointed.
                    CHORUS
                            Sister Gabriel
Is right.
            Yes, she is right.
                    A SISTER
coming forward
                            My dream . . .
                                    My dream
Is out

SISTER STANISLAUS

Your dream is out . . .

What do you mean?

THE SISTER

When Sister Gabriel

Was speaking, all came back to me.

with growing excitement

I dreamed

Last night the convent had been decorated

Again. As I leaned across the bannister

The walls were mirroring the white paint

And in every room, every passage of the house,

Electric light was wasting by itself

So that I thought the workmen had gone home

And left the bright enamelling . . . But I

Could hear somewhere, stripping behind a panel,

The dull roar of a spirit lamp.

SISTER STANISLAUS

impatiently

Yes. Yes.

THE SISTER

Then all was different . . .

For we were waiting in this very place,

The bell for prayers began to ring, each light

Become a glowing wire and, like a statue,

Sister Eucharia was standing there

Alone.

pointing to the central doorway

Three candles guttered from the iron heart

Below that shrine . . .

O then I saw her shake.

I heard her moaning — and may God forgive me

For saying what is on my tongue —

But in that dream, I thought, I thought

That she had made a bad communion.

a murmur of consternation

SISTER GABRIEL

Something

Was on the tip of my tongue too, all day,

Something I dared not tell to anyone

Until this very minute.

CHORUS

What is it?

What is it?

SISTER GABRIEL

Only a night ago
I met her on the stairs just as the clock
Was striking in the hall below. She swayed . . .
I caught her arm and . . . Sisters . . . It was not
A human arm.

SISTER STANISLAUS

Now, Sister Gabriel,
That is sufficient.

SISTER GABRIEL

I tell you it was

No human **arm**

slowly

. . . so stiff . . . so hard . . . so cold.
All lumps and knobs in her half-empty sleeve.
I thought of a door knocker hidden in crepe
And then I thought that I had put my hand
Within the railings of a vault.

SISTER AGNES

Sister

Your mind has been upset. You should not say
A thing like that.

SISTER GABRIEL

I tell you it is true
And something horrible is going to happen
To her, because we are afraid. I say
Again that she should be anointed.

CHORUS

Yes,

Yes. Sister Gabriel is right.
We are
Afraid. We are afraid of what is going
To happen here this night.

SISTER AGNES

aside

The house is out
Of hand. O what are we to do now?

SISTER STANISLAUS

                                   Send

For Reverend Mother.
Sister Jerome enters. She is aged and walks slowly.

SISTER AGNES

                        Here is Sister Jerome.

SISTER STANISLAUS

Thank God for that.

SISTER AGNES

to Sister Jerome
O Sister, what are we
To do?
          We should be in the chapel now.

CHORUS

                                        Yes, yes.

We should be in the chapel.

SISTER JEROME

looking towards central doorway and nodding

                                        Is she

The same?

SISTER AGNES : SISTER STANISLAUS

together
              Yes, she is praying, praying
Still.

CHORUS

          Praying, praying.
                    All night,
All day.
              She is praying, praying still.

SISTER JEROME

What is the time, please, Sister Agnes?

SISTER AGNES

taking watch from pocket in habit concealed by cape
                                        Five
To eight.

SISTER JEROME

              This is disgraceful. In my day
The young were always humble at their prayers
And silent at the stations of the cross
As if they heard the sighing of poor souls
In Purgatory; and we never knew

How many times they did the sorrowful round
Morning or evening, but this nun, whose name
I have forgotten . . .

SISTER STANISLAUS

prompting

Sister Eucharia —

SISTER JEROME

ignoring

. . . This nun has turned her back upon the lesson
We learn and made the holy offices
Her own.

SISTER AGNES

Reverend Mother thinks
It is the will of God.

SISTER STANISLAUS

No, Sister is right.
The sacred name is loud upon her lips,
She kneels in dread of the Eternal Fire
And ends the world upon a cry. Indeed
The convent has been scandalised.

SISTER AGNES

I feel
Ashamed as if at every sob she took
A ladder from the cross and our own prayers
Were not enough.

SISTER GABRIEL

joining in

That is uncharitable.

SISTER JEROME

Order and discipline must be restored
At once.

turning, as lay sister enters, right, front

Who's that?

CHORUS

Here is the little lay sister!
The little lay sister!

*single voices rise, but we cannot tell who is speaking,
as the sisters are thinking aloud*

What can she want?

Her nose is very red.

She has a cold

Again.
                    And she's been crying in
The kitchen.
                          LAY SISTER
she is dressed in a grey habit and wears a small check
apron. She hesitates between Sister Agnes and Sister
Stanislaus
                    Sister, am I to ring the bell?
                          SISTER AGNES
kindly
          We don't know.
Reverend Mother is not here.
                          LAY SISTER
O sister, I forgot to do it to-day —
To ring the Angelus, I mean.
And Reverend Mother was to send for me
But it was not my fault.
                          No.   No . . .
I couldn't help it, I couldn't help it.
All this dreadful day of accidents, the cooking
Has been upset, the damper will not work,
The sink is choked . . . Sister Eucharia
Has eaten nothing for two days . . .
I burst out crying every time I see
Her plate.
                     SISTER AGNES
           We are all troubled, Sister.
                      LAY SISTER
Oh! It is terrible.
weeps

                      SISTER AGNES
                There, do not cry.
Reverend Mother is not vexed with you.
                     SISTER JEROME
She should control herself.
                       LAY SISTER
confused
                             I'm sorry, Mother.
lay sister hesitates at exit and comes back timidly
      And the bell? . . . am I to ring the bell for prayers?
         SISTER AGNES : SISTER STANISLAUS
      No.   No. Reverend Mother must decide

That question.
lay sister bows and hurries out
SISTER JEROME
It is disgraceful. In fifty years
I have never known the like. What is the name
Of the young nun who keeps us waiting here?
SISTER STANISLAUS
Sister Eucharia.
SISTER JEROME
In my opinion . . .
*She lowers her voice and the conversation with Sisters
Agnes and Stanislaus is heard as a murmur, accompanied
by much shaking of the three heads.*
CHORUS
rapidly and tensely
What are they whispering?
What
Are they whispering?
Whispering . . .
whispering . . .
*The words of the Chorus become a mere sibilance. Sudden-
ly Sister Angelica, who has been standing by herself at
the extreme right in increasing agitation, steps forward.*
SISTER ANGELICA
Stop! Stop!
I cannot bear it any longer.
SISTER STANISLAUS
What do
You mean, Sister Angelica, by this?
What do you mean?
SISTER ANGELICA
I mean the three of you
Are wrong, are wrong, hooding yourselves together.
Sister Eucharia is holier
Than all of us.
SISTER AGNES
Good gracious! *You* were
The very first to blame her.
SISTER STANISLAUS
Last week
You said that she was selfish and

SISTER ANGELICA

Self-willed.

May God forgive me for those words.
I did not know what I was saying. Just now
As I stood there —

Pointing

Sister Eucharia
Seemed, seemed to smile at me and then I knew
The truth.

CHORUS

What can have happened,
Sister Angelica?

Her face is drawn
And pale.

She must be ill.

Her hands are trembling.

SISTER ANGELICA

addressing all

Come, come into the chapel now
And pray with her.

Are you afraid because
She tries to stay in daily adoration
And her sweet breath lingers in every word
Or sigh, when she has given up her soul
To God.

Recital of a single prayer,
Appointed both for the living and the dead,
Can save us from the pains of Purgatory
Though seven years and seven quarantines
Come, then and pray.

SISTER JEROME

This, this
Is spreading quicker than a common cold,
A cough that tickles every throat in church
Before the Gospel has been read. It is
Ridiculous and order must be kept
Here.

SISTER ANGELICA

turning to her

Rules and regulations, Sister Jerome.

as if by rote

Get up at six o'clock
And go to bed at ten
An hour for meditation
An hour for recreation
Dead silence in the house
When all the lights are out.

SISTER STANISLAUS

Have you no shame,
Sister Angelica?

SISTER AGNES

This quarrelling!
This quarrelling!

SISTER ANGELICA

turning towards central doorway with out-stretched hands
Sister Eucharia,
Our sister in religion, pray for us
Because we do not understand. I know
That they are wrong. I know you are a saint.

SISTER JEROME

grimly
A saint!

CHORUS

in wonder
A saint!
Ssssh!

Here is Reverend Mother,
Reverend Mother!
Reverend Mother enters

REV. MOTHER

What does this disturbance
Mean?
A few sisters lead Sister Angelica back to her place

A SISTER

aside
Nothing, Reverend Mother, nothing.

Sister
Has spoken just a little sharply. Her nerves
Are all on edge.

SISTER JEROME

grimly
What are we to do now?

REV. MOTHER
I sent for Father Sheridan.
He should be here at any minute.
SISTER JEROME
You should have sent for him before.
REV. MOTHER
I know. I made a great mistake.
SISTER JEROME
I warned you what would happen.
SISTER AGNES
shocked to Sister Jerome
Sister, you
Forget yourself.
REV. MOTHER
No, she is right. It was my fault.
SISTER JEROME
Moreover, everyone is saying
You gave this young nun special privileges,
The key of your own bookcase, holy leaflets
And she had too much time
On her hands.
REV. MOTHER
dreamily as if she were speaking to herself
Ah Sister, it is hard to hold
The difference in mind, when we ourselves
Were young and every book was edged with gold,
How at the stroke of early bell, we sighed
All in a tremble at the chapel door
As if it were the first time or the last
In life, how in the year we were professed
We never heard the sound of our own footstep,
We clasped the silence in the corridor,
We did not raise our eyes . . .
she pauses
but when
At evening time the beeswax on the floor
Became too bright, we knew the sun was shining
Between the sashes. Month by month we paced
The corridor and it was best to tell
The season by the flowers upon the altar! . . .
But sometimes when I sit, with pen

In hand before my writing desk, busy
With bills, accounts and printed forms, I think
Of that.
                    Got knows if I am wholly to blame
Because I thought this child, so serious
Beyond her years, so pure in every act
Of love, might teach a lesson to us all.
                              SISTER JEROME
bluntly
Well, now you know the truth.
                              SISTER ANGELICA
coming forward
        O Mother, let
Me speak.
                    Sister Eucharia is wise
For her soul is sighing in the hands of God
All day.
                         REV. MOTHER
thoughtfully
        If she were right.
                              SISTER JEROME
        Right! Right!
                        This house
Has been distracted. Order and discipline
Must be restored.
                        SISTER ANGELICA
                        O Mother, hear me
                        REV. MOTHER
                                    I cannot
Now.
        Sister Jerome is looking down
The years.
                        SISTER ANGELICA
                        But, Mother—
                        REV. MOTHER
                            Silence, Sister
Angelica!
                        SISTER JEROME
                This, this
Is spreading like a common cold, a cough
Behind the hand . . .

A SISTER

I hear the hall door bell.

CHORUS

The hall door bell!

REV. MOTHER

Pray, it is Father Sheridan

At last.

LAY SISTER

entering excitedly

Reverend Mother!

REV. MOTHER

Who is it?

LAY SISTER

Father Sheridan and he says . . .

REV. MOTHER

Where is he?

LAY SISTER

In the parlour.

REV. MOTHER

I'll come and speak to him.

changing her mind

No. No. I'll see him here.

She calls Sister Agnes and gives her instructions. Sister Agnes goes out followed by the lay sister.

REV. MOTHER

You may all leave now, Sisters.

The nuns are in a flutter of excitement but they leave quietly, left, right.

Enter Sister Agnes and Father Sheridan. The latter is tall, handsome and of refined appearance. He is a city priest and his black clerical clothes are excellently cut so that he has the general air of being well turned out. He still carries his tall hat and gloves which Sister Agnes takes with great respect. She leaves, bearing the precious objects with great care.

FATHER SHERIDAN

I got your letter, Reverend Mother, only a quarter of an hour ago.

REV. MOTHER

It was good of you to come here at once, Father.

FR. SHERIDAN

in a low tone
    This seems serious.

REV. MOTHER

We do not know what to think, Father. It has all
happened so strangely, so suddenly.

FR. SHERIDAN

Where is she now?

REV. MOTHER

In the chapel.

FR. SHERIDAN

Has she been there long?

REV. MOTHER

All day.

FR. SHERIDAN

Well, well!

REV. MOTHER

What do you think of it, Father?

FR. SHERIDAN

In cannot say as yet. In such a case we must consider
everything very carefully.

REV. MOTHER

Nothing like this has ever happened in the convent
before.

FR. SHERIDAN

It's most unusual, certainly. But I have known such
cases. We have to be very careful, however. We
must not be misled by mere delusions and the folly
of self indulgence. The Church warns us in such
cases that . . .

REV. MOTHER

almost in a whisper
    Father.

FR. SHERIDAN

What is it?

REV. MOTHER

I think I hear her.
She goes over to steps
    Yes.
Cautiously
    She has left the chapel. She moves as if she were

in a trance. She is coming this way.
Leaves steps
What are we to do?

FR. SHERIDAN

I'll talk to her.

REV. MOTHER

But if she is in this strange kind of trance—

FR. SHERIDAN

Yes, yes. You are quite right, Reverend Mother.
We must be cautious. I'll observe her first and see
what she does.

REV. MOTHER

I'll stay here, Father?

FR. SHERIDAN

No. It would be best if I were alone. But remain
within call. I'll step in here and watch her first.
*Reverend Mother goes out left. Father Sheridan goes to
right exit and stands within doorway so that he is not
seen. The stage gradually darkens and for a few moments
there is a complete blackout.*

SCENE II.

*The action is continuous and the stage is in darkness
but we are aware of some change in the setting which
indicates that the scene is beyond time and place. For a
curtain has been drawn across the central doorway and
gradually we see Sister Eucharia standing in light on the
steps. In front, obscurely seen in a greyish light are the
two Speakers, dressed in conventual robes and with heavy
hoods. Their words are slow and significant.*

BOTH SPEAKERS

Sister Eucharia!
Sister
Eucharia!

FIRST SPEAKER
Why do you hesitate
Again? Are you afraid to-night?
SECOND SPEAKER
Are you
Afraid, Sister Eucharia!
Pause
BOTH SPEAKERS
Pray, pray
For your own soul.
FIRST SPEAKER
softly
Before it is too late.
*Sister Eucharia has remained motionless but now raises
her head*
SISTER EUCHARIA
Too late?
BOTH SPEAKERS
Too late.
SISTER EUCHARIA
Poor souls in Purgatory
Why are you calling me again? Have I
Not prayed for you? Have I not offered up
My own intentions for your sake at Mass?
Why do you come at such a time?
She waits but there is no reply
Morning,
Though dark, delights the living and the dead
When angels cluster in a great cathedral;
O had we their faculties, who wait from day
To day for that half-hour, we too might share
In seven Masses at one time, be fast
Or slow, bow down before the Elevation
At the high altar, kneel where the pillars
Have catacombed the glitter of a shrine,
Follow the Gospel, changing place
On the side altars, glorify the end
In the beginning of the Sacrifice.
FIRST SPEAKER
Pray, pray to-night for you will never see
The morning.

SECOND SPEAKER
Pray for your own soul.
SISTER EUCHARIA

No! No!
Not that familiar fear to catch my breath
With cold. I have too much to do
For my own soul.
to herself

How many moments I
Have lost each day in idle breath that might
Have been the sum of holy aspiration.
Only the saints who stand before all time
Can know the total, see tremendous days
Of faith and mercy going down with flame
And coffin to the dark.
FIRST SPEAKER
urgently

These, these
Are mortal fears.
SECOND SPEAKER
Pray, pray for your own soul
Before it is too late.
SISTER EUCHARIA
pleadingly

Not yet. Not yet.
I am not worthy to obey the Son
Of Man.
FIRST SPEAKER
His love is young as your own soul.
SISTER EUCHARIA
softly
As young?

SECOND SPEAKER
Yet He has suffered on this earth
Two thousand years.
FIRST SPEAKER
In every violent act
Of men, and cities that, in changing, build,
Unbuild, His word.
SISTER EUCHARIA
half to herself

Two thousand years . . .
And yet poor fast can bring me to my knees
Though not in prayer and a pain in my back
Unstay me. Fear, fear, not faith still holds me down
With iron arm and pincer, heats the pitch
Of frenzy, strips me for the martyrdom
Of shame. The saints are their own example
And when we die in thought, the senses are
Our executioners.

FIRST SPEAKER

Let the dead speak.

We have gradually become aware of the presence of others, the souls of the sisters in Purgatory. They are grouped left and right and some of those who speak singly are in a kneeling attitude below the central figure of Sister Eucharia. They divide the words among each other as if they were desirous of expressing the mystical unity of their painful, yet joyful existence in Purgatory. They are lit from below so that their up-raised hands and sleeves move in and out of that silver radiance.

BOTH SPEAKERS

alternatively

Sisters of this convent,

twenty

thirty

A hundred years ago.

Were you afraid?

CHORUS OF SOULS

We were afraid.

BOTH SPEAKERS

And did you fail?

CHORUS OF SOULS

We failed.

BOTH SPEAKERS

Are you in pain?

CHORUS OF SOULS

We are in pain.

SISTER EUCHARIA

O they

Are joyful in their pain.

CHORUS

left

Yes, we
Are joyful in the flame of Purgatory.

CHORUS

right

And feel in every pang the striking love
Of God.

SINGLE VOICES

alternatively

I was so timid in my life
I did not hear the little cough that killed me.
But I am brave now, I am brave.

I was
So happy, so contented that I never knew a pain
In all my time on earth.

My hands
Are memory but they are burning holes
Shaped by the nails —

That pierce my hands —

That break
My feet.

Ah! I am wounded in the side.
I share the blood and water.

I am saved
By incorruption of that holy matter.
My soul is purified by flame.

I am
Halfway to Heaven in my pain.

One speck,
One speck of venial sin —

Too small, too small,
To stay the inquisition of a scruple
Can keep the soul impure.

CHORUS

But we begin
Our gleaming for the heaven-set jewels, the rings
That shone upon the fingers of the great
Dominican will fit at last our humble
Love.

receding

                    Yes, we are joyful in the flame
Of Purgatory.
                         SISTER EUCHARIA
                    O do not leave me, blessed souls. I am
Afraid no longer. Let this be my last fault
On earth, to be impatient for that love
And pain. O tell me, tell me what I am
To do.
Only the speakers are now seen.
                         BOTH SPEAKERS
                    Gain absolution for the sins
Of your whole life.
*The speakers vanish and Sister Eucharia is seen alone in
an attitude of trance. Voices of sisters far-off:* Sister
Eucharia! *Voice of Priest off stage:* Sister Eucharia!

                         SCENE III.

*The action is continuous and the scene is the same as
Scene I. The light gradually rises to normal as Fr.
Sheridan steps forward from right.*

                         FR. SHERIDAN
firmly
          Sister Eucharia.
                         SISTER EUCHARIA
suddenly seeing him
                         Father!
She comes down the steps

                                              God
Has sent you here to-night. I want to make
A general confession.
                         FR. SHERIDAN
That is an unusual request, Sister. Didn't you make
     one last year before you took the veil? Is anything

troubling your mind? You know, of course, that a
general confession is only for a very great occasion.

SISTER EUCHARIA

softly

This is a great occasion.

FR. SHERIDAN

Something has been on your mind, Sister, something,
perhaps, you would like to discuss with me first . . .

Try to concentrate

And tell me as your spiritual director.

SISTER EUCHARIA

I am dying, Father, I am dying.
But O because I have prayed incessantly
For all poor mortals lying at death's door,
Absolve my sins, and then remember me
In your own prayers. When you ascend
The altar steps and all the congregation kneels
And after the first Gospel, remember me.

FR. SHERIDAN

kindly

Come, my child. Your mind is disturbed. You are
upset. You have been under some terrible strain. You
need rest and sleep . . .

All, all of us must wait our time

Until God calls us to Himself

SISTER EUCHARIA

I have

Been called.

FR. SHERIDAN

firmly

We must beware

Of spiritual despair.

SISTER EUCHARIA

I have been called.

FR. SHERIDAN

What do you mean?

SISTER EUCHARIA

They have told me so.

They have told me so to-night.

FR. SHERIDAN

What do you mean? Who told you so?

SISTER   EUCHARIA

The voices.

FR. SHERIDAN

What voices are you speaking of?

SISTER   EUCHARIA

Voices

That are in Purgatory.

FR. SHERIDAN

startled

But Sister

Eucharia . . .

SISTER   EUCHARIA

rapidly
Believe me, O believe me
Is not each sacrament an outward sign,
Visible action, plain to all the senses
And yet divided from them by the meaning? . . .

FR. SHERIDAN

interrupting her
Yes, yes, but what about those voices,
Those voices you were speaking of?

SISTER   EUCHARIA

Father,

Can you not say two Masses on a Sunday
And three on All Soul's Day, renew the fast,
The miracle . . . and are you not ordained
To move at day in mysteries of joy
And pain that the poor napkin, we
Embroider in our awe, can hide upon
The altar?
She comes forward rapt
                    I see, I see the impassioned cope!
O shoulder thrust into the tabernacle
At evening time to put God from our reach
And strengthen faith again!
*She turns to him and sees his hand, half-raised in protest,
as it catches the light. She points to it.*
                              Believe me, O
Believe me by this hand that can bestow
Our daily blessing, by this mortal hand

That touched the Sacred Body in the tomb
To-day.

FR. SHERIDAN

withdrawing

Sister, Sister.

SISTER EUCHARIA

suddenly kneeling at his feet. Stage gradually darkens around them so that all light is focused on the two figures:

Bless me, Father,
For I have sinned.

FR. SHERIDAN

Sister, Sister, listen to me.
This is most irregular.
This is not the place for confession.

SISTER EUCHARIA

unheeding

*Confiteor Deo omnipotenti, beatae
Mariae semper*
*Virgini, beato Michaeli Archangelo, beato
Joanni Baptistae, sanctis Apostolis Petro et
Paulo, omnibus sanctis, . . .*
her voice sinks to a murmur, but rises again as she strikes her breast three times
mea culpa, mea culpa, mea maxima culpa.

FR. SHERIDAN

You are overwrought, Sister. Your mind is disturbed . . .

SISTER EUCHARIA

The sins of all my life are here, terrible
As the foresight of God accusing me.
When I was in the world,
A looking-glass could keep me late for Mass
Or send my mind on idle messages,
A holy picture in a book distract
My fancy under eastern arch and palm.
I ruck the linen band and yet my thoughts
Are inattentive . . .

FR. SHERIDAN

I cannot listen.
I cannot now.

SISTER EUCHARIA

I have been disobedient
To my parents, ungrateful for the dowry
They gave me, indifferent at the swinging door.
Last night, thinking that I had never been
Professed, that I was still Elizabeth
O'Connor . . . I hurried from street to street, in coat
And skirt, with high-heeled shoes . . . I saw
A tram, shining with angels, at Harold's Cross
And then I saw the Hospice for the Dying . . .
I stood beneath the iron gate, unveiled,
Vocationless, in all that dreadful dream . . .

FR. SHERIDAN

I cannot give you absolution now.

SISTER EUCHARIA

O let me not be lost.
I repent, I repent, admitting
With all my heart and soul
The mortal sins I have committed.
O let me not be lost.

FR. SHERIDAN

Sister. You misunderstand me. You must try to be
calm and control yourself. A solemn occasion
requires proper preparation.

SISTER EUCHARIA

I repent, I repent.

FR. SHERIDAN

To-morrow, perhaps, when you have examined your
conscience more quietly, I will come here specially
to hear your confession in the chapel and give you
absolution.

SISTER EUCHARIA

faintly
Too late. Too late.
Falls at his feet

FR. SHERIDAN

alarmed
Reverend Mother, Reverend
Mother! Come quickly!
Reverend Mother hurries in followed by Sisters. They bend

*over the prostrate figure of Sister Eucharia, who is now
hidden from our view. Normal lighting.*

REV. MOTHER

coming forward

She's only fainted, Father.

FR. SHERIDAN

Do you think a doctor should be called?

REV. MOTHER

I don't think it's necessary. This sudden weakness
may be the best thing possible for her. She will
have to rest now and take nourishment.

FR. SHERIDAN

I shall call again in the morning after first Mass.

REV. MOTHER

Thank you, Father, for all your trouble and goodness
to-night.

*Sister Agnes comes forward with his hat and gloves. She
leads the way and he follows, obviously with considerable
relief. A pause.*

SISTERS

Reverend Mother!
Look! Look!

*The sisters are grouped at each side and behind chair
supporting Sister Eucharia who is recovering. They have
removed her hood and cape and rolled back the sleeve of
her habit, so that her arms are bared. On her arms are
thick, knotted chains. Her cropped head adds to her
strange appearance.*

SISTERS

Look at the chains!
Look at the chains!
Where did she get them?

A SISTER

She must have found them
In the carthouse.

SISTER

Look at the bruises!
Terrible bruises on each arm.
O the pain she must have suffered!
The pain she has endured!

SISTER ANGELICA
with tears of joy
> Was I not right, Mother?
> She is a saint. She is a saint.

CHORUS OF SISTERS
> Yes. Yes . . . A saint!

Sister Eucharia opens her eyes slowly as if she were still in trance, her head raised, her body seems to become strangely rigid. As if compelled the sisters slowly withdraw. She is now isolated in light and the community is grouped in the surrounding dimness.

CHORUS OF SISTERS
softly, following each gesture and action
> She is getting up.
> She is getting up.
> She cannot see us now.
> All, all is dark
> To her unseeing eyes.
> Angels are supporting her.
> She turns, she turns.
> Angels lead her to the chapel.
> Her feet still know the way.
> Why does she stop?
> Why does she stop?
> Why does she hesitate?
> She is listening.
> She is listening.
> Her soul must wait

almost in a whisper
> For a sign, for a sign
> From God

The chapel bell sounds a deep solemn note

CHORUS
in wonder
> The bell is ringing by itself!
> A miracle! A miracle!

Sister Eucharia hesitates, turns and, as if following each stroke of bell mounts the steps and disappears. There is silence, broken only by a few sobs. The tension becomes intolerable

SISTER GABRIEL

suddenly coming forward
>God help us all, to-night!
>I am afraid, I am afraid that
>Something will happen. I know
>That something will happen.

CHORUS
>We are afraid. We are afraid.

REV. MOTHER

taking control
>We must be calm. This is God's will.

*The light gradually has become normal. Rev. Mother
beckons to Sister Agnes and Sister Stanislaus and gives
them instructions. Sister Angelica comes forward.*

REV. MOTHER

gently, to Sister Angelica
>Not you, Sister.

*Sister Agnes and Sister Stanislaus go up steps swiftly and
silently towards chapel. Once more there is an uneasy
silence.*

CHORUS
>O why are they so long?
>O why are they so long away?

*Rev. Mother motions to sisters for silence. Sister Agnes
and Sister Stanislaus appear again at central doorway.*

BOTH

in broken voices
>Sister Eucharia is dead.

*For a moment there is complete silence followed by a
murmur of consternation and grief. Rev. Mother signs
significantly to the two sisters. They go up the steps
again and turn right. During the subsequent scene they
pass along corridor towards chapel bearing a folded pall.*

REV. MOTHER

motions for silence and comes forward
>Why are you crying? Why are you crying?

She pauses until all are attentive again
>Sister Eucharia is now in Heaven,
>God called her quickly to Himself; she was
>So pure in every act of love,
>Could not delay. The rubbings of this world

Are ignorance of soul and when we have
That lesson off by heart, our daily thought
Is suffering.
                              The repetition, always
The repetition of the truths we know!
And yet we fail each time in practice, fail
In thought, forget, as inattentive children,
And head like a poor duster carries in
Confusion all that has been written plainly
On the blackboard.

slowly
                              This extraordinary night
Something has happened which we do not understand,
Some wonder that our senses have refused
To know. But we believe in humble faith
That God at last has granted to our order
A saint, a saint to stand within His Presence
And plead for us.

A murmur of joy

REV. MOTHER

admonishing
                              No, no, do not rejoice
So soon.
                    Have we not doubted?

CHORUS
                              We have doubted.

REV. MOTHER

Did we not fear?

CHORUS
                    We feared.

REV. MOTHER
                              Our faith was weak.

CHORUS
Our faith was weak.

REV. MOTHER

pointing towards the chapel
    Let us pray.

*Slow action. The Rev. Mother, followed by the nuns in
procession, mounts steps. Sister Angelica is last. Lay sister
enters, right.*

LAY SISTER

cautiously

    Sister! Sister!

Sister Angelica comes down steps.

     LAY SISTER

weeping

   I couldn't help it! I couldn't help it!

    SISTER ANGELICA

  What do you mean?

     LAY SISTER

        Sister, I rang the bell
But it was not my fault, no, not my fault.
I saw the bell rope and it seemed to move . . .
Then something made me put my hand upon
The second knot and something made me ring
The bell. But it was not my fault, no, no,
Truly, for I have not been my own self
To-day.

     SISTER ANGELICA

pausing and then gradually with a smile of inspiration

      This is a lesson for us all.

     LAY SISTER

puzzled

  But Sister . . .

    SISTER ANGELICA

  Because you are humble and always willing,
  God chose you for His will to-night.

*The Litany for the Dead is heard without. The lay sister
looks at Sister Angelica in wonder and alarm, but the
latter takes her arm quietly and both mount the steps.*

CURTAIN

BLACK FAST

A POETIC FARCE

IN ONE ACT

CHARACTERS

In the order of their appearance:

Man Servant	Blanaid Fairnape, his Wife
Steward	Mahan, an Adviser
Girl Servant	Cummian and his Monks
Connal More of Ulster	Romanus and his Monks

Cogitosus

Men and Women of the Household

BLACK FAST

The seventh century controversy over the exact date of Easter had its lighter moments according to the Venerable Bede. The culinary complications in this play were suggested by some pages of his ecclesiastical history. But the episcopal challenge used in the play has been taken from a debate between an Ulster saint and a Munster saint on this vexed subject of Easter observance. The scene is the judgment-hall of Connal More in Ulster. On the right, dais and two chairs of state. Entrances, front, right and left. At the back, through a lofty doorway formed by two transverse curtains, can be seen part of the supper room and the long table. The judgment-hall is partly in shadow; the supper room is cheerful with lighting. A man servant comes in, left, carrying a large basket-dish piled high with apples. He crosses the stage with great care and places the dish in the centre of the table. He puts out his hand to re-arrange the king-apple at the top, then hesitates, as if he were afraid even to touch it. He moves the dish a little, stands back, moves it again, stands back to admire. The light seems to become intensified around those magnificent apples. Pleased with himself, the servant turns to cross the stage. Immediately the dish moves mysteriously along the table and disappears from sight. The steward comes in, right, carrying a small dish. He sees the empty table, lays down the dish on dais and calls after the servant in great excitement.

STEWARD
Where are the apples?
Where are the apples from Armagh?
SERVANT
outside

Upon

The table.
STEWARD
running and bringing him back
Where did you put them?
Where did you put them? Twenty times I told you

To keep your mortal breath from them,
To carry in that dish as if it were
Your soul.
With emotion
                    Frecklings of honey in their shadow!
The last in the winter loft! I polished them
As a special treat for Connal More himself.
My darlings brought the summer back: they bore
The branch away!
desperately
                    Tell me the truth. You let
One fall . . . two . . . three . . . or half a dozen, hid
Their bruises in an overall?
                    SERVANT
                                        I swear
I didn't let a single apple fall.
I put them all on the table.
                    STEWARD
sarcastically, turning and pointing to table
                                        My sweet ones turned
To cookers, peeled, pipped, pied themselves or soured
Into a stew!
                    SERVANT
running to table
                    They're gone!
They're gone!
*Searches, then looks up towards heaven and comes back
in alarm*
                    It is a miracle!
                    STEWARD
Aye, somebody has cut the apron string
And they have tumbled into the next world
That saints may pick them up in Paradise!
Tell that to Connal More when he is asking:
grimly
    'Where are my favourite apples from the sunyards
Of ecclesiastical Armagh?'
                    SERVANT
                                    It is a warning,
A warning from above.
                            Major, I've seen

Strange things before my time that put the fear
Of God in me. Last year I saw a saint
Darken the sky with his stick, crackle a rock
As quickly as a rotten hazel-nut
And put a swollen river back to bed again.
This is a warning, a terrible warning to those
Who break the fast.

STEWARD

mocking

Abstain from apples, twice
A day, before and after . . .

SERVANT

earnestly

You forget
The big joints sitting up before the fire now,
The stirabout soup, the boilers and the rounders
Of crusty ham. Is this the way to keep
The fast?

STEWARD

The seven weeks
Of Lent are passed.

SERVANT

Our mistress says that this is Lent,
According to the scholars from the south.

STEWARD

indignantly

I say that our own clergy ought to know.
They celebrated Easter a month ago.

SERVANT

Major, those scholars must be right.
Heaven is warning us to-night.

STEWARD

excitedly

This house
Has been distracted by religion, late
And early. The Ri says this . . . his wife says that . . .
And everybody quarrels at the grace
Before the fry skips off the fire. The milk
Won't yield, the dashing butter is afraid
To turn. The cooks are scalding their own tears
In suet puddings, they lard the leeks, they skewer

The sausages. Both high and low complain:
' Who put the mutton fat into the pot
The fish was cooking in? ' ' Who saw my ham? '
' Who boiled the cabbage with that sinful bacon? '
The wind of indigestion bangs the door,
And when the salmon smokes upon the grill,
The spiced beef turns to penitential ashes.
Enough of this.
With determination, as an idea occurs to him
                              I'll show you miracles.
Taking up the dish
Here, put this dish of chitterlings
On the table

                              SERVANT
                    . . . and see an angry messenger
From the Almighty snatch it up in smoke, while
Board and joining roar in a single draught
Down to the water butts! Upon my soul,
I won't!

                              STEWARD
              I'll do it, then, myself.
                              SERVANT

edging away

                                        Come back!
              Come back!
*The steward places the dish on the table, walks back with
heavy steps to left exit, then creeps back to the transverse,
bringing the unwilling servant with him. A hand is seen
stretching towards the dish. The steward pounces and
drags forward a girl servant.*
                              STEWARD
                    Here is your miracle!
                              SERVANT

catching her

                                        You think
That you can steal the breath out of my body
And take my living from me while my back
Is turned!

                              STEWARD
                    Where are those apples?
Where are those apples?

GIRL

Let me go!

struggling

ah . . .

let me

Go now!

STEWARD

Hold her tight!

She escapes

SERVANT

discomfited

They learn that double trick
Struggling with stableboys until they snap
Their blessed scapulars.

GIRL

I'll tell
My mistress on you both. She ordered me
To take those apples from the table.

STEWARD

Wait

Until the master hears of that.

GIRL

What right
Has he, my mistress says, to break the fast
And eat those apples for dessert to-night?

STEWARD

The seven weeks of Lent are passed.

GIRL

They're not.

This is a day of total abstinence
According to the scholars from the south.

STEWARD

Can you stand there and have the impudence
To doubt my word before it leaves my mouth
And contradict what our own clergy tell us?

GIRL

My mistress says . . .

STEWARD

My mistress says . . .

Will you deny the Lenten pastoral
In which our Bishop, speaking from the altar,

Denounced all women who have shortened skirt
And petticoat . . .
                    SERVANT
                         . . . till every tuck becomes
A sin.
                    STEWARD
         They listen to new doctrines, he
Declared . . .
                    SERVANT
                         . . . and all respect for modesty
     Is gone.
                    STEWARD
              Where are those apples now?
                    GIRL
saucily

                                             Find out!

They seize her again
     Help! Help!
                    SERVANT
triumphantly
                    I've got a couple of big apples.
                    STEWARD
anxiously
     Be careful with them.
                    GIRL
                    Stop.   Those aren't apples!
*Connal More has come in. At the same time the hall
becomes brighter though the change to normal lighting is
imperceptible.*
                    CONNAL
loudly
     What shameful immorality is this?
Servants retreat respectfully
                    STEWARD
breathlessly
     She took the apples, sir, the apples from Armagh.
                    GIRL
frightened but sullen
     My mistress ordered me.
                    CONNAL
                    I'll see to this

Blanaid Fairnape, his wife, has come in
BLANAID
Yes, Connal,
I told the girl to take them.
CONNAL
dismissing servants and turning to her angrily
What do you mean
By giving orders to your women servants
To steal the courses from my table?
BLANAID
Connal
For three weeks now or more, on every fish-day,
You have deliberately mortified me,
Sitting behind a roast with noisy fellows
Who eat their way into your favour, calling
Your carvers in with swear-words, honeying
The champion's portion, hurrying each mouthful
With toppings of sweet ale. You clap late hours
Together, devouring, drinking, till every hiccough
And story is a shout.
CONNAL
Can anybody say
I do not practise my religion? All
Through Lent, I kept the days of abstinence,
Both black and white. I made my Easter duty
And that is more than you have done. When I
Was fasting, you ate meat. You picked a wing
Of devilled chicken twice upon Ash Wednesday.
You scandalised my cook and made him heat
The grill again.
BLANAID
I said repeatedly
It was an ordinary Wednesday. You
Began the Lent a month too soon.
CONNAL
I tell you
That Easter's come and gone.
BLANAID
This is a fast day.
CONNAL
I say that it is not

BLANAID

It *is* a fast day
And what is more, you think of other ways
To shame me in this house, humiliate
My feelings and distract me from devotions.
You treat me worse than any common woman,
Start quarrelling when we retire to rest,
And in the small hours waken up the baby.

CONNAL

It is your duty to obey me.

BLANAID

                              Not

In Lent.

CONNAL

        That is untrue.

BLANAID

                        Then tell me why
Are weddings never held in the holy season?

CONNAL

I say that Lent is over. Our
Own clergy ought to know. Year in, year out,
Our fathers, our grandfathers, all observed
One date. Am I to resurrect their dust,
Scribble the altar book with this new ink
You have a fancy for?

BLANAID

                    Romanus says
Our clergy are in error, that we should follow
The calendar of Gregory.

CONNAL

                        Put back
The sun a month, melt down the moon for wax
And stick a newer wick in it! I say
These converts are the curse of Ireland.

BLANAID

leaving

                                        Say
Your worst. Romanus and his company
Are coming here to-night and rigid fast
Must be observed while they are present.

CONNAL

calling after her

I

Refuse to fast.

I do not want them here.

BLANAID

at door

Remember what I say now. Rigid fast
Must be observed by everyone to-night.
She goes out, left, leaving Connal speechless with anger.
Mahan, his advisor, comes in, right.

MAHAN

Saint Cummian and his deputation are here

CONNAL

O tell them I am busy.

I cannot see them.

Confusion outside. The Abbot-Bishop, carrying his pastoral
staff, enters rapidly with his monks. They are in white
robes

CUMMIAN

Connal More, I have come
To warn you solemnly and for the last time
That these disturbers, these strangers from the south
Must not be heard in any diocese
Within my jurisdiction. Caillin who called
An angel to his flinty pillow, Gillabocht,
Who heard at night the people talking in heaven,
Were my own ancestors and these poor veins

holding out left hand

More knotted than the roundstone of their graves
Are scored with chalks of pain. But I remember
My uncles and grand-uncles held the crook
In true humility, inheriting
The harvest charities, the unwritten dues
And rentals of this land. Have I not kept
The simple from themselves, firmly denounced
The sins of immorality and pride
In every pastoral? On Easter Sunday
I mentioned from the altar foolish women
Who dig up beauty from the very clay,
Redden their lips, unbar the modest stitch

At neck and ankle that the eye may find
A short-cut to false Edens. Now these strangers,
These unfrocked clergy, who have sent loose tongues
Ahead of them, are coming here to unbury
Our past and, with a wicked doctrine, spread
Dissension through the countryside, upset
Authority of church and state.

CONNAL

What can

I do? You know it was my wife
Invited them.

CUMMIAN

You have authority

And in all lawful matters she must obey
Her husband.

CONNAL

excitedly

Nothing is sacred to her now

Since she became a theologian! Early
And late she quarrels with my fonder wishes.
She sends the servants to remove the dishes
From my own board, expostulates in bed . . .
Father, she makes a mock of matrimony
And scorns the sanctity of family life.

CUMMIAN

This is what happens

When women listen to the Adversary,
Borrow bad tongue and open every satchel.
But Connal More, you have yourself to blame.
I warned you solemnly two months ago
And now I warn you solemnly again
That these disturbers from the south, these strangers
Must not be heard in any diocese
Of mine.

CONNAL

helplessly

What can I say, your Holiness?

My wife insists.

CUMMIAN

Then I

Must do my duty.

to monks

> Put on my cope, please.
>
> CONNAL

What are you going to do?

> CUMMIAN
>
> Place all

This household under interdiction.

> CONNAL

angrily

> You

Would dare to threaten me.

> CUMMIAN

to his coadjutor

> The handbell, quick.
>
> MAHAN

aside

He is in earnest, Con. Remember how
Your second cousin was cursed right, left and centre,
For pitching a psalter into the lake. His shirt
Blew off and, springing from her cheeky bed,
His wife ran to the door and saw him pelting
Along the tree tops. After that, he had
To beg his daily bread from passing crows
That pitied him.

> CONNAL

angrily

> Well, let him do his damnedest!
>
> CUMMIAN

to monks
The breviary!

> MAHAN

aside

> You know that scratching stone
At Inishmore, the one the spotted heifers like
The best.

> CONNAL

uneasily

> I do.
>
> MAHAN
>
> Men say
It is your grandfather, the pagan one,

That he was turned to granite by a saint
When he refused a site for a new church there.
CONNAL

Stop, Cummian!
I give in.
to Mahan
Call up my men.
Bar every door.
*Confused sound of happy voices outside. Blanaid comes
in with Romanus and his monks. The Munster monks are
dressed in blue or black robes*
BLANAID

sweetly
Dearest,
Romanus and his monks have come, hasty
As angels and indeed, much earlier
Than we expected. But their holy news
Can scarcely wait. They carry information
And spiritual benefits for all.
How can we welcome them enough?
ROMANUS

Connal,
We thank you for this hospitality.
Your noble wife has told me in her letters
Of your anxiety to promulgate
The truth in Ulster.
CONNAL

You are welcome. Just now
I was in consultation with my soul-friend,
My spiritual adviser —
quickly presenting him
Most Reverend
Lord Bishop Cummian.
Romanus and Cummian bow stiffly to one another
ROMANUS

to Connal, smiling
I must explain
The meaning of this sudden visitation.
I have obtained, in fact, a dispensation
To travel even on a day of fast.

CUMMIAN

sternly

> This is a feast day, sir

ROMANUS

politely

> I fear
>
> That you are misinformed. It is
> A fast day.

ULSTER MONKS

> No, a feast day . . .

MUNSTER MONKS

> a fast day . . .

ULSTER MONKS

> A feast day . . .

The two parties of monks approach each other and begin to argue excitedly.

CUMMIAN

to his monks

> Come back, have you forgotten all respect?
> All discipline of foot and mouth?
>
> Connal,
> I warned you. Now I will pronounce
> A challenge.

CONNAL

startled

> A challenge?

ALL

echoing

> A challenge!

CUMMIAN

> Yes,
> A challenge to the strangers in our midst.

slowly

> Let two books, one of the old order, another of the
> new, be cast into the fire and let us see which of
> them will escape the flame.

He pauses but there is silence. He continues, with a smile

> Or, if you have no books, let two monks, one of
> yours and another of mine, be shut up in the same
> house. Then let the house be set on fire and we
> shall see which of them will escape the flame.

The Munster monks look at one another anxiously

AN ULSTER MONK

O Father, let me go into the flame
Again to see the terrors of the past,
The trumpet-scattered armies of Canaan,
The iron pits, war prisoners polishing
The brasses of the Moloch . . .

ANOTHER

No, it is

My turn.

ANOTHER

No, mine!

CUMMIAN

in a firm but kindly tone

Be patient

addressing his opponent

If

You fear the flame,

impressively

then, let us go to the grave of a deceased monk and
raise him up to life and he will tell us which order
we ought to observe in the celebration of Easter.

CONNAL

good-humouredly

That is a sporting proposition. I
Will gamble on my Battle Book, Romanus,
Or if you wish, wager my capuchin
Will not be fried before his time.

ROMANUS

quietly

What

Is the name of the little hill we passed
Above the holy well?

BLANAID

Slieve Corry.

ROMANUS

Thank you,

Lady.

I have no doubt that, Heaven willing,
Cummian could rock that hillside with his staff,
Such is his holiness, his practical
Renown. So how could I, a simple schoolman,

A humble servant of the Lord, compete
With him in wonder-working? Rather let us
Discuss the matter quietly. Connal,
Your judgment is respected far and wide.
Your word is law. Attend each argument.
Detect each fallacy. We are your books.
Decide among us like that Emperor,
The famous Constantine, and so restore
The faithful to one service.

CONNAL

flattered, consulting his wife

                                        I agree.
And furthermore I am prepared to stake
My supper on the scholarship of Ulster.
Will you support me, Cummian?
*The Abbot-Bishop hesitates, consults senior monks, yields
to their urgings.*

CUMMIAN

                    I will.

CONNAL

Then choose your two word-champions.

ROMANUS

                                        I, myself,
Will speak.

CUMMIAN

consulting seniors

                                        We choose
Our classic scholar, Cogitosus.

OTHERS

                    Yes,
Yes, Cogitosus.

CONNAL

briskly, giving orders

                                Set the supper.
                                        Lay places
For all.
            Ignorant fish and joint must come
To trial.
*With some ceremony, Connal More and his wife take
their places on the dais. Men and women of the house-
hold assemble. The monks group themselves, left, right.*

*Trumpets outside. During this scene servants place dishes
on table for supper.*
                          CONNAL
            The conference may now begin.
    We call on Cogitosus.
*Monks bring forward Cogitosus, a tall, lean man, slightly
greying around the tonsure and obviously absent-minded.
He begins to speak, as if he were unconscious of his sur-
roundings and lived in the spacious past which he evokes
but gradually his voice changes and quickens as he be-
comes aware of the suave opponent facing him.*
                         COGITOSUS
                    White-robed Patric
Preached to our people by the lake-shores, bright
With baptism and when the branch at evening
Became a tent and berries seemed larger than
The birds that pick them now, he sat among
His new disciples, listening with a smile
To ancient stories of Oisin, but heard
None greater than his own.
                              The glens sprang up
With gospelling until the faith had come
To rest. How often in her old age, Brigid,
Herdswoman of heaven, gazed across her plain
In happiness: for praise found residence
In gold that ran the river, mortar made
With milk. The churchmen called on architects
To marry broad and slender, take by sleight
The crooked from the straight. O not from plan
Or parchment but by the holy rule of thumb
The tower was capped, the arch was sprung!
                                        Who cupped
The inner sacrament with scope of chasings
That angels had foreseen? Who multiplied
The letterings of books? Go ask the bell-ringers
Of Cluanbeg, eye-straining copyists
Beyond the Shannon reed-beds. Ask the child—
Who hides the night-spark on the hearth? Who makes
The glad sun dance on Easter morning? Simple
Or wise will tell you all. For we maintain
The gospel truth that the Evangelist,

John o' the Holy Bosom, propagated
Among the deacons and the presbyters
Of Asia Minor.
A murmur of admiration from the northern monks
               And shall we extinguish
The Pentecostal fire, huddle together
Within a lower story, shaken by street-noise
Of cities, ancient in their wickedness,
Where countryfolk lose faith?
             ROMANUS
                        Will you deny
What all men practise now in Rome? In Gaul?
In Greece? . . . Dispute in Antioch? . . . Or come
Again to Carthage? In the Libyan desert —
Where noon is falsifying, the very plants
Stuckful o' pins and needles — contemplatives
Pick out the opposites of thought, distinguish
The substance from reality. The truth
Is voiced in solitude, in Lower Egypt,
In Alexandria. Your nettled hermits
Assume, no doubt, that God Almighty rests
On the Old Law. Borrow these eyes that saw
Last year the wonders of the New. Beyond
The isle of Golden John, our pilgrim ship
Was stopped by darkness on Good Friday. All
Could see the alp that opens into flame
At the Third Hour. Believe me, I have sponged
From this poor body, this passing dust, the pock
Of cinders flying from the lower regions
Where the lost souls are tortured.
murmurs of astonishment

             BLANAID
                     And you saw
The wonders of the Holy Land, too?
             ROMANUS
                  Lady,
I did, for I was in Jerusalem
At the last annual fair. Crowds basketed
The Gate of David, stalls were everywhere,
The cattle backed against the shuttered sills,
The prices rose and fell. And, saving your presence,

Those streets are never staled with donkey dung
Or camel drench, for when the fair is over —
A sudden clap of cloud comes down to cleanse
The cobbles. I sheltered from that miracle,
I heard it pass the arches of a bridge,
Roar from the rocky gutters, vanish down
The valley of Jehosophat.

                    COGITOSUS

                                Come

To your point.

                    CONNAL

intervening

                    This is most interesting.
And did you see Mount Olivet?

                    ROMANUS

                                I did.

And Brother Diuma was with me.

indicating a monk

                                We climbed
The rocky pathway to the last basilica
Of all. We saw the sacred circle of air
No roofing stone can vault. We stood in fear
And trembling there for the gigantic lamp
Swung back, the pulleys creaked and we ran with
    others
To pray in the portico, cried out and our sleeves
Were plucked apart by the miraculous blast
That passes on the Night of the Ascension.
And many other things I saw, showing
The active Hand of God . . .

                                But who will dare
To contradict what is decreed by councils,
Deny what is believed by all the faithful
From Palestine to Rome?

                    COGITOSUS

drily

                                We have a saying
That those who go to Rome might well have stayed
At home.

                    ULSTER MONKS

excitedly

And why did Patric bring to Ireland
The relics of the apostles?
                    The bones
Of Stephen . . .
                Martin . . .
                        and the other martyrs?
Cummian silences them with a gesture
                    ROMANUS
                        Will you deny
That Peter, preaching in the capital,
Reckoned his candle from the waxing moon
Upon the fifteenth night, the seventeenth,
The twenty-first, according as the Lord's Day
Occurred?

                    COGITOSUS
            I say that John began
His midnight fast upon the fourteenth moon
But did not calculate the Easter date
Beyond the twentieth. Will you admit
That he ignored the Lord's Day in that sum?
                    ROMANUS
Of course.

                    COGITOSUS
            And yet he was the favourite
Disciple?

                    ROMANUS
                Granted but he paid respect
To the Mosaic Law. And what of Paul?
Did he not practise circumcision, shave
His head at Corinth, go up to the temple
With gum and spice for fear of giving scandal?
                    COGITOSUS
A clever quibble, friend.
But I will stand within your camp. Do you
Approve of Anatolius?
                    ROMANUS
                Truly,
A learned father . . .
                    COGITOSUS
                    most respected?

ROMANUS

yes . . .

COGITOSUS

Completely orthodox?

ROMANUS

Agreed.

COGITOSUS

And yet,
He calculated Easter in his writings,
As we do here.

ROMANUS

I have you by the horn
Of that dilemma, for he reckoned twice
According to the old Egyptian figures,
Acknowledging the fourteenth risen moon
To be the fifteenth in our calendar.

MUNSTER MONKS

He tosses on our bull!

He is impaled!

COGITOSUS

Repudiate my premises.

ROMANUS

Will you
Deny the cycle of Vitruvius
By which we reckon from the Flood?

COGITOSUS

scornfully

Unflatten
The earth, revolve it round the sun! Unfix
Creation's date!

ROMANUS

Not only that, I hear
You sometimes reckon from the thirteenth moon . . .

COGITOSUS

That is untrue . . .

ROMANUS

. . . forget the Older Law,
Despise the New.

ULSTER MONKS

That is untrue.

We count

The fourteenth to the twentieth moon.
MUNSTER MONKS

> We count

The fifteenth to the twenty-first.
COGITOSUS

> I say

That Ambrose, Cyril . . .
ROMANUS

> Dionysius

Exiguus . . .
OMNES

the fourteenth . . .

> fifteenth moon

The twentieth . . .

> the twenty-first moon . . .

Complete confusion and noise of argument
CONNAL

rising and clapping his hands

> Order!

Order!
> This house
Has been distracted by religion, night
And day. I cannot sleep in any comfort
Until this matter has been solved. I will
Acknowledge, Brethren, that accuracy
Is everything. It keeps the soul and body
In space and time, directs the mineral
And plant, upholds the double heavens. I
Respect theology. I do not think
That we can make the soul into a parcel
And tie it up with simple heart-string, save
Ourselves by common ignorance.

suddenly addressing the auditorium

> But some

Among our audience grow restless . . .

a loud cough from auditorium

> . . . sound

The chest as if they were at church.

> So now

Let Cogitosus give his final speech,
Our guest reply — and let them both be brief.

Why need I fast in public here? And if
I should decide this is a feast day
indicating with some relish, the laden supper table
                                        — must

The mutton roast be spoiled?
                    COGITOSUS
                                I have but little more
To say. Three hund d years have come and gone
Since Columcille di . / the breath of life,
Moving among the mysteries of earth
As we do now, the patron of our hopes
Beyond the grave. Three hundred years, Brethren,
We have observed his strict monastic rule
Within the north. His word of mouth maintains
The islands where he sang the matins. Nettle
And briar remember how he lived. Shall we
Forget when the poor husbandmen can tell
His blessing on the buckle strap and women
His prayer that protects the churn? The books
Of his biographers attest in full
The wonders he performed. The night he died
The coasts were shining, invisible messengers
Were heard at every crossroad. Shall we say
This man who talked with angels in his sleep
And penned the painful gospel in his cell
Too near to heaven, could not calculate
Exactly from the changes of the moon
The true date of the Resurrection?
                    ROMANUS
                                Many
Who have worked wonders, Cogitosus, shown up
The vanities of air, will not be recognised
Upon the Judgment Day. I have no doubt
This elder you praise,
                    this . . .
one of his monks prompts
                                Columcille . . .
                                    thank you . . .

This holy Columcille lived in truth
According to the knowledge of his time

But fear you have not proved your point. I will
Explain once more.

CUMMIAN

He has insulted us!

ULSTER MONKS

Attacked our faith!

CUMMIAN

We will not stay
Another minute. Connal More, I warned you.
And now I place your household out of bounds.
Come, brethren.

He walks out, followed by his monks. General confusion

CONNAL

gloomily

This is the frypan!

BLANAID

Give
The verdict for Romanus now.

CONNAL

listening, in alarm

What's that?

What's that?

*A distant rumbling is heard. Lights dim, complete black-
out in supper room, nearer rumbling of thunder, clattering
of dishes and plates. Lights up. The table is seen to be
completely bare.*

ROMANUS

A miracle!

OMNES

in awe

A miracle!

BLANAID

The joints have disappeared.

CONNAL

The very plates are gone.

ROMANUS

Yes, they are gone,

Connal.

solemnly pointing upward

This is a warning from above,
A terrible warning to all unbelievers

Who scorn our holy fast. Proclaim the truth
Before we kneel in prayer.

CONNAL

rising

I here proclaim

This is . . .
distant rumble

BLANAID

prompting

a fast day.

MAHAN

rushing in

Stop! It is a feast day.

CONNAL

What do you mean?

MAHAN
Another miracle!

CONNAL

Another miracle?

MAHAN
I saw with my own eyes
Your dishes steaming through the air!

CONNAL

amazed

Where did

They go?

MAHAN
Down to the monastery.
general astonishment

Our monks

Are laying them on their table.

ROMANUS

A sign
Of Evil. Powers of wickedness have come.
Let us all pray.

CONNAL

indignantly

Why should the Devil dish up
Late dinner for my venerable Bishop?
I say that you are wrong.

BLANAID

Were it my last day
On earth I would maintain it is a fast day.

CONNAL

turning to her
You mean a feast day

BLANAID

. . . a fast day . . .

CONNAL

a feast day . . .

BLANAID

. . . a fast day . . .

The wrangling voices of Connal and his wife are lost in the general confusion and noise of argument as the curtain falls.

THE END

THE KISS

A LIGHT COMEDY IN ONE ACT

AFTER THE FRENCH
OF
THÉODORE DE BANVILLE

CHARACTERS

PIERROT
UIRGEAL

Time: A sunny morning last May.

Place: A wood near Clonsilla.

THE KISS

As the curtain rises, the wood is still in shadow. But the
morning sunlight has reached one spot, just in front of
the mossy trunk of a fallen tree, left, downstage. Imagine
birds are twittering but cease as Uirgeal comes on, right.
She is wrapped in a ragged cloak with a heavy hood and
drags herself forward as if under the weight of centuries.

UIRGEAL

Why must I hobble, shudder with old age,
Wrinkle the raindropped pools in tiny rage,
Bedraggle the spine of the bramble rose,
When by the very whiteness of the clothes
He wears and their big buttons, I can tell
Pierrot will surely break the wicked spell
That keeps me old? What is the only cure
For me? The first kiss of his life, so pure
He has not dared to dream of that first kiss,
And if I steal what he will never miss
Until he looks for it, no tongue will blame
My meanness, so I can escape from shame
And anguish. I have only half an hour
Or less to save my being from the power
Of evil. First touch of mortal innocence
Belongs, all say, to spirit, not to sense.
I'll catch him by that sweetness of the heart
Before his senses have had time to start
From me. But will he pity my distress?
How can his young eye know my ugliness
Is only skin deep?
Peering round
                Now I see him run
Between the ivy shadows and the sun.
  I'm frightened, frightened to the wings.
going right
                              I'll hide
A moment, watch those lips that have not lied
  As yet to any girl.
She conceals herself among the trees. Pierrot enters,

carrying a luncheon basket. He is young and ingenuous
PIERROT

to audience
What's in the basket?
That is your question and before you ask it,
I'll answer everything. But let me take
My luncheon out.
Suiting rhythmic action to word
First, an old-fashioned cake.
What are the specks? You've guessed it — caraway.
Some muscatels,
a cake knife,
corkscrew, —
— Pray
Excuse the tissue paper and the twine —
Together with a bottle of light wine,
For when I drink, I love to see the grape.
A napkin —
I can wrap it round the nape.
Two little glasses, one inside the other
For company.
You ask why do I bother?
Well, anything can happen in a wood
Like this.
*Uirgeal appears from behind a tree, but is unseen by
Pierrot*
UIRGEAL

aside
My Pierrot, when dare I intrude?
PIERROT
I'll pick a nosegay, while the dew is wet
On lily o' the valley, violet.
UIRGEAL

aside
My favourites!
PIERROT
But first, in case of theft,
I'll hide my luncheon basket in a cleft
Among the oaks or — safe as sound — under
A rock that has been shattered by the thunder.
He runs out, left

UIRGEAL

appearing for a moment
    I must be brave, and take him by surprise.
Pierrot comes back, brushing his sleeve

PIERROT

    This is a spot for laughter not for sighs.
    Had I a sweet companion, dark or blonde,
    I would not care if only she were fond
    Of me and very brave and when she flung
    Her arms around me I would hold my tongue,
    Though I could gossip on this heavenly morning
    With the devil himself, in spite of every warning.
Catching sight of Uirgeal stooping on right
    I see a country girl beside that stream,
    Her cheeks, no doubt, beetroot and double cream.
    She stoops to gather twigs. When she turns round,
    I may be disappointed.
                H'mm.
                  Confound
    It! Why, her nose is tippling with her chin,
    The poor old creature — and her ancient skin
    Is tougher than a taproot.
Uirgeal approaches slowly
                I must talk
    To her. She may be ill, can scarcely walk,
    A centenarian. She must have known
    The years of peace. I wish I were alone
    Eating my seed-cake, cracking my bottle of wine,
    For who could call that one a Columbine?
As Uirgeal totters, Pierrot runs to her

PIERROT

Pray, madam, take my arm.

UIRGEAL

               You are polite,
    Sir, I am faint. I have not had a bite
    Of food for days.

PIERROT

           Come, Madam, you must rest
    Upon this moss. I'll bring you cake, fruit, best
    Of all, a glass of wine.
He runs off

UIRGEAL
                    His kiss is mine.
Pierrot returns with basket and busies himself
                              PIERROT
        Now eat and drink,
                            I'll sit upon the grass,
        Elbow the early sun and take a glass
        With you.
A pause
Making conversation
                  This wine is not so bad.
                                        Another slice
        Of seed-cake?
                              UIRGEAL
                        No, thank you.
                              PIERROT
                                  Weather has been nice.
Uirgeal nods
        I hope that you are better now.
                              UIRGEAL
                                        I feel
        The centuries are going back. I reel
        With hope since I have had some food to eat.
        Dear child, how fortunate it was to meet
        You in the sunshine. Picnics are so few
        Now.
                What's your name?
                              PIERROT
                              Pierrot.
                              UIRGEAL
                                        What do you do
        For a living?
                              PIERROT
getting up
                        Nothing much, I fear, delight
        In momentary fancies, dress in white.
                              UIRGEAL
        May-blossom in the hedge! Yes, white is pretty
        And suits the country better than the city,
        My Pierrot.

PIERROT

shyly

White looks well on me, I think.
Uirgeal sways as she rises to her feet
But what is wrong? You're faint. More wine.
Please drink
It.

UIRGEAL

No. No. I am trembling. I am chill,
But there is something that can save me still,
Hobbling into the shadows
Something that I am ashamed to ask of you.

PIERROT

puzzled but polite
If I have got it, it is yours.

UIRGEAL

I knew
That you would save me.

PIERROT

But what is it? Tell
Me, have I got it?

UIRGEAL

solemnly

Swear by book and bell
To give it to me first.

PIERROT

gallantly

Madam, I bare
My head to Heaven. May I go in black
And all salute the serge, if I take back
My word. But tell me, is it far or near?
I'll race your wish and bring it to you here.
The electric clock upon my mantlepiece?
It's yours. A gigue from Italy or Greece?
I'll dance it. Sign a cheque . . . without a blot?
Snatch the last sovereign from the melting pot?

UIRGEAL

I only want a moment. Swear to give it.

PIERROT

It's yours, although I never can relive it.

By my own sister, the snow, and my brother, the
                                                         swan,
I shall be happier when it is gone!
                              UIRGEAL
clutching him
     Then give it to me quick.
                         PIERROT
                                   How?
                         UIRGEAL
                                        In a kiss.
                         PIERROT
withdrawing, aside
     Her eye is catching fire ... her tongue's a-hiss.
                         UIRGEAL
pleading
     What only takes a moment will not hurt you.
                         PIERROT
coming downstage, to himself
     This strange old woman has alarmed my virtue.
     My heart is jumping. I can feel it dash,
     (A frightened swallow at the window sash).
     Must my first joy be broken on the wing?
     Disgust unsparkle the engagement ring?
     But no, I must be kind as I am pure
     And this good deed will help me to endure
     What's horrible. Horatio held a span
     Across the Tiber. Am I not a man
     And why should I be so afraid of her?
     Scævola, scorning agonies of fire,
     Branded his own right hand. Did Theseus blench
     When he went down to Hell for all the stench
     Of sulphur?
                         UIRGEAL
calling
                         Dear.
                         PIERROT
aside, wavering over his oath
                                   Did heaven hear me swear?
                         UIRGEAL
     Dearest.

PIERROT

without turning
  What?

UIRGEAL
  Kiss me.
PIERROT
  I . . . I . . .
UIRGEAL

Kiss me.

PIERROT
running to her, with sudden determination

There!
*The moment he kisses her, the stage becomes fully lit
and Uirgeal is transformed into a young girl. Still masked,
she appears as the ideal Columbine of his thoughts. Pierrot
is overcome with wonder and delight*

PIERROT
  Heaven and earth! Is there a catechism
  Of kissing? Are the gay tints in the prism
  Pure science or the lingerie of light?
  Were our First Arts and peaceful Ovid right?
  Can lap of water, flame, trees, money, snore
  Of bull, conceal the shape that we adore?
  And do we wake or dream, when we lie down?
  Love is a proper, though a common noun,
  So let *me* be the gentle verb to *live*
  And rule *you* in the sweet accusative.
  Plural or singular, can I decline
  Your loveliness, if you are Columbine?
UIRGEAL
  No. No. I am a creature of the air
  Light as your syllables. Why should I care
  Whether you see me only in the shape
  Of Columbine or not? I can escape —
  A poet loved me once when he was young
  And foolish. He spent half his time among
  The woods with me. In fact we were engaged.
  But he grew famous and the more he aged,
  He dealt in rags and bones, in dirty delph,
  Then seized and tried to make me like himself.
  I am most grateful, Pierrot, for you gave me

Quite willingly the one thing that could save me
From fate.

PIERROT

But is there something else you need?

UIRGEAL

No. Thank you. Thank you very much indeed.
leaving
And now, goodbye.

PIERROT

calling after her

Madam, you've dropped a glove,

I think.

UIRGEAL

turning

What do you mean?

PIERROT

I am in love

With light of hand.

UIRGEAL

I do not understand.

PIERROT

sarcastically

All property is sacred in this land.
When patriots can pick the public purse
But not the private pocket, what is worse
Than petty larceny? To rob mere pence
And not a bank increases the offence.
If company directors are promoted
For fraudulence and deputies have voted
Large pensions for possession of a rifle.
It is indictable to steal a trifle.
Your takings are too modest, Madam . . . Miss . . .

UIRGEAL

indignantly

In that case, I will give you back your kiss.

PIERROT

One kiss to set my heart and mind at rest!
Lady, however business men invest
Some fraction of their total, they insist
On quick returns. Would the industrialist
Compete, when he can have monopoly

Of tariffs and unship the Irish sea?
The poor ratepayers groan, are apprehensive?
Dam every river, make their light expensive!
Charity fund and social service bless
Obedient rollers of the printing press
Until the Constitution shakes with laughter.
What did I say? This country makes me dafter
Than my own heart. I touch a floating mine.

UIRGEAL

What do you want?

PIERROT

All, all, my Columbine.

UIRGEAL

If love were fancy, given for the asking
How could I hope to please you?

PIERROT

By unmasking.

UIRGEAL

You want too much.

PIERROT

And what do you suppose is
The reason of your own metempsychosis?
If one plain kiss return you to the sky,
Dare we in one another's arms be shy?
Whisper to me of all that whiteness none
Have been but airmen, flying past the sun
Through icicles, before the lever drops
The high explosive, whiteness that never stops,
Whiteness from which the moon is shining back,
Although the clouded skies we know — are black
With horror.

UIRGEAL

In a happier, peaceful time
We'll talk of love.

PIERROT

Say I were past my prime,
Grown old, what kiss could make a younger man
Of me? Let us be happy while we can,
Wander among the woods, do what we please.
The sun is most discreet among these trees
And never goes too far lest hidden flowers,

That show their paleness at unearthly hours
And fear the day, might come to any harm.
So be my Columbine and take my arm,
Where none can see us, you shall pay that debt
With lily o' the valley, violet.

                              UIRGEAL
moved
    I think you love me, Pierrot.

                              PIERROT
                                             Dare I tell
How much I do?

                              UIRGEAL
                              Let us be sensible.

                              PIERROT
Of course.

                              UIRGEAL
                    What is my nature, Pierrot? Light
And innocence, perhaps love at first sight.
But mortal longings are the deathward flight
Of midges towards the dusk — and must I sigh
For transitory pleasures, learn to die
When all my sisters are content to be?
Only the adolescent mind can see
By that forgotten faith men dare not name
Since they inherit consciousness of shame.
Pierrot, those first impressions cannot last,
This blazing universe goes much too fast
And men exchange so soon the startling presence
Of all the heavenly bodies for sad lessons
In dualism.

                              PIERROT
                    Spiritual change
Is more important. Do you fear the strange?
Despise the marvellous experience.
Of life upon this earth, spirit and sense?
You were engaged once. Love can bring all nearer
The farther that it seems and men hold dearer
What they must lose too quickly.

                              UIRGEAL
                    Though you tempt
Me, Pierrot, with your thoughts, I am exempt.

PIERROT

Not from my love. This fire-clay world's not yet
A cinder track.

UIRGEAL

But, Pierrot, you forget
One thing.

PIERROT

What is it? Let me know the worst.

UIRGEAL

Morality. We must be married first,
If I am to be yours.

PIERROT

Then be my wife.

UIRGEAL

You really mean it?

PIERROT

Darling, share my life.

UIRGEAL

pleased

That would be very charming, Pierrot.

PIERROT

I would
Purchase a caravan of painted plywood,
All weather white, with cupboard, pantry, shelves,
A tiny sitting-room just for ourselves.
With innocent amusements we would pass
The summer, chaining daisies in the grass.

UIRGEAL

I'd wash your white clothes by a river's edge
And hang your pantaloons —

PIERROT

upon a hedge?

UIRGEAL

I would not send them to a common laundry.

PIERROT

They'd dance in sun there. Could my brother swan
dry
His wings as quickly?

UIRGEAL

We would both be white —

PIERROT

As our reflections —

UIRGEAL
white as the distant sight

Of snow —

PIERROT
in April —

UIRGEAL
white as avalanches

That veil the Alps.

PIERROT
At midnight, barely conscious
With pleasure, dream how all that whiteness stole
Around the globe once —

UIRGEAL
lingers at the Pole —

PIERROT
And on the heads of the Academicians,

UIRGEAL

In Paris,

PIERROT
London,

UIRGEAL
make as quick decisions.

PIERROT

And have a villa,

UIRGEAL
vegetables,

PIERROT
fence.

UIRGEAL

Large family —

PIERROT
regardless of expense.

UIRGEAL

A gardenful of columbines

PIERROT
— and pierrots.

UIRGEAL

We'd teach them Irish.

PIERROT

Tell them of the heroes —

UIRGEAL

Of Easter Week.

PIERROT

My heart is beating fast.
Say, say you love me.

UIRGEAL

Yes, I do.

PIERROT

At last!
We are as good as married, darling. Kiss
Me.

UIRGEAL

withdrawing

But there must be something more than this?

PIERROT

You mean?

UIRGEAL

O nothing in a wrong or sly sense.
Something, I think, they call a special licence.

PIERROT

I have a fountain pen, if it will write.
produces one and shakes it
It does.
takes out a small diary and starts to scribble on a page
Our marriage lines in black and white.

UIRGEAL

Not that. Some person in a domino
Performs the marriage service, people throw
Confetti at us afterwards and drink
Our health in noisy glasses.

PIERROT

Let me think.

going aside

Is this a question of Ne Temere?
Mixed marriages with the ephemerae
So serious, when those who live on air
Can find the finches nesting everywhere?

coming back

Dear, in these woods where strangers do not stray

Only the birds can give a bride away.
The blackbird is their senior. He will bless
Our happy union if you murmur ' yes '!
                    UIRGEAL
But is that ceremony recognised?
                    PIERROT
Of course, it is, dear; no one is surprised
By what can happen nowadays.
eagerly

                                        Consent!
                    UIRGEAL
        I do.

                            Then let us marry —
aside   as in Lent!
he leads her to the tree trunk, goes down on one knee
Dear, if in fancy I have made too free,
Forgot the long wars of the apple tree,
What harm have hasty lovers ever done
Who only want to be alone with one
Another? Has not every young man tried
To find the woman taken from his side?
                    UIRGEAL
You speak so strangely, Pierrot.
                    PIERROT
jumping up
                                    I will dare.
To call our witnesses out of the air.
We imagine we hear the singing of birds
They've come already.
                    UIRGEAL
                        I can hear the dotes!
                    PIERROT
They bob, flip, hop it.
                    UIRGEAL
                            Dash off little notes.
                    PIERROT
Congratulate us on our private wedding.
                    UIRGEAL
alarmed
But what has happened to me?

PIERROT

You are shedding
A tear for the first time. Take off your mask
That I may catch it.

UIRGEAL

Pierrot, do not ask
So soon. I only hear finch, sparrow, linnet.

PIERROT

The blackbird will be here at any minute.
Look! Wagtail, pipit, yellowhammer, perch
On branches. Show me all your beauty.

UIRGEAL

Search
The wood first, Pierrot. Somebody might pass.

PIERROT

The wood is empty.

UIRGEAL

Try the meadow grass.

PIERROT

aside

But can I dare to let her out of sight?

UIRGEAL

Go. Go.
Pierrot runs off
Alone, unmasking
I wonder am I doing right
To marry him? It is no harm to flirt in
The sunshine for a while. But am I certain
I love him? Must I weep . . . weep . . . come to earth?
How can I tell the facts of life are worth
Acquiring? I must weigh the pros and cons.
For if his nearest relatives are swans
He may be flighty, have too much in common
With them. What shall I do? They say a woman
Can never be too careful. I refuse
To give my hand. No. No. I love him, choose
All the responsibilities of life.
Yes. Yes. I love him. I will be his wife.
Quickly masking herself as she hears his step

PIERROT

returning
We're quite alone, dear. Come into the shade.
A sound of distant spirit voices

UIRGEAL

alarmed
What's that?

PIERROT
The blackbird. Do not be afraid.

UIRGEAL
No. No. I hear my sisters calling.

PIERROT
Stay
With me. I love you, Columbine.

UIRGEAL
wavering   Delay
Is dangerous.

PIERROT
I will not let you go.

SPIRIT VOICES
off
Uirgeal!
Uirgeal!

UIRGEAL
They call me.

PIERROT
Now I know
Your name, Uirgeal, I love you more.

UIRGEAL
They miss
Me.
running to him with a sob
Darling, I must give you back your kiss.
*She kisses him quickly and as she disappears through the
wood turns for a moment*
Goodbye.

PIERROT
running and looking up
She's gone.
craning
She's smaller than a fly
Now.

Coming downstage
>   Gone . . . and that first tear was scarcely dry.
desperately
>   I will destroy myself with such a stir
>   And upshot, she will know I follow her.
knowingly
>   There's bound to be an ammunition dump
>   Within this wood. My friends will hear the bump
>   And guess at last that Pierrot is no more.
considering
>   But firearms are illegal now. A door
>   Should shut more quietly.
Looking round and selecting a tree
>   and so I'll choose
>   That tree instead, if I can find a noose,
>   Cast off my holiday clothes for the circus clown
>   Who tickles village better now than town.
sadly
>   But who will wash them by the river's edge,
>   Hang them unseen upon as white a hedge
>   In Maytime?
firmly
>   No. I'll keep them, brace the sleeves
>   Into a lover's knot among the leaves.
begins to take off his jacket, then pauses reflectively
>   But let me think. This may be serious
>   For when the brainpan is delirious,
>   The mind repents of all that it has been.
>   Man finds no comedy in the unseen.
>   What shall I do?
slowly
>   To be or not to be? . . .
Takes out a large claspknife and feels the blade.
>   This pocket knife is stronger than a tree,
>   And since all human shadows fear the dark,
with a sudden smile of relief
>   I'll carve her name and mine upon the bark.
*He goes over to the tree and begins to trace and cut the
initial letter U as the curtain slowly descends.*

THE END

AS THE CROW FLIES

A LYRIC PLAY FOR THE AIR

DRAMATIS PERSONAE:

Father Virgilius

Brother Manus

Brother Aengus

The Eagle of Knock

Her Eaglets

The Crow of Achill

The Stag of Leiterlone

The Blackbird of Derrycairn

The Salmon of Assaroe

AS THE CROW FLIES

SCENE ONE

An evening in late summer, on the Shannon, in the seventh century. A boat, in which there are two monks, is moored in a creek.

MANUS
softly
    Father Virgilius . . .
                      Father
    Virgilius . . .

VIRGILIUS
waking
    God bless us all. I must
    Have nodded again. My head was in the sun . . .
    My eyes are gilded by it.
happily
                      Brother Manus
    The best of spirits came upon this journey
    With us to-day.

MANUS
                Father, I am uneasy
    Now. We've been resting on our oars too long
    And Brother Aengus is still away.

VIRGILIUS
                        We've time
    Enough upon our hands. We can be back
    At Clonmacnoise before the midnight bell rings.

MANUS
    But you don't know the Shannon, Father. This boat-load
    Of rushes will be heavier than our faults
    The more we pull against it. Brother Aengus
    Should never have gone into the forest
    Alone.

VIRGILIUS
    God will protect him.

MANUS

obstinately
> But why did you let him go?

VIRGILIUS
>   Because he is young.
> And the young see but the eye in every bolt
> That keeps them from the meaning of Creation.
> Yes, they want all that breathing space
> Before bird, beast or reptile had been named
> And pain started the first rib.

MANUS
>   But, Father . . .

VIRGILIUS

good-humouredly
> I know too well what you are going to say,
> Manus. For twenty years you've chased the raindrops
> From Clonmacnoise with crossbeam, patches, gluepot.
> Whenever we dare to sneeze, you give a nail
> Another rap and heal us with your hammer;
> And if our old bones creak too much in church,
> You hurry up the rungs to mend a joint
> Or clap a comfortable cap of stone
> About our chilling pates.

MANUS

pleased, puzzled
>   That's true.
> But why did Father Abbot send me out
> To cut him rushes in the wilderness?

VIRGILIUS

quietly
> Perhaps he sent you here
> To learn the mercy of the elements.

MANUS

> Well, maybe so.

VIRGILIUS
>   Do take
> Another look at those gigantic reeds.
> Whoever saw green toppings half their size
> On any roof? They might have been cut down
> To floor the heel of Finn. The very Salmon
> Of Knowledge mentioned by the storytellers
> Could scarcely jump their height.

MANUS

                                    I do not like
The look of them. They are unlucky, Father.
                    VIRGILIUS
Well, then, we'll bless them in the shed
And sacristan will dip a few for me
When he has fired our own fascisculi.
Good soul, he hates to see me annotating
A manuscript at night. But they will strengthen
My hand and dry my ageing eyes . . .
                    MANUS

                                        Pardon
Me, Father. I see big clouds upon the hob.
We should be gone.
                    VIRGILIUS
                    Call Aengus. He is sure
To hear you from that rock there.
                    MANUS

                                    I will.

at a distance

                                    Aengus!

Aengus!

                    There's no reply.
                    VIRGILIUS

                                    Call, call again.
                    MANUS

Aengus!
                    Aengus!
a far shout

                    MANUS
coming back

                    Thank Heaven he is safe.
But why is he waving to us? Something
Has happened.
running steps
                    What is it, Aengus?
                    AENGUS

breathlessly

                                    The cave, Father

    Virgilius, the cave!

MANUS

impatiently

What cave?
VIRGILIUS

Brother
Has been uneasy at your absence.
AENGUS

Forgive
Me, Father, if I have been late.
The forest
Was dark as Doom. I groped from age to age,
Among the knottings of each century;
And then my eyes were opened
So suddenly by Heaven, it seemed their dust
Had risen and this everlasting body
Was glorified. Humbly I prayed, I ran . . .
My habit tripped me on a chiselled step
Beneath a cliff . . . and I saw the cave.
Father, a hermit must have lived there all
His life, it was so full of thought.
I could not catch up on my breath again
Because I was too happy with my spirit
In that heart-beaten solitude.
MANUS

drily

You heard
No stir of beetle, bird or beast?
AENGUS

No stir.
No stir.
MANUS

I told you, Father. Every creature
Is hiding from the sky.
VIRGILIUS

Brother
Is troubled, Aengus . . . fears a storm. So let
Us go.
They get into the boat
AENGUS

I'll take the other oar.

MANUS

We must be cautious with that heavy load
Of cuttings.
Are you ready?

AENGUS

Yes, yes. I
Am ready.

MANUS

Pull now . . .
One . . two
One . . two
One . . two.

*The voices and splash of oars recede and only the quiet
river is heard. Gradually the dipping of the oars is heard
again, then stops suddenly.*

MANUS

Listen! Listen!

VIRGILIUS

What is it?

MANUS

The wilderness
Is stirring.
A faint sound of wind.

AENGUS

And look, look at the forest.

MANUS

We must turn back before the furrl squall
Strikes down.
The wind rises
There, there it is!

VIRGILIUS

What shall we do?

AENGUS

I know, I know, Father Virgilius.
Take shelter in the holy cave.
*Their voices are swept away by the sudden storm which
rages with ever-increasing fury.*

SCENE TWO

Inside the cave.

AENGUS

from the cave
                                    Father, can you hear
        Me?
                        VIRGILIUS
below
                Yes.
                        AENGUS
                Give me your hand. I'll help you up
        Into the cave.
                        VIRGILIUS
panting
                        Bless you, my pupil. That climb
        Was heavier than my years. Heaven be thanked
        That we are safe at last.
anxiously
                                But where is Manus?
                        MANUS
        Beside you, snug as your own Latin books
        At Clonmacnoise.
                        VIRGILIUS
                God sent us to this cave.
                        AENGUS
        And Father, the rock is dry.
                        MANUS
                                A bad night, surely
        For lath and latch. Can you remember, Father,
        So sudden a storm?
                        VIRGILIUS
                        I can remember the Night
        Of the Big Wind and that was fifty years
        Ago, the very week that I had passed
        My first examination. The Shannon rose
        Three times and locked us in the chapel. Blocks
        Of mortar fell and the foundations moved
        Beneath our knees. Those hours come back to me

Again. We prayed together, sang in turn
The greater psalms and all that night in dread
We heard the roar of waters multiplying
As if God called His creatures from the deep
But in the morning, happy youngsters paddled
The trout, indoors, with dish or pannikin, caught
Our dinner in the refectory and went
To class by boat. Thanksgiving services
Were held at ebb. But never have I known
So bad a night as this.

A VOICE

outside

*Never have
I known so bad a night.*

MANUS

alarmed

What's that? Who spoke?

VIRGILIUS

Nobody.

MANUS

Listen. Listen!

ANOTHER VOICE

Never have

I known so bad a night.

MANUS

I hear the voices
Of demons talking.

OTHER VOICES

Never have we known

So bad a night.
peal of thunder

AENGUS

Father, are you near me?

VIRGILIUS

Yes, yes.

AENGUS

I crouched behind a chink of rock,
And clearly in that flash of lightning saw
A demon bird with eyes of glassy fire.

VIRGILIUS

Where?

MANUS

Where?

AENGUS

Sitting upon the cliff top.

MANUS

We
Are lost.

AENGUS

Father, Father, I am afraid.

VIRGILIUS

calmly

And yet
Aengus, you want to be a hermit.
God
Has let us hear the voices of the fallen.
His pleasure is revealed by miracle.
Kneel down, kneel down. The three of us will pray
Together.

They murmur in prayer as the storm rises again.

SCENE   THREE

In the eagle's nest

EAGLETS

Mother, mother, something wicked,
Something cold is in our nest.
Catch it and kill it, kill it quickly!

EAGLE

Come under my wing and try to rest.

EAGLETS

Mother, mother, can you hear us?

EAGLE

Yes, yes, my children.

EAGLETS

Are you near us?

EAGLE

What is it children?

EAGLETS

Something wicked,

Something cold is in our nest.
Catch it and kill it, kill it quickly!

EAGLE

Rain is drenching every stick
And stone we own. Keep close together
With every feather.

EAGLETS

But the thing

That freezes underneath your wing
Is shivering. It must be sick.
Catch and kill it!

AN EAGLET

Kill it quick!

CROW

Don't be frightened, little chick,
Because your mother doesn't know.
Chuckling

I am a crow, a poor old crow.

EAGLE

What do you want?

CROW

You are annoyed,

Eagle. But feel me, now! Destroyed
I am this night, blown helterskelter.
Give me an inch, a pinch of shelter.
I am so weak, I can hardly speak,
So very cold, I cannot build
A nest: and this big wind that filled
My wingbones blew me into the trees,
For the first time in centuries.

EAGLE

Where do you live?

CROW

I hop and pop

Into a hole before I drop,
As best I can on my bad leg.
And I am baldy as the egg

That hatched me out, so long ago
I cannot count.
                              EAGLETS
                         But has she known
So bad a night, mother, so bad
A night as this one?
                         CROW
                              Clouds that shadow
The Shannon dripped into the nest
I used to have. The sudden west
Would come at day with flap of waters.
But I was strong as my own daughters,
Though they were greedy of claw and craw.
I kept the air. One time I saw
The tree-tops bending back to snap
Their joints below. From pit and trap
The wild pigs came up with a bound,
Then hurried, grunting, underground
Again. Eels glided on the flood
With grassgreen skin through every wood.
The holy man who lived alone
Upon an island, threw no stone
At birds but fed them every morning,
Was carried off without a warning.
                         EAGLE
What did he do?
                         CROW
                         He gave a screech,
Clutching at reeds beyond his reach
And vanished down a mighty hole
Among the waters. Salmon pole
And netting took the river races
And after, came pale floating faces
And painted timber, cattle trussed
In their own muscles.
                              Another night
When no house in the glen had light
But hers, I flew from salt and shingle
And foam to see the Hag of Dingle.
                         EAGLE
For what?

CROW
I was her messenger
That time. Every two-hundredth year
In storm, she casts another skin.
I saw her do it as I came in,
Step out of it on younger toes,
Quickly as someone changing clothes;
And brighter than a brand-new pin,
She shone from nape to slender shin,
Naked and shameless as a sin.
That night, there was no mortal caller
To see that woman stand there, taller
Than any man. Well might she stoop
To hoop the silk into a loop
And rummage in her box of treasure
Till she had found an old tape measure;
And as I nodded on a rafter
I heard her quiet, sinful laughter.

EAGLE
Why does she change her old skin?

EAGLETS
                                Tell
Us. Why she does it, dearest Crow?

EAGLE
Yes, tell us.

CROW
            I know what I know.
But ask some hermit in his cell
How thought can keep his body warm.
I'll only say that this bad storm
Has come that she may change her form
Once more.

EAGLE
            You have experienced much.
But can you not remember such
A night?

CROW
        Eagle, I never knew
So bad a night since I first flew.
But I grow sleepy.
                    Ask the stag

Of Leiterlone. He saw the hag
When she was young before that.
                    EAGLETS

                                        Mother,
Dear mother, ask the stag.
                    EAGLE
                              Don't bother
Us.
      Where is he, Crow?
                    CROW
                                Beneath that jag
Of rock and furzebush.
                    EAGLETS
                              Has he seen
So bad a storm?
                    EAGLE
                        Keep quiet!
                                        Stag
Of Leiterlone, beneath my crag
And furzebush, have you ever been
In such a downpour?
                    STAG
                                'Twas I who warned
Diarmuid and Grainne, night and morning.
I knew the larger winds that roar
At daybreak, saw them butting shoreward,
Shadowing Shannon, clapping horns
Of ice, but I was never cornered:
For when they came before the winter
They blew my scent away through mint
And garlic. Over pebble and tussock,
Deer leaped along the summer rock,
But in bad weather, wandered freely
Feeding beneath the forest trees,
Before the Fianna could fire
The cooking pits they hid in briar
And ash. I led my herd of does
To quiet glens beneath the snows.
But men were ever on our track;
And when the thawing pools were blacker,
One time, I ran their mighty dogs

A fortnight through the rainy bogland,
Never snapped a fallen branch
Or struck the brown leaf with my antler
As I went past it. Caoilte swore
To pull me down when I had worn out
The heart of Bran, seethe me for supper
And fling my humbles to his pups,
But I got wind of him. At dawn, once,
The woman who became a fawn
Fled with me to the grassy lairs
And heather tops. Though I was wary
And in my prime, it was her son
Who wounded me with woman's cunning.
Where are the proud that never brandished
A head like mine? And where is Flann
Or Bran? Many a time they started
The chase and yet I broke their hearts.
Believe me I have seen the Christians
When they were ambushed in a mist
At Tara change into a herd
Of deer — and yet they have not spared me.
By night and day, I am pursued
With pain and terror in the wood.

EAGLE

But, Runner, have you ever heard
So loud a deluge?

STAG

       Ask the Blackbird
Of Derrycairn for it is perched
Upon my antler.

CROW
Live and learn!
EAGLE

imperiously
  A song! —

        Blackbird of Derrycairn!
BLACKBIRD

Stop, stop and listen for the bough top
Is whistling and the sun is brighter
Than God's own shadow in the cup now!

Forget the hour-bell. Mournful matins
Will sound, Patric, as well at nightfall.

Faintly through mist of broken water
Fionn heard my melody in Norway.
He found the forest track, he brought back
This beak to gild the branch and tell, there,
Why men must welcome in the daylight.

He loved the breeze that warns the black grouse,
The shouts of gillies in the morning
When packs are counted and the swans cloud
Loch Erne, but more than all those voices
My throat rejoicing from the hawthorn.

In little cells behind a cashel,
Patric, no handbell gives a glad sound.
But knowledge is found among the branches.
Listen! The song that shakes my feathers
Will thong the leather of your satchels.
                        EAGLE
But have you ever known a night
As bad, Blackbird, in all your life?
                        BLACKBIRD
Stop, stop and listen for the bough top
Is whistling and the sun is whiter
Than God's own shoulder in the cup now!
Forget the hour-bell . . .
                        CROW
                                    O that bird
Will drive me foolish. Late and soon
More grace notes but the self-same tune!
                        EAGLE
We *must* find out.
                        CROW
                                    I am disturbed
But let me think . . . Hm! Hm!
                                    There is another
Yes . . . he will know.
                        EAGLETS
                        Then ask him, mother,
This very minute.

CROW

Go and visit

His home.

EAGLE

Where is it?

EAGLETS

O where is it?

CROW

Under the falls of Assaroe.
The ancient salmon there will know
The answer rightly if you call him
For he is wiser than us all.

EAGLE

How can I go on such a night
And leave my children?

EAGLETS

Race the lightning,

Dear Mother.

CROW

eagerly

Do. Now I am warm
I'll tuck them in despite the storm　.

EAGLETS

And be our grannie.

CROW

Yes, dears.

EAGLETS

Hurry,

Now, mother, hurry. No need to worry.

EAGLE

The north is dangerous and darker.

EAGLETS

You will be back before the lark-cry
Has made us hungry.

EAGLE

doubtfully

Can I peer
Into the foam of the salmon-weir?

CROW

Fly down, fly down, but do not look.
His name is stronger than the hook

Men use.
chuckling
            It broils him like an ember.
    Call Fintan.
                        EAGLE
                    Fintan?
                        CROW
                    Yes.
calling after eagle
                                Remember
    The name is . . .
                        EAGLE
faintly far away in storm
    Fintan.

SCENE   FOUR

Inside the Cave

                        AENGUS
softly
    Father, are you awake?
                        VIRGILIUS
    Yes, Aengus, I am still awake like you.
    Only the young and old are troubled at night.
    God has been merciful to Manus. He
    Is fast asleep.
                        AENGUS
                But were they really there?
    The voices, Father, that we seemed to hear
    Despite the storm.
                        VIRGILIUS
                    I am inclined to think
    They were delusions of the senses,
    Secular follies of the mind.

AENGUS

If so,

What is their meaning?

VIRGILIUS

They were sent to try
Our faith to-night.

AENGUS

in fear

But that name, Father, that name.

VIRGILIUS

Come close. Why do you tremble at a name,
My son?

AENGUS

I heard that name before.

VIRGILIUS

alarmed

But where?

AENGUS

In class ... Our teacher quickly turned the page.
Father ...

slowly

Is Fintan still alive?

VIRGILIUS

Of course not.

He went to Limbo.

gravely

Knowledge is old, my son,
Older than us and there are thoughts men suffer
Which are not fit for books. But try to go
Asleep now.

AENGUS

Father, I will try to.

Silence
softly

Archangels, pray for me to-night that I
May sleep like Manus on this pillow of rock.
Let me not dream of evils that afflict
The young, and by your intercession, save me
From the dreadful voice beneath the waters.

The storm rages more shrilly through space now.
Gradually it deepens again and far below is heard the
thunder of a waterfall.

SCENE   FIVE

The Falls of Assaroe

EAGLE

above
     Fintan . .
                    Fintan . .
                              Fintan.
                              SALMON
below
                                        I
     Am here.
                         EAGLE
               Where?
                    Where?
                    SALMON
               Beneath the Falls.
Who is it calling from the sky?
What spirit cries my name?
                    EAGLE
                              Eagle I
Of Knock.
                    Through leagues I fought, I dared
Unearthly waters flooding the air,
To find your home beneath the foam-pit.
                    SALMON
Why have you come?
                    EAGLE
                    To ask a question.
                    SALMON
What is it?
                    EAGLE
               Tell me of a tempest
At any time, as sudden, dreadful
As this?
                    SALMON
               I knew the muddy beds
Beneath the Bann, the Suck, the Barrow,
Leaped up the narrows where Shannon topples

In miles of thunder, by torch-lit caves
Of Cong, half choking in the sunlight
And bellied by the Atlantic waves
Plunged down . .
                    down . .
                              sank into the deeps
Of darkness to a primal sleep.
I dreamed of horrors that had shrieked
Before creation. There the sightless
And deafened creatures grope to life
With deathly gulp: the giant claw
Searching the forest of the fronds.
In pulps of sperm, the shapeless maw
Swam slowly past me and mute monsters
Uncoupled one another's armour
Though they were blind.

EAGLE
                    I kill at sight,
For I am fearless.

SALMON
                    How can you guess,
Poor bird, dressing your carrion meat
With highflown feet, that every creature
We know is eaten by disease
Or violent blow! We are unseasoned,
Unsensed, unearthed, riddle-diddled
By what is hidden from the reason.
How can the forethought of defilement
Be reconciled with any faith
That teaches mortals to be mild?
A thousand years, I waited, prayed
And all my fears were only answered
By agony of ignorance.
How must reality be named
If carnal being is so shamed?
From this humiliating body
And brutal brain, these loathsome scales
Itching with lice that no salt water
Can purify, I cry to God
To pity my madness.

EAGLE
                    What are you?

Pause
                                              Answer,

    Great Salmon.
                        SALMON
              I am a man.
                        EAGLE
                                    A man?
                        SALMON

        A man . . .
kindly
                        your enemy, poor bird.
        The selfsame instinct that has stirred
        Your wing is stronger than our will.
        Innocent infants trying to kill
        A bot or housefly know as much
        As their own father.
                        EAGLE

from storm
                                    Icicles clutch
        My pins. Shout, shout, for I am hurled
        Down gaps of hail.
                        SALMON
                              I saw a deluge
        Destroy in rage the ancient world
        And millions perish in the surge
        Hugeing above each mountain refuge.
        I could not keep my subterfuge
        By mortal shape. Yet I escaped
        Into another consciousness
        That did not know me. I lived on.
        Men called me blessed. In the west
        I prophesied to Partholan,
        Divined the arts but knew no rest.
        The very plague-pit in my breast
        Widened my time. How can I find
        In all the ages I have known
        The dreadful thought that slowly brought
        My consciousness beneath these waters
        Where memory unrolls the mind

In chronicles of war, greed, slaughter —
Unchanging misery of mankind!

EAGLE

joyfully

The night of the Great Flood! I know
The answer now.

SALMON

Before you go
One word.
How did you bait the hook
That I must bite, if pious monk
Pumice my name from lessonbook?

EAGLE

A scaldcrow told me.

SALMON

Was she shrunk
And old?

EAGLE

Yes.

SALMON

Baldy as the egg
You lay?

EAGLE

Yes, yes.

SALMON

And did she beg
For shelter?

EAGLE

True.

SALMON

That was the Crow
Of Achill and well I know her ways.
Mummified fingers of the plaything
She gave her children with the great ring
Carbuncled by the jewellers
Of Egypt — that was the hand of Nuadha.
Aye, at Moytura, she despoiled
Many a hero. In his boyhood
Cuchullin was her friend. She croaked
Three times upon the pillarstone
Before he died. She was alone

With him in his last moment. Mist
Of blood had hid her from his fist.
She ripped the lashes from each lid
And blinded him.
                              Homeless with age,
Her food has changed but not her guile.
On stormy nights when she has crept
Upon her belly like a reptile
Into a nest and the frightened chicks
Cry out that some thing cold and wicked
Is sticking to their mother's wing,
eagle cries out
She tells her story, makes excuses
(if they are very small and juicy)
To send their parent far away,
That she may overlay and kill them.
The eagle cries out again
What is it, Eagle?

EAGLE

far away in storm
                              O my children,
My little children!

SCENE SIX.

Early morning: the monks are rowing up the Shannon.
They pause to rest and look round them.

VIRGILIUS

Who would have thought there was a storm last
    evening.
The gravels run so softly.

MANUS
                              When we are safe
At Clonmacnoise, I will be more myself.

This wilderness is not for journeyman
Or scholar.

VIRGILIUS

　　　　How can we convert you, Manus?
Look at that wild-thorn on your left. I hear
An early blackbird in it praising Heaven
Above.

as if despite himself

Stop, stop and listen for the bough top
Is whistling . . .

MANUS

alarmed

Father.

VIRGILIUS

　　　　What did I say just now?
Illusions of the night are still upon us.

half to himself

But why should they conspire against the east?
Well might the ancients warn the fortunate:
'Cave cavernam!'

AENGUS

excitedly

　　　　　　No, Father, you were right.

VIRGILIUS

What do you mean?

AENGUS

　　　　Look . . . Look . . . that speck within
The sky.

VIRGILIUS

　　Where?

AENGUS

　　　　Coming swiftly from the north.

VIRGILIUS

I cannot see it.

AENGUS

　　　　Now a cloud
Has hidden it.
　　　　There, there it is again.
It is the eagle.

MANUS

　　　　Aengus is right. It is

An eagle. Never have I seen so fast
A goer.
                    VIRGILIUS
          I can see her now above
Us.
                         MANUS
          She is turning.
                    She is striking from
The air.
                    AENGUS
          No, she is swooping to the cliff
Above the cave-mouth.
                    VIRGILIUS
uneasily
                    This is very strange.
But why is she hovering so heavily?
Why does she dash her wings against the rock
Like that?
                         MANUS
          She must be wounded in the breast.
                    AENGUS
I know. I know.
                    VIRGILIUS
          What are you saying, Aengus?
                    AENGUS
I've known it all the time.
                    She is too late.
Her little ones are dead.
                    VIRGILIUS
               What do you mean,
My son? Why is your habit shivering?
Why are you frightened?
                    AENGUS
               Father, Father, I know
The ancient thought that men endure at night.
What wall or cave can hide us from that
   knowledge? . . .
     The voices are fading in the distance.

                    T H E   E N D

THE PLOT IS READY

A PLAY

IN FOUR SCENES

CHARACTERS

Muriadach Mac Erca

Crede, *his Wife*

Osna, *his Mistress*

Murna

Fergus

Abbot Cairneach

Old Monk

Young Monk

Brother Malachi

First Narrator

Second Narrator

Monks

Grave-Diggers

THE PLOT IS READY

SCENE I.

The play is based on one of those semi-historical tales of the Irish kings, which exemplify what has been called ' the drama of conscience,' The action begins after night-fall on the 3rd November, 534 A.D., at Cletty, beside the River Boyne. The first scene is played at the proscenium and, if there are proscenium steps, partly on them. As the curtain rises, the stage is in total darkness. Monks gather from left, in moonlight, and are met by the Old Monk, carrying a cruse of oil; he crosses front stage from left. In the performance at the Peacock Theatre, Dublin, the monks entered from the auditorium. Some mounted the steps, while others remained grouped below them. Muriadach is pronounced mur-ëë-a-doch; Crede: Cräy-day.

OLD MONK

slowly
     Will the plot
Be ready soon?
     YOUNG MONK
     Father, you never saw
Such blessed work.
     OTHER MONKS
     Gravediggers sharing one
Another's breath —
     and shovelling faster than
Their lives.
     They know Muriadach Mac Erca
Must die to-night.
     The burial pit is deep
As mortal pride, for when the moon came up
We saw the mound —
     blackening as their heads
Went under ground.
     OLD MONK
     God grant us in our need
The mastery of minutes!

MONKS
                    When will he die,
Father? When will the Ard-ree die,
To-night?
                        OLD MONK
              Our holy abbot cannot tell
The moment of his death.
                        MONKS
                              What can
We do, if *he* is still in doubt?
                    YOUNG MONK
              What can we do but pray now, wait
Another sign?
                        OLD MONK
              Brother is right.

expansively
                              All, all
Salvation is a darkening riddle, no soul
Can read by the mind's eye. The holy texts
Themselves are so obscure with paradigm
And parable, the learned scarcely dare
Expound them. Very words of Revelation
Increase through centuries of explanation.

sadly
The great vine thickens among its leaves, hiding
The sky.
              We must be patient . . . pray.
                                        I brought

The oil.
Gives oil to young monk
                    Keep charge of it, my son.
                    YOUNG MONK

Yes, Father, yes.
                        OLD MONK
turning to another monk about to speak
                    What is it, Malachi?
                        MALACHI

puzzled
Father, we only know Muriadach
Must die to-night. We know no more, for true faith
Is buckled by the sharp spike of ignorance.
How, therefore, can we think of him, absolved,

Anointed, if the seven doors of Cletty
Are closed against us
lowering his voice

— and that woman rules
His sickbed, night and day? And if it is true
No consecrated hand has ever graced
Her forehead or her lips, what heavenliness
Can flow within her nature, touch the parts
Of speech? They say she has authority
Beyond the household now. She has expelled
His wife and children, friends, all his advisers . . .

MONKS

Yes, banned the holy writings . . .

hidden away
The Great Book of the Boyne.

OLD MONK

Let Malachi speak.

turning to him

What is your argument?

MALACHI

Eight nights, nine days,
We have prayed about the house at Cletty, camped
As soldiers under a thatch of thorn, when raindrops
Have drowned the spark at every flinting, felt
The watery side of rock — our knees in mist —
The daylight wound us in our thinning sleep.
Eight nights, nine days, we have prayed about this
      house
And still Muriadach is obstinate.

OLD MONK

What then?

MALACHI

May this be not another warning?

OLD MONK

Another warning?

MALACHI

Yes, that he may die
As his own father died.

OLD MONK

You mean?

MALACHI

I mean . . .

slowly
> Without **repentance.**

General murmur

OLD MONK
> Mortal argument
Is vain, Malachi, when the night brings back
The mysteries of the spheres. I served beside
Our holy abbot, yet I heard no sound
When he sank down, beyond all genuflection,
Churched by the voice above him. His senses lightened
Three times and he cried out to me in anguish . . .
And yet he knows that Heaven will have mercy.
Must we not pray as he is praying now
By the shaken river? We cannot tell what shape
The spirit of evil may put on, what tickle
Of sight or sound . . .

YOUNG MONK

interrupting

> Father, I hear a step.
There, there it is again.

MONKS
> Yes, someone
Is coming up the path.

OLD MONK
> It is
An idle motion of the night. No layman
Would break our holy circuit, marked nine days
By bell and staff.

YOUNG MONK
> No man has broken it.

OLD MONK
What do you mean?

YOUNG MONK
It is a woman. I saw
Her breast-brooch in the moonlight.

OLD MONK
> Are
You sure?

YOUNG MONK
> Yes, yes, the trees have hidden her
From us.

A MONK

jubilantly

> Father, our prayers have stood in Heaven,
> Taller than tonsured men! The doors of Cletty
> Open at last!

OLD MONK

> We must be very cautious.

> We must . . .

The woman, cloaked and hooded, enters rapidly from proscenium

WOMAN

> I want to see the Abbot,
> Please.

They remain silent and she turns impatiently to the senior monk

> Where is the Abbot, the Abbot? I
> Must speak to him at once.

The voice of the Abbot is heard as he enters, right, behind the group of monks

ABBOT

off

> This place
> Has been forbidden to the laity.

MONKS

murmuring

> Father Abbot! Father Abbot!

The monks withdraw slightly to right and allow Abbot to pass

ABBOT

> What do you want? Who are you?

The woman throws back her head, revealing her fair hair, and, as her cloak swings back, her rich robes are seen. Bring up spotlight on both. Other monks remain in shadow

ABBOT

astonished: urgently

> The Ard-ree's wife!
> Lady, you cannot stay.
> Call, call your women, kinsfolk, servants,
> Go back with them to Tara, for the night
> Is dangerous to soul and body. In

Their little houses, men and women fear
And in their lofty dwellings, held by wonder,
The gospel nuns have veiled their eyes.
                         CREDE
                       No. No.
I came alone and I must speak to you.
                         ABBOT
Not now, not now, while Ireland prays.
                         CREDE
                                      My prayers
Have brought me here to-night. Rain-floated floods
My only hedgerows and the strong messengers
That passed the shadowy mounds along the Boyne —
The beatings of my heart. Cairneach, we learn
To think when conscience has tormented us,
Singled the bed and flung sleep down. Believe me,
For I have suffered in that rage of being
Until the thought which stripped my mind at night
Had grown impatient of the day and sent me
Here.
                         ABBOT
                    What do you mean?
                         CREDE
                         I mean that you must go
In God's name, Cairneach, from this place.
                         ABBOT

indignantly

                                           Remove
    The interdiction?
                         CREDE
                      Yes, yes, no other act
Can save Muriadach.
                         ABBOT
                      Affliction, Crede,
Like cunning flattery conceals a sweet
The palate recognises but too well.
Have you forgotten that Muriadach
Has justified his conduct, cherishes
This churchless woman as the breath taken
Beneath his ribs, priding the house with craftsmen,
Musicians, storytellers, who can please

His weariness with shape, air, speculation:
The very scholarship of sin? Shall we
Confuse the present with the past? Reward
The bardic college? Must there be two Patrics?
Another Paschal fire at Slane? No. No.
You wrong your grief by this impatience.

CREDE

Pride

Is louder than the holy offices
And when I hurried to you at first, Cairneach,
For help and counsel, daring at night to spike
The crozier in my thoughts, to fire the camp
And sudden right-of-way, monsters had dashed
The spirits from my sight.

ABBOT

You did your duty

As I do mine.

CREDE

pleading

I know Muriadach

Will change. His folly has had too many fathers,
The generations quarrel in his veins
And write their secret annals there. I am
His real wife. No arm, however young,
Can break that sacrament. His pleasure alone
Supports the thickening wall, gathers the metal
For bell and neat to bind each book, taxes
The north and south.

ABBOT

And so the lawful wife

Connives at his adultery, consents
To a licence that makes marriage easier
And in this new obedience finds, no doubt,
A scandal in our lack of sleep?

CREDE

Cairneach,

Hate keeps a vigil of its own, speaking
Another language of the dead. Too well
I know his guardian enemies, too often
Have feared the holy word, the hasty blessing
That changes all to blood.

ABBOT

                              And if the angels
Have fought with one another in heaven — can
We hope for peace on earth? What, what is the time,
My child? Rebellion in eternity.
And what can arm the soul but the decrees
Of knowledge? Ancient temples by the Tiber
Flower again in stone and their stories sink
Below themselves. But have fire, deluge, war
Destroyed the documents that were transcribed
For our salvation? No. The written pages
A scratch might nullify, outlast the ages
And a frail feather copying the hand
Carries the gospel into every land.
Why, therefore, should faith fear the physical,
Respect it?

CREDE

                    Father, believe my ignorance,
          Believe it by these teardrops,
kneels

                                        fiery teachings
No cheek can catch too soon. Had there been nothing
In marriage but obedience, how could I
Have broken the ninth commandment, coveted
My husband? What if the knowledge we gain in blush
And downward look corrupt us, unawares,
And jealousy become our hidden lover?
Believe me I have suffered in the darkness
All, all that torment of the naked pupil,
For demons held the lashes back and I saw,
In smiling act, the last indulgence
By which the soul is lost. Why must I blame
Muriadach, if my own shame at midnight
Has sent me here before it is too late?

ABBOT

raising her, in moved tones
          Crede, it is too late. May God forgive
          This mouth and all that takes the breath away!

CREDE

alarmed
          Father, what do you mean? What do you mean?

ABBOT

slowly

> Muriadach must die
> To-night. These are the tents of prayer, the camp
> Against God's enemies.

CREDE

incredulous

> He cannot be sick
> As that. He has an iron constitution,
> Eats well, is stronger than the men that praise him.
> He will forget his pride, strike gold from arm
> And wrist, plate every altar. Have I not
> Forgiven him that God may show us mercy?

ABBOT

> It is too late.   His grave is opening.

CREDE

wildly

> His grave...his grave?...Death cannot take him...
> like
> That woman, his mind, his senses all aflame
> With living thought.

ABBOT

aside to monks

> The moment may
> Have come.

Monks begin to move quietly across the stage and off

> Crede, God sent you here to save
> Your husband's soul.   Our fasting, discipline
> Are less to Heaven than your heart.

beckoning all monks

> Go, go
> With Brother to my oratory beside
> The river, kneel there and pray alone.

The moonlight begins to fade and Crede is seen staring in front of her

CREDE

to herself, with sudden vehemence

> No.   No.
> Death cannot strike
> As softly, softly as that woman.

slow black-out

SCENE II.

The action is continuous. Murna enters in the dark, right, back stage, carrying a small medieval lamp showing a bead of light. The stage brightens gradually and reveals the inside of the house of Cletty. A few steps lead up to central doorway at back, beyond which can now be seen moonlit sky. On right, Muriadach is lying asleep on a flat couch or bed. He is half dressed and partly covered by a great hide cloak. Murna places the lamp on a table, on which are a vessel of oil and a phial. She sits down on a bench at the foot of the bed but arises anxiously as she hears an angry murmur of men's voices outside. Fergus enters quickly from left, front.

MURNA
What is it, Fergus?
What is it now?

FERGUS
Another war of words!
The Leinstermen are angrier than horseflies
Unblooded by the whip. They're swearing on
God's doom.

MURNA
What do they want?

FERGUS
They want to see the body.

MURNA
puzzled

The body?

FERGUS
Yes.
They swear Muriadach is dead — and his
Successor named. I cannot keep the bolt
Much longer, Murna.

MURNA
But you must, Fergus,
You must until the others come at midnight,
Carry Muriadach to safety, hide him
From handbell, Latin book . . .

FERGUS
No man will stir
His spittle's length for fear the chambered earth crack
And vault his bones into dust. The river rose
In flood, they say, when Cairneach raised his voice
Last night beyond the doorpost, lengthening
His shadow through the house.

MURNA
But where are Rinn,
Criven and Turlough?

FERGUS
Capped upon their knees
Because they think no man on foot can fight
The empty stomach of a saint.

MURNA
Men! Men!
Finding salvation in the nettle seed,
Forgiving only when the trespasses
Are burning on their last breath.

FERGUS
How can we blame
The ignorant when their own master is raving
Like a poor student fondled by the plague,
Creeping upon all fours into a cell,
To hide his filthy fever from the daylight.
lowering his voice
Worse, worse . . . They say that *she* is from the
earth-mound
Of Dowth and never screamed above the font
That dandles natural infants into grace
But has been limbed in darkness. When his strength
Flows back in sleep, they say she wakens the great
man
By shadowy caresses, fires his throat
With stink of orchis, cattle-muddied water.
She lifts a naked light, she makes a sign
And he believes that it is blessed wine.

MURNA
The house is full of shaven spies! Osna
Must never know.

FERGUS
Where is she?
MURNA
                                        Lying down
She too, has fasted, night and day, to save
Muriadach.
FERGUS
going over to bed and coming back, gravely
                    Half dressed for the wrong journey!
This, this is the last pillow-fight all dread.
No hand can wipe the centuries from his forehead
Now.
MURNA
hotly
                                So the Abbot has your ear at last.
Run, run to him before the earth crack, confess
The headstrong silence of our kisses, late
At night, whisper the words of blame too long
Delayed within your mouth. His books have taught
    him
All that a woman's tongue can do.
FERGUS
catching her in his arms
                                        But, listen,
Murna . .
MURNA
half relenting and then breaking away as she hears a step
    Not now. Not now.
                        I hear her step.
pushing him out, right
    Quick. Quick. She mustn't see you here.
*She goes back stage, then turns to meet Osna who comes
in, left
reproachfully*
                        Madam
You promised me . . .
OSNA
                    Don't blame me again, Murna.
How can I close an eyelid now?
coming forward, to herself
                                        Is sight

Our only friend and not the will? Who knows
The common answer?
turning anxiously

Has he stirred?
OSNA

Not once.

as they turn to the bed
Not once.

OSNA
taking the phial from the table and gazing at it
How strange it is — this midnight plant
We measure by tears.

MURNA
Yes, stronger than the hot root
Of life itself.

OSNA
But shrivelling too soon.

anxiously
He may need more before the journey, to-night.

MURNA
I counted every weeshy drop. Seven, no, nine
Are left.

*Osna leaves down phial, listens, hurries up the central
steps and looks out*

MURNA
What is it, what do you hear?

OSNA
Look, Murna, look at those two monks.

MURNA
on second last step

Where?

OSNA
Climbing
The ridge into the moon-grass.

MURNA
Yes, I see them.
They're stopping to rest now.

OSNA
puzzled

They have spades with them!

MURNA

They huddle their hoods, unstraw their shins.

OSNA

still puzzled

Have they
Been digging for a penance in the dark?

MURNA

as they turn from the doorway, gossipy, yet half in a
tone of wonder

It's more than that. I heard the women say
That Cairneach came at dawn to chase away
The mist with holy smoke. He had his book
With blue, red, glassy knobs. They saw him look
Twice at the east and slowly staff his hand,
Calling the sun to shine at his command;
While clerks were estimating tree and stone,
Pegging the ground as if it were their own.

OSNA

grimly

I see. He means to build a church here.

MURNA

Yes,
They say he has designed and circled half
A hundred churches.

OSNA

scornfully

Shall we cry or laugh
Because this abbot, sheltering in a hovel
Beside the jetty, thinks that he can shovel
The clay from Cletty in the night-time, trip
The sinful into terror when they kiss,
And dedicate his trowel here? Is this
A mission booth? Where are the Leinstermen?

MURNA

nervously, as she turns to table

The Leinstermen?

She busies herself filling lamp

OSNA

coming near

Yes, yes. Why does your hand shake?

The light of the lamp increases and Murna hurries to draw

the curtain across the central doorway, speaking casually
over her shoulder
MURNA

Nothing. Nothing. You know
They are afraid of him.
OSNA

staring at lamp

Shadows of a threat
Scorching behind his busy finger tips
Have ferretted their fears upon the wall.
I had forgotten that.
half to herself

What am I saying?
Sleep clappers my mind with the noising of a bell
No saint has ever blessed.
MURNA

Lie down, lie down
And rest a little.
OSNA

I dare not, Murna.

Ssh!

He's stirring.
MURNA

Only in a dream.
OSNA

A dream . . .
Though I were wasted to a thought, how could I
Fumble that narrow doorway in the darkness
Through which no body squeezes. Last night he
    kicked back
The blanket, called for his wife and when I touched
His fiery skin mistook me for a monk
Absolving him.
MURNA

admiringly

Yet when the lying sweats
Shone with a thousand eyes last week, storied
The men that held him, flung gigantic foreigners
From mountain fort and shore, it was your hand
And voice that quietened him.

OSNA
bending over the bed, softly

                Muriadach.

MURNA
Look how his sleep obeys!

OSNA
              Muriadach,
Though Ireland pray against us both to-night,
We'll leave this fallen house forever, be far
From handbell, Latin book and all this new
Discourtesy to hearts in pain.

She motions to Murna, who tiptoes out, left
                We'll find
Great friends, armies that can protect your sleep.
We'll make our bed again at Tara, knowing
That all we have believed and done is right,
Though Ireland pray against us both, this night.

She comes downstage, obviously in a state of perplexity
and distress. Then, as if she had suddenly made up her
mind, she turns and takes the lamp from the table, crosses
slowly, and comes round to the far side of the bed. She
holds up the lamp and gazes at the sleeping Muriadach.
Then very deliberately, she extinguishes the flame, and
puts the lamp away. She kneels down by the bed, and
only her pale face is seen now in the moonlight as she
speaks in a low passionate voice.
                Darling, my darling,
I have lied to you, deceived you, night and day,
With merry words. Men cover with fallen leaves
The pit they dig to catch wild animals
In. Those who fear your name have baited one
No deeper than my mouth. They hurry behind
The chapel door. They take you in a kiss.
You smiled one evening, questioned me:
                      " Deirdre,
A tear, Osna, a sigh. Who gave you that
Unlucky name? "
               How could you know my finger tips
Had learned far more than needlework in the night
    time
Or little prayers they had forgotten, learned hate

And cunning from the Lower Tribes of Tara?
Too long my fosterparents, brothers, cousins
Had plotted every move, before my hair
Was pinned up, fought again in each embrace
The war in which your father had defeated them
Completely.
                    Why did I wear a leaf-shaped belt
Half fastened by a single jewel that time
My women left me at your hunting-mound
Ten miles from Tara? You saw me in the twilight.
You crossed yourself in superstitious fear
And I laughed, having my lesson off by heart.
You promised me a hundred jewels, bigger
Than pheasant's eggs, a hundred rings, a crowd
For merrymaking every other night
At Cletty, would have borrowed my body in your
Impatience. But I said:
                                    "No other woman
Must sit beside you every second night
When I am present."
                              "Easier to give away
The half of Ireland to my enemies
And yet I promise everything." — you cried.
But when we pledged that kiss, my people died
Upon my lips — and both of us were lost.
Was it wrong, if for a month we scarcely saw
The daylight, wearied of flattery around us,
Longed for the hours of silence, when we could wait
On one another, hand and foot? Is no
Mistake allowed by spiritual law?
You said that you would summon the bishops and
    scholars
To Cashel, annul by many arguments
A marriage contracted in force, not consummated
With true consent. Together we would repent,
Obey the holy orders of the church,
Repeat and solemnise our happiness
In the binding word that must be heard in Heaven
Once it is spoken on earth.
                                    But, darling, can
That second marriage save you now? Last night

You blamed me in sleep, counted your enemies
Upon my very breast, counted them, counted them,
Until my straining heart could scarcely beat
Their numbers for you.
                                    Why was I afraid
To tell you everything? Is bitten tongue
The best, now all the lies are gone? No. No.
Our love is stronger than the fit of sleep.
Forgive my fear, forgive it to me now
Before we leave this house forever, knowing
That all we have believed in must be right,
Though Ireland pray against us both, to-night.

*Her voice has become a murmur and her head sinks
wearily on his breast. There is complete silence for a
few moments and darkness*

VOICE OF MURIADACH

Osna! Osna! Where are you? Why must
I suffer in a dream?

SCENE III.

*The dream-scene. The curtains are slowly withdrawn from
the doorway and the Abbot is seen standing on the threshold. As he moves aside to left of doorway, the monks
enter, left, right, from the wings in dim moonlight. Both
groups move to centre and cross. As they withdraw
again, left, right, Muriadach is seen kneeling in centre of
stage. His eyes are closed and the moonlight shines on
his pale, rigid face. The features of the monks are
shadowy, concealed by their drawn hoods, but, as the
feverishness of the dream increases, the words spoken
have a suppressed intensity.*

ABBOT

Muriadach.

pause
                          Muriadach
Mac Erca.

MURIADACH

dully
Who is calling me?

ABBOT

softly
Think. Think.

MURIADACH
> I know that voice. Thought strikes
At me across the Shannon.
> > Solinus,
You taught me all the mysteries
Of faith. But Isaac and Jacob fade
In rain, the carven stone is faceless,
The manuscripts and lesson-books
Decay. You said men's minds were fierce
As bush and weed. So many stone-crops:
Philosophy could never stop them.

ABBOT

urging
Think. Think.

MURIADACH
> Your voice is different.
Is there no quiet clay in Connaught
Now?

pause
> Why are you waiting here?

Opening his eyes in sudden recognition but without turning
> Cairneach !
Is this another trick to harm
My name?
> Leave, leave this house!

ABBOT

God sent me

Here.

MURIADACH

trying to raise his voice

> Leave it at once.

ABBOT

> You cannot shout

For mortal help.

slowly
                              You are about
      To die, Muriadach.
                              MURIADACH
                              You lie.
      My men are here.
                              ABBOT
                              You cannot stir.
      The everlasting cold, the fire
      Beneath it — stranglehold of Asia
      And warring Europe —
                              think of it, think
      In that awful moment on the brink
      Of your own grave.
pointing
                              Look!
*Muriadach closes his eyes, as the two gravediggers are
seen passing with spades outside*
                              MURIADACH
                              Who are they?
                              ABBOT
      Your last servants on earth.
urging
                                    God sent
      Me here, Muriadach. Repent.
                              OMNES
echoing
      Repent, Muriadach.
                              ABBOT
                              The name
      Of your successor bears no shame.
      Before it is too late, disown,
      Disown the woman you would marry
      By forcing the sacred law.
                              MURIADACH
                              No . . . No . . .
      The brain of man must carry all
      That it has found. Though sinew slacken,
      Memory unravel, I'd call back
      Every devil of thought again!

                                 ABBOT
    Then you are lost, Muriadach!
                                 OMNES
echoing softly
    Lost, lost, Muriadach!
As Muriadach leaps up and dismisses them with furious
gestures, the Abbot and monks begin to recede and the
stage gradually darkens
                               MURIADACH
                                Must I
    Be double-crossed for Paradise
    Because this mad ecclesiastic
    And his fantastic followers
    Think that my heart is at its last tick?
    You are nothing . . .
                           nothing . . .
                                    but shadowy blurs
    In a dream that is fading.
There is a complete black-out and his voice is heard calling
from the bed
                         Osna . . . Osna . . .
    This is the bottom of the cup.
    Kiss me. I want to waken up . . .

                             SCENE IV.

Confused and angry noise of crowd. Muriadach is seen
standing on the top step in a spotlight. Osna runs from
right and, half prostrate on steps, clasps his knees, as he
shouts deliriously. Very rapid action. Two monks, as
Narrators, are on left and right outside the proscenium.

                               MURIADACH
    Maelgarrive . . .
                    Fergus . . .
                              Duv-da-rinn . . .

Quick! Quick!
The painted missal is shoulder-high. Shannon
And Boyne catch more than salmon in their mouth.
Quick! Quick! Our enemies are marching south.

OSNA

entreating
Muriadach! Muriadach!
Fergus and Murna rush in from opposite sides

FERGUS

taking in situation instantly and calling over his shoulder
Surround all Cletty!
*He rushes forward but is held by Muriadach's silencing
gesture and whispering tone*

MURIADACH
Listen! Listen! They
Are praying.

OSNA
Dearest, you are dreaming, dreaming
Still.

MURIADACH

despairingly
Clergy bless our arms. The camps
Are crucified. Can there be peace if men
Must fear the bed that makes them weak, prefer
To rage themselves into eternity?
Repulsing Osna and shouting as he rushes out
Maelgarrive . . .
Fergus . . .
Duv-da-rinn . . .
Quick! Quick!
Our enemies are marching south. Shannon
And Boyne catch more than salmon in their mouth.
*Fergus catches Osna as she reels back, steadies her and
dashes up steps. Murna reaches doorway before him*

MURNA
Quick, Fergus, he's running down
The slope.

FERGUS

confidently
The Leinstermen are closing
In.

Look! They have him now.

              MURNA

                       No. No.

He's scattered them.

              FERGUS

               He's turning back.

They're heading him from the Boyne.

              MURNA

                      He sees

The clergy at their little fire
And halts.

            FIRST NARRATOR

        Our holy people are coming
To meet him now with lighted candles.

              MURNA

He thinks they are the foemen . . .

              FERGUS

                   charges

Across the grass.

          SECOND NARRATOR

          Cairneach has raised
An awful hand in warning.

              FERGUS

            Nothing

Can stop him now.

*Osna, who has stood staring in front of her, screams out
in warning as if she saw what was about to happen*

             OSNA

collapsing

          Muriadach!

Pause

             FERGUS

amazed

   He's gone.

             MURNA

         The earth has opened up
And swallowed him! Pray, pray, Fergus,
   Before we are destroyed.

turning

          My God!

FIRST NARRATOR

slowly
>Muriadach has fallen —

SECOND NARRATOR
>>into

His own grave.
Pause

NARRATORS
>>Gently, gently, dark
And moonlit hands are lifting him
Beyond the housing flame of candle.
The abbot murmurs in his ear.
His wife is kneeling at his side.

MURNA

stooping over Osna
>God help her now. We must escape
While there is time.
Fergus nods grimly, as they help Osna out, right

NARRATORS
>>Our holy people wrap

A pall around the body —
>>>carry it

In state —
>>and now, a slow procession, come
At last into the mournful house of Cletty.
The murmur of prayer is heard gradually approaching.
Monks enter, bearing the body, followed by Muriadach's
wife, the Abbot, and monks with lighted tapers. The body
is draped on the bed as on a bier

ABBOT
>>Crede,
Be comforted. Our fast, our discipline
Were less than your forgiving heart. Believe
As I do that your prayers have saved a soul
To-night — your husband's soul. His death was
  fearful
And sudden, yet I know that he repented,
Repented just in time. What would be faith
Religious action, if the final moment
Could not outweigh the errors of a lifetime
In the disappearing scale of consciousness?

At his last words, Osna enters right, walking as in a
trance. Fergus and Murna follow her but remain at wings
MONKS
following her movements
    Father . . .
          the woman . . .
                the woman . . .
                          She sees
    The pall that hides his face —
                  a face
    On which the clay has left its mark
    Of recognition.
              She's going up
    To it.
        She hesitates.
    She turns away.
              Invisible grace
    Prevented her.
ABBOT
warningly
              Unhappy woman,
    Pray, pray before it is too late.
    Kneel down and pray.
MONKS
             She cannot hear
    Or see us now.
OSNA
centre, looking towards doorway
             Muriadach!
    Muriadach!
Pause

NARRATORS
            A shadowy form
    Is waiting by the grave.
              It turns
    Impatiently.
          It glimmers to the ground
    Shaping itself from memory —
                 begins
    To move more rapidly across the grass.

The spirit of Muriadach Mac Erca
Is coming to this house.
                    ABBOT
                    Pray, pray for him!
A murmur of prayer. The stage begins to darken
                    NARRATORS
We cannot see his face, so glorious
The heart is shaken with tears.
*Tense silence. The doorway brightens until the light is
dazzling*

                    VOICE OF MURIADACH
outside
                                        Osna!
She moves towards the steps
Osna!
*She is seen at the doorway, glittering in the light, her face
radiant, her hands outstretched*
                    OSNA
                    Muriadach!
*Her hands are caught by unseen hands and she is drawn
slowly into the light*
                    ABBOT
loudly
                                Close, close
The doors!
*Monks instantly draw the curtain across the doorway.
Normal lighting again*
                    CREDE
distractedly
                    Pity me. Pity me, Father, in this anguish.
I do not understand.
                    MONKS
                    Pity us, Father.
We cannot understand.
                    ABBOT
                    Be calm.   Be calm.
The danger is past.
                    What have you seen, heard, known
To-night?
                    OMNES
                Father, we are afraid to say.

ABBOT

Then I will tell you now —

plain devilry.

The terrible assumption of that woman,
Drawn soul and body from our midst — unspaced
In a second — is a warning to the faithless.
I speak of things not known in nature.

More than

Five thousand years ago, measured by sun
And moon and working star, archangels, angels,
Revolted from their spiritual being,
And theologians say their headlong flight
Continues still through conscious time —
slowly

and as

They pass —

the brightness of those heavenly bodies
Destroys the unprotected.

Let us pray.

*Crede kneels beside the bier and, as the monks begin to
pray, Murna kneels at wings while Fergus stands, with
bowed head.*

CURTAIN

THE VISCOUNT OF BLARNEY

A PLAY FOR RADIO OR STAGE

IN ONE ACT

CHARACTERS

Cauth	Pooka
Woman	Fostermother
Husband	Jack O'Lantern
Old Man	Gallant

THE VISCOUNT OF BLARNEY

*The action starts on a lonely road near the Blackstairs
Mountains, after nightfall, seventy years ago.*

*As the curtain rises, the stage is entirely dark except for
a spot, down, centre. There are two small stools, one on
each side of proscenium. Angry voices of men and an
elderly woman are heard from one of the entrances of
the auditorium. ('Put her out,' 'the lazy get,' 'bad cess
to her impudence,' 'chase her out of sight.') Cauth
Morrissey, a young girl, runs through the auditorium to
the stage, centre, down. She has a small fringed shawl
around her shoulder and carries a bundle wrapped in a
coloured handkerchief. She wears shoes but not stockings.*

CAUTH

to audience

> The moment that I got my toes
> Inside that house, pots came to blows,
> The ash-hole dog began to bark,
> The turf fell out, bog-flame and spark
> Smoked up the flue and red stars of smut
> Shot down. I knew it was a witch
> Had done it, but they called me — slut.
> That woman was beside herself
> Chasing my elbows round the delf,
> Through rings of old potato peels.
> Her sons came at me from the door
> But I showed a cleaner pair of heels
> Than they had ever seen before.
> I thought they wouldn't leave a stitch
> Upon me as I sprang the ditch,
> Except the fancyings of my shawl!

sagely

> They say when people use bad language
> The devil scribbles on their wall,
> Empties his sack of sins, kicks back
> A dozen hoofs in every stall!

yawning

> I'm half asleep . . . Will no one help

A poor young orphan going out
On service, give a little shelter
Until the day peep. Is there no house,
No house in all this neighbourhood
Will take her in without a line
Of reference?
starting back

                              What's in the wood there?
A wicked tramp . . . must find a rock
And hide from him.
crouches down
A woman comes out, down, right, and sits on stool, before
red glow of fire

                    CAUTH

looking right
                    A lamp is shining
Behind that window pane. I'll knock.
She makes a gesture of knocking. The sound of the
knocking is heard, off

                    WOMAN

Who's there?

                    CAUTH
          It's me, ma'am.
                    WOMAN
                              Who?
                    CAUTH
                              Cauth Morrissey.
An orphan going out on service. I'm lost
Entirely.
                    WOMAN
          Lift the latch and walk right in.
                    CAUTH

O thank you, ma'am.
                    WOMAN

rising
                    God bless me, you're exhausted.
Sit here before the fire and rest a minute.
What can have happened you?
                    CAUTH
                    Such a to-do, ma'am
I looked into a shanty near the roadside

And saw a pothook coming down the flue.
It jumped at me and changed into a cartload
Of sooty sparks. The place was smothering.
With smoke and stink of ash and boiling mash,
And seven fellows bawling for their mother.

WOMAN

Good gracious!

CAUTH

                        Big galoots in hobnailed boots!
Tried to play tig with me around the pighouse,
Over a drain and through a patch of furze!
And ma'am, the cursing!

WOMAN

                        Must have been the Quigleys,
Fighting and running to solicitors
With every shillingsworth they cut or dig.
You're safe now, Cauth. Is that you're name?

CAUTH

                                Yes, ma'am.
And . . . could I stay the night?

WOMAN

hesitating, then making up her mind
                                I'll do my best
For you. Himself's a bit cantankerous.
leads her, anxiously, right, down
In here and don't disturb the childer.

CAUTH

                                Thank
You, ma'am. May God reward your kindness.

WOMAN

                                Hurry.
The bed is in the corner. He may be back
At any moment now. The crack in the door
Will give you light and when I hear him snoring,
I'll bring you a drop of new milk.
Pushes Cauth off, right. Michael, her husband, comes,
down, from the dark stage, lifts latch

HUSBAND

in a surly tone
                        What's your worry?

                              WOMAN
    Nothing.
A noise off
                              HUSBAND
                            Who's that?
                              WOMAN
                                    Tim had a little pain
    Just now. I'll take him into bed with us.
A louder noise
                              HUSBAND
grimly, going right
    He's learned to walk.
                              WOMAN
                              Stop, Michael, I'll explain,
    You can't go in. She may have nothing on.
                              HUSBAND
    Who?
                              WOMAN
        It's an orphan girl . . . she lost her way.
                              HUSBAND
    She can't sleep here.
                              WOMAN
                    Michael, Michael.
                              HUSBAND
                                        I say
    She can't sleep here.
                              WOMAN
                        You'll have remorse of conscience
    For this.
                              HUSBAND
                I'll have no hop-the-hedge or stray-
    By-night inside this house.
                              WOMAN
                        But listen, Michael.
A crash, off, and howls of children
        Merciful Heavens!
following him off
                    Stop, stop! Don't strike the girl.
    Don't strike the girl.

off
HUSBAND

I'll cook her goose!

*Cauth runs in with clothes disordered, catching her shawl
as it is flung after her*

CAUTH

to audience
   I'm back again!
Am I to blame
Because the knobs and screws were loose?
I hardly sat upon the bed
Before the mattress, spring and frame
Fell down.

As she fastens her clothes
No thought stays in my head.
I toil and moil. It's all the same.
Foot-water tries to come to the boil
And scald the basin. Sticks want breaking.
The turf is damp. Paraffin oil
Upsets the lamp. The dough won't rise,
The currants come out in the baking;
And onion choppings skin my eyesight,
   Although I drop them in the bucket.

sagely
   They say the third time must be lucky.

*An old man comes out, left, spot light, sits down on
stool with a book*

CAUTH

looking round
   An old man reading at a doorway.
   He wipes his spectacles . . . schoolmaster . . .
   Respectable. I'll ask once more.

approaching
   God save you, sir.

OLD MAN
God save you kindly, child.
What is your name? . . . don't know your little face.

CAUTH

Cauth Morrissey, Sir.

OLD MAN
The people here are wild

And dread to see a stranger round the place.
Where are you from?
> CAUTH

Sir, if it does not vex you,
I'm only an orphan going out on service,
Walking the road all day from County Wexford
And now I'm lost.
> OLD MAN

smiling

A most deserving case
For supper, bed and breakfast.
sternly

But you must earn
Them, Cauth.
> CAUTH

Yes, sir, I darn and mend.
> OLD MAN

My wife
Does that. You'll have to earn them with a story.
> CAUTH

I've no book learning, Sir.
> OLD MAN

But you have life
And all of us are on our way to glory —
half to himself

Although the old must riddle their own ashes
To find what's hidden in them, . . . senseless work . .
The lashes of the Turk.

But awake, my Cauth, or
Asleep, a story stirs the porridge in
The pot. Now listen to this ancient author:
reading from book

" The mind's of such a noble origin,
Man is condemned to see his own blood flow;
Obey that dreadful state or dare to ask —
Impatient in the courtyard, far below,
The executioner puts on his mask."
You understand the sentence?
> CAUTH

No, Sir.

OLD MAN

Just

     As well, poor child.
rising

                    And now to earn your crust.
     Here is a lantern.
Gets it off stage

                 Go into the barn—
     It's part of an old castle — and bring me back
     Five sods of dry turf and a story.

CAUTH

Yes, sir.

OLD MAN

     But don't go near the corner where the sack is.
     Upon your life, Cauth, don't go near it.

CAUTH

                              No, sir.
*Old man goes off, left. Cauth comes centre, down, shading
lantern with her shawl, looking up and around*

CAUTH

          I never saw so big a barn
     Before. What's shining there? A harness
     And there's the sacking. Daren't look
     Into that corner. Five . . . five sods
     Of turf, he said . . . a story . . . a book.
finding a tool-box, left centre
     I must sit down, my head is nodding.
     I think I'm half asleep already.
Yawns
     Or is the lantern wick unsteady?
*Her eyes close. Gradually the cyclorama brightens until,
at back, centre, through a wide and lofty doorway, can
be seen a starlit sky of Spring. The barn remains in
shadow. Sacking in corner over a box or crate, heap of
turf left. Far away are heard light hoof-beats and a faint
tinkling sound. As the sound comes nearer, Cauth opens
her eyes. During this scene, the words of the unseen
Pooka can be followed in the childlike intensity and eager,
changing expressions of the girl's face*

                                   CAUTH
in delight
    The Pooka! The Pooka! I must be asleep now.
    The fishermen know by the bubbles and frothing
    When he snorts in his shadowy water-hole, deep
    Under Shannon. But why is he stopping?
                              VOICE OF POOKA
right, outside, cautiously
    Cauth . . . Cauth . . .
    Is there anyone there with you?
                                   CAUTH
rising

                        No, not a soul,
    Dearest Pooka.
                                   POOKA
    Then come to the doorway.
                                   CAUTH
to audience
                            I must
    Have a peep at him.
She runs to doorway, leaves lantern just outside it, left,
her face gleaming in starlight
              Nothing . . . nothing but dust
    And gray docken.
                                   POOKA
    You're wrong. I am here on my shoes.
importantly
    They have thousands of sparks that can hop in the
                                  dark
    Whenever I choose.
                                   CAUTH
    But where can I find you?
                                   POOKA
    In the silver of sight. Now shut both your eyes,
    Cauth.
    What can you see?
                                   POOKA
slowly
                Something that's bright . . .
    Moving . . . and mooning along the ground.
turning, as if impelled, until she is facing audience again;
puzzled

I must be looking at a lake
And yet the water makes no sound.
Alarmed, opening her eyes
    It's at my feet.
catching up her skirt and turning
                It's all around
    Me.
Facing around again
             Water, deep water.
screaming

                   I'll be drowned.
POOKA
Quick, close your eyes again.
CAUTH
             The lake
Is gone!
POOKA
      I know. Why are you shaking?
CAUTH
I saw it twice when I was smaller,
Rising from mud floor, sill and wall.
What was it, Pooka?
POOKA
         Noah's flood,
That's sent to castigate the young
At night. They huddle half asleep
Because their minds have grown too big
For them and keep on falling, falling
Into the pit their terror digs.
Then, wide awake, all of a sudden,
They see that flood-gleam, hide their heads
Beneath the bedclothes, see that flood-gleam
And are so much afraid of it,
They cannot scream until the fit
Is over.
farther away
      Open your eyes.
CAUTH
turning
               I see
The moon shining on rock and tree,

Gray docken . . .
A faint tinkle

POOKA

nearer

What else?
CAUTH

A tiny horse.
It must be you, dear Pooka !
POOKA

Of course,
It is.
CAUTH

in admiration

All silvery and speckled.
POOKA

coaxing
Come, put your arms about my neck,
Cauth. Pet me. pat me for a while.
I see you smiling.
pleading

Cauth, be kind.
CAUTH
Poor Pooka, why are you so sad?
POOKA

indignantly
I'm treated badly, north and south,
Especially on Sunday nights
At closing time. Carousing crowds
In public houses struggle and roar
Around the door-bolt while the barmen
Put back the bottles on the shelves.
The married men are much the worst
And women who take a drop themselves,
Singing till twelve o'clock and cursing
And using filthy language.
CAUTH

I know
Too well, for when I lived with grand-dad,
They used to wake me, stumbling home,
Swearing like mad.

POOKA

Just think of it!
When I have found a drunkard sitting
Upon the ground beneath a shutter
I have to scare his living wits —
As if I were a common nightmare;
And lie beside him in the gutter,
Then trundle like a whiskey keg
Between his bow legs, carry him
For miles and be his boon companion
Until the shouting moon is dim.

CAUTH

Poor little Pooka.

POOKA

Hug me, tug
My curly mane, Cauth. Let us snuggle
Together closely, rubbing noses,
Your little one and mine. No leather
Or saddle girth has ever pressed me
And when you've fondled and caressed me,
Away we'll go.

CAUTH

doubtfully

You will not bite,
If I come near.

POOKA

I won't.

CAUTH

You might.
So promise me.

POOKA

I promise, Cauth.
She puts her hand past doorway, starts back with a cry
What is it?

CAUTH

Your mane is wet and cold.
It makes me shiver.

POOKA

Only froth,
My dear.
in a sinister voice

The river Shannon rolled
A dreadful wave above my head
And drove me from its ancient bed,
To-night.
pleasantly

You must be brave and dare
To come with me.

CAUTH

recovering

I'll try. I'll try.

POOKA

We'll gallop off, but do be careful
For when I mount into the sky
You'll have to lie along my back
And grip me tightly with your knees.
The hollowing of air is black
At first, a wind comes from the tree-tops
But when the mountains stop their nodding,
We'll see a croppy moon in water
And then look down on field and townland.

CAUTH

Counting the miles —

POOKA

Laughing and talking —

CAUTH

Above the heads of everybody —

POOKA

In Ireland.

CAUTH

Wait, dear Pooka, wait.
I'll leave the lantern just inside
The doorway for old baldy pate.
coming back
Now tell me, will we see all Ireland?

POOKA

Why not?
Mount Leinster is on fire
Since dusk. I saw upon Slieve Bloom
A jig and reel of yellow sparks —
The gorse was not more gay at noon.
Friends of the dark, the loop of wire

Stretching across the rabbit-run,
The night-line twitching in the pool —
All still.

CAUTH

But are there cunning witches?

POOKA

Of course. They gather up the smoke,
Hide in the stable, chain the smoke,

CAUTH

Creep to the cowshed—

POOKA

Dry the udder,
And hurry to sour the milking can.

CAUTH

They have big humps?

POOKA

They'll make you shudder.
They've nothing on those hairy lumps
And bumps but smouldering red flannel,
And when they turn in cartridge wheels —

CAUTH

I'll make you gallop all the quicker,
By drubbing gently with my heels —

POOKA

Disturb the birds in every thicket —

CAUTH

And never hear the wicked words
Of witches —

POOKA

leap the iron gates
And hurry up the avenues
Of big estates where nothing stirs
At night but grass, waken the mews
And kennel yard —

CAUTH

But trespassers
Are prosecuted —

POOKA

landlords thinking
Evicted men have come to shoot them;
And when we leave these mansions, number

As many little lakes as they
Have windows. All will quickly link
Their arms and light us on our way
To see that place where finch is caught
At last. There, there upon Mount Nephin
All lovers can be safe in thought,
And cap in hand is head in air!

CAUTH

Let's hurry!

POOKA

     If I go too slowly
Spur, spur me with your little toenails.

CAUTH

Must I take off my shoes?

POOKA

         Yes, dear.
Then stoop and whisper in my ear.

CAUTH

And when my breath is tickling in it?

POOKA

I'll gallop at a mile a minute.
She runs off right
The Fostermother appears in barn from left, back. She
wears a short cape and jet bonnet, and carries a small
black bag

FOSTERMOTHER

Cauth Morrissey, come here.

CAUTH

coming to doorway, picking up lantern
    Who's calling?

FOSTERMOTHER

You wicked girl, I'm just in time . . .
I jumped the cemetery wall
At Cleggan, straddled a tombstone, climbed
The quarry until that lantern shone
Outside the door.

CAUTH

        Yes, ma'am.
tinkle, sound of hoofs
            He's gone . . .

FOSTERMOTHER
coming between Cauth and doorway
    Aye, gone. I've saved you from the Devil.
CAUTH
desperate
    No. No. It was the Pooka.
FOSTERMOTHER
                        Be civil
    And please remember who I am,
    Cauth Morrissey.
CAUTH
           But, ma'am . . .
FOSTERMOTHER
                    Now hold
    That lantern up. Do what you're told.
    No . . . higher . . . higher than that.
                      Dear me!
    You've grown much faster than your pimples.
    Keep still . . . respectable appearance . . .
    Firm chest . . . the arms a little skimpy.
    Cauth Morrissey, you'll come to harm.
CAUTH
    Let . . . let me go. I do not know you.
FOSTERMOTHER
    You know what brought me here so quickly.
CAUTH
    No. No.
FOSTERMOTHER
          Your wicked thoughts. Don't dare
    To contradict. Too fine a comb
    Will break its teeth in that wild hair!
    When you were small I took you home
    And dirty bottle was your mother.
    I tried to send you back to heaven
    And save the angels all this bother
    Before you reached the age of seven.
    But you grew faster than the lie
    That hid your birth, with every cry
    Struggled for foolish life on earth.
complainingly, leading girl to tool-box
    Nurse children all forget my kindness.

sitting down with horrible affection
>   Who turned you up when you were bold,
>   Gave you a scolding for your supper?
>   And when you fell, have you forgotten
>   Who kissed the spot and made it well?
>   CAUTH

ın terror
>   Your eyes are staring through the shadows.
>   FOSTERMOTHER

fiercely
>   Because I've seen young girls, half maddened
>   By grief and terror do queer thing —
>   CAUTH
>   You squeeze me tightly —
>   FOSTERMOTHER
>   wizen the string
>   Of life, sentence themselves to prison.
>   CAUTH
>   What have I done?
>   FOSTERMOTHER

half to herself
>   My lap is weary
>   With all the labour of the years.
>   Let the unhappy fill with sighs
>   The charitable institutions,
>   Wash, wash and scrub without a wage,
>   For melting crystal purifies,
>   Yet hear in mockery the hiss
>   Of scalding pipe: their clock—the steam-gauge,
>   Their refuge — a laundry.
>   CAUTH

stopping her ears
>   I will not listen.
>   No. No. I dare not.
>   FOSTERMOTHER

whispering
>   Premature age . . .
>   Paralysis . . . Think of the lost
>   Raving at night in hospital
>   From lock to lock, until their screams
>   Are certified . . .

What's that? Sssh! Hide.
The lantern flame.
to herself

The plot's the same,
Misery of fields and little farms.
Look, tell me who is passing by.
A girl and woman pass outside

CAUTH

A girl with something in her arms.
I cannot see it but she is crying.
puzzled

Maybe the fairies stole her child,
And put a changeling in its place.

FOSTERMOTHER

Who follows her?

CAUTH

A woman.

FOSTERMOTHER

Wild?

Purse-lipped?

CAUTH

I cannot see her face.
What is it makes me so afraid?
Tell me, tell me.

FOSTERMOTHER

A tiny soul
Has gone to Limbo.

CAUTH

Limbo?

FOSTERMOTHER

Yes.

It's dark there, darker than a hole
Dug in the ground. No prayer or blessing
Can reach that place where nothing sighs,
Wakes, sleeps, for ever.

CAUTH

kneeling and tearfully

I've learned my lesson.
I will be good, never tell lies
Again, if you will only save me.

FOSTERMOTHER
raising her up, cheerfully
  Of course I will. We'll cut the cards
  And cheat the Joker, call on knave
  And queen to play their ancient part,
  Shuffle with hearts, laugh at all danger
  And catch the dark or fair-haired stranger
  Before his tricks begin. We'll fix
  The future in the present, glue
  The dirty Devil, hoof and horn.
      CAUTH
O thank you, ma'am.
      FOSTERMOTHER
       The pack of cards
  Under the sacking in that corner,
  Quick, get it now.
Cauth goes with lantern, then hesitates
      CAUTH
         I beg your pardon,
Ma'am.
    FOSTERMOTHER
    What is it?
      CAUTH
      I quite forgot . . .
The man . . . he warned me of that spot.
      FOSTERMOTHER
What man?
      CAUTH
    The man that read the book
And gave me the light. I daren't look.
      FOSTERMOTHER
You're dreaming.
      CAUTH
     Maybe a black hound
Or something cold that makes no sound
Is waiting to pounce. Or a corpse might raise
A coffin lid and slowly gaze
At me.
      FOSTERMOTHER
    Nonsense. Do what you're bid,
Cauth Morrissey.

*As Cauth goes to corner, Fostermother points at her, winks
grotesquely at audience, then steals out, left. A small
figure with horns and demi-mask peeps in and whistles
softly, then withdraws. Cauth turns but sees no one.
Figure re-appears at doorway and whistles. He is dressed
in Tudor green and terracotta, with a buckle belt*

STRANGER

She's gone.

CAUTH

alarmed

Who are you?

STRANGER

Don't you know

Me, Cauth?

CAUTH

No.

STRANGER

I'm the Pooka. Yes,
Your little Pooka. Didn't you guess?

CAUTH

You're not the Pooka. You are old
And hairy with crooked horns. Please, Sir,
Please go away.

STRANGER

with a few dance steps

I'm hot and cold.
I'm drizzly and dry, a born teaser.
For when I show my fiery spot
To straying eyes at night, beware
The sudden splash of bog-pool. Mist
And darkness are my doubtful lair
For I am quicker than the kiss
That needy bachelors try to snatch,
As tricky as their coaxing hand,
But stinking as a sulphur match.

darting out a finger at her

What is my name?

CAUTH

recoiling

You're Jack o' Lantern.

JACK O'LANTERN
That's right. No, now give me back my flame.
I want to know what's happening
To-night outside the fairy ring.
Two women, who had hid a spade there,
Put something small into a hole
And it was waxen as a candle.
Foul Jack must learn their secret.
He grasps at lantern

CAUTH
                                        Stop.
The man that gave it to me . . .
JACK O'LANTERN
                                        stole
My property. Let go that handle.
Let go!

CAUTH
          Help! Help!
*A Gallant in eighteenth-century riding costume appears
at doorway*

GALLANT
melodramatically
Villain, you dare
To molest a young lady!
                              Take that now.
Cuffs and chases him out

                                        A pair,
A pair of smoked glasses to strengthen my sight!
bowing
Say! Are you Aurora, that early riser?
Her cousin, Flora, who fears the hailstones?
Venus herself — surpassing thought?
Or the fairest daughter of Granuaile?

CAUTH
Oh, no, Sir, I'm only an orphan from Wexford.
GALLANT
The light of her sex, then! I cannot be wrong —
That grace, that modesty, noted in song,
Must surely belong to — Miss Morrissey.
CAUTH
Your honour is joking me.

GALLANT
> Do I make bold?
> You cannot deny your own name. It is known
> Far and wide, both to poor folk and wealthy.

CAUTH
> But how can my name . . .

GALLANT

smiling
> You are back in the past
> Where all boxes are crammed when the future is
> doubtful.

with a sweeping gesture
> And I swear by this barn that only last week
> The Viscount of Blarney was speaking about you
> And drinking your health in his castle.

CAUTH
> The Viscount of Blarney!

GALLANT
> Guests were assembled,
> The chandeliers burning — I remember distinctly —
> The pledge they were drinking was flavoured with
> lemon,
> Demerara and nutmeg. The fair were concealing
> Each blush with a fan for the gentlemen showed them
> A dashing fine leg as the dancing began,
> But every proud lady that kirtled her petticoat
> And led up the set was soon brought to heel
> For the tune that was played was — *Miss Morrissey's
> Reel.*

Music of a reel is heard

CAUTH
> I can hear it, so softly.

GALLANT

to audience
> The young find a riddle —
> Existence! The old give it up.

CAUTH

to herself
> . . . so softly . . .

GALLANT

to audience
> And the answer is?

to orchestra
                              Fiddlesticks! Play with more feeling.
Italian music
to Cauth
        Cupids that cluster on a lovely ceiling
        With tiny darts gilded above each lustre,
        The cloud-born Goddess revealing her body,
        Awaken mere sighs. True modesty flying
        To closet or screen still fears to be seen,
        Because the first lesson in joy must be tearful.
Music fades out

                              CAUTH
        O what do you mean?
                              GALLANT
                              I'll tell you my secret.
        For fear of offending you, dreading refusal,
        His Lordship has sent me ahead of his carriage,
        To post without stop, with spurring of topboot,
        To beg and implore your consent — as I live —
        To give him your fair hand in marriage.
                                            As token
        Of deepest respect, this heirloom —
presenting a tiara, confidentially
                                    worth more than
        A thousand in guineas.
                              CAUTH

rapt
                        All shiny.
                        GALLANT
                                    Accept it —
        A trifle of rubies and diamonds.
                              CAUTH
                                    I daren't.
                              GALLANT
        Put it on for a moment.
*As she does so, he conjures a satin cloak from behind
the tool-box and slips it round her*
                              The night air is cold.
                              CAUTH
        A cloak!
                              GALLANT
                And a ring.

CAUTH
Two hearts made of gold!
GALLANT
It comes from the Claddagh.
Your finger . . .
Not the second . . .
Third.
Thank you . . . fits perfectly!
CAUTH
But how can I wed him
With nothing, no nothing at all, for a dowry?
GALLANT
Such silking of panel and spreading of gown
On sofa and bed, the latest from town,
And milliners feathering hats by the dozen.
I swear, as first cousin, he loves you.
CAUTH
dreamily

He loves me!
He nods
And he's tall?
He nods
And handsome?
He nods
And darkhaired?
He nods
Truly?
He nods
suspiciously
But is he . . . a Protestant?
GALLANT
shakes his head vigorously — then confidentially
Convert . . . newly
Received!
CAUTH
clasping her hands and looking upwards
And his eyes?
GALLANT
Their colour?
she nods
He'll tell you

Himself if you dare him. And now a surprise.
Can you guess it?

CAUTH

I cannot.

GALLANT

      Impatient to welcome
The Bride, he is waiting outside in his carriage.
Black horses, scarce seen in the fleering of tallow,
A pair neck to neck . . . runaway marriage —
Mad kisses through Carlow, breakfast in Mallow!
Sssh!

CAUTH

  What is it?

GALLANT

      People are stirring outside.
 Not a sound. Not a spark —
He takes lantern and as he leads her to left corner, up
stage, lowers the light
      We'll grope here and hide
 Until they are gone.
Extinguishes the lantern

CAUTH

alarmed

    You've put out the light.

GALLANT

 Of course. Elopements are always kept dark,
The crying girl and the woman pass slowly outside on
their homeward journey

CAUTH

 The pale girl again. She trembles . . . She stumbles . . .
 The woman is helping her on.
      Where are you?
 Where are you? I'm frightened.
Cauth is seen running across the stage, past doorway,
without the cloak and jewels

GALLANT

outside

    The Viscount is coming!

A DEEPER VOICE

announcing
 The Viscount of Blarney!
Bass music, multo agitato, as the cyclorama begins to

change to a red glow. A figure appears, tall and hand-
some, in travelling cloak with tricornered hat. As the
newcomer raises his face, he holds a small gold devil-mask
and looks at her through it with a quizzical smile. The
red glow deepens until it is like the background of an
ancestral painting

CAUTH

The Devil Himself!

As she screams, there is a black-out. Shuffling steps are
heard, left, downstage, and the Old Man comes in with
a candle calling her. She runs to him for protection

CAUTH

Where am I?

OLD MAN

You're safe now. The lantern went out.
You were gone but a tick when herself heard you
calling.
I caught up the candle-stick, came out to look.
Don't cry, child. Don't cry. Sure it's nothing at all.

CAUTH

dazed

I remember . . . the Pooka . . . the Pooka.

OLD MAN

You saw him?

CAUTH

Yes, truly.

OLD MAN

You looked in that corner —
pointing finger in playful reproach

CAUTH

protesting

I didn't

OLD MAN

Good girl. Herself has a clutch in the straw there
And the brown hen is on it.
Some turf for the fire.

Giving her sods

CAUTH

in terror

That woman . . .

OLD MAN

excited

Respectable? Wearing a bonnet?
I know her . . . the night-hag. She fills the next world
With sorrow. Her bag — ssh! — the secret of Ireland.

CAUTH

almost letting turf fall, feeling her brow
The jewels are gone!

OLD MAN
And the heir to the Earldom
Of Hell!
Quick, bring in the turf,
I'm in glory,
For that is a story I heard as a boy.
Not a word now to spoil it.

calling
Wife, put on the kettle
And take out the china.

leading Cauth off, left, down stage
We'll draw up the settle,
When I wind the repeater. But mind you don't utter
A word, keep it all in your head, like a play,
Until you have eaten six slices of bread
With plenty of butter — and saucered your tay!

CURTAIN

THE SECOND KISS

A LIGHT COMEDY IN ONE ACT

CHARACTERS

| Pierrot | Harlequin |
| Pierrette | Columbine |

THE SECOND KISS

SCENE: An open space near Templeogue, or any other English-speaking district outside Dublin.

*The stage is set with black curtains. On left, front, the garden gate of a villa, bearing the name, ' Cosy Nook ';
on right, front, a painted cut-out of a small tree. Right, near centre, a grassy bank. The kiss, with which the play commences, should exceed by three seconds the emotional duration allowed by the Film Censor, for there is no Irish stage censorship yet. As the curtain rises, all is in complete darkness, so that Pierrot and Pierrette cannot be seen but their voices are heard in a loud stage whisper.*

PIERROT

Darling . . .

PIERRETTE

Darling . . .

Spotlight gradually rises, showing them clasped in a long
kiss

PIERROT

turning

Look! the moon at last.

PIERRETTE

Our clock was right.

PIERROT

smiling

Only our hearts were fast.

PIERRETTE

Let us go home now, Pierrot, forget the moon.

PIERROT

Why do you want to go to bed so soon?

rapt

All maps are silver now. Go where thought will,
Midsummer fills a million miles of space.

PIERRETTE

peeved by his reverie

Pierrot, the moon is rude. It makes your face —

249

PIERROT

waking up

      Too pale?

PIERRETTE

No, blue.

PIERROT

rubbing his chin

             Did I forget to shave?

PIERRETTE

You're laughing at me.

PIERROT

        True.

catching her around waist

          Let's misbehave!

Do something shocking!

PIERRETTE

withdrawing

           Quite impossible !

We're married now.
suppressing a little yawn

        Come home to bed.

PIERROT

teasingly

              Who fell

Asleep at nine last night?

PIERRETTE

playfully

        I did.

PIERROT

         Then stay

Up late to-night . . .
striking an attitude

      and we'll perform a play.

PIERRETTE

surprised
A play?

PIERROT

nods and points to moon
    Our spotlight.

PIERRETTE

      But we left the door

Wide open, dear.

PIERROT

What matter to the four
Of us?

PIERRETTE

The four?

What do you mean?

PIERROT

Look round.

PIERRETTE

There's nobody.

PIERROT

Our shadows on the ground!

PIERRETTE

happily as they both mime

I know. We'll chase them to the garden wall,
Pierrot, and make them very big —

PIERROT

and small.

PIERRETTE

For comedy can prove by night —

PIERROT

that black —

PIERRETTE

Is white.

PIERROT

hopping

Poor Pantaloon, who finds a tack
In every carpet slipper.

PIERRETTE

Columbine?

PIERROT

The dance that hides the clothes peg on the line!

PIERRETTE

considering

No, all that jumping round would weary us.
We must walk on like this — be serious.

PIERROT

Gesticulate?

PIERRETTE

— like actors that we know.

PIERROT

I'll be an elongated Romeo —

PIERRETTE

tenderly

Stooping to kiss me, dear —

PIERROT

in silhouette!

PIERRETTE

leaning on his shoulder

What shall I look like as your Juliet?

PIERROT

caricaturing in air

Victorian Virtue —

catching up her clothes

To run —

all bustle —

bandy whatnots—

nose

More pointed than my own —

and such a chin.

PIERRETTE

bursting into tears

I hate your nasty play. I'm going in.

runs left

PIERROT

following her

But listen, darling. Don't you understand!

*She dabs her eyes with a tiny handkerchief. He goes on
one knee and catches her other hand.*

PIERRETTE

You do not love your wife. Let go my hand.

PIERROT

rising, pleadingly

Pierrette !

PIERRETTE

at gate

Last night you said that you adored

My shadow in pyjamas —

turning as she closes gate

now you're bored.

PIERROT

centre alone, to audience
I meant no harm. I hate domestic dramas.
moving left, looking
The windows flash —
                                two —
                                        three —
                                                six startled eyes
Across the trellises and lawn. She flies
Upstairs and down again to every switch in
The drawingroom, hall, the bathroom, pantry, kitchen,
As if the house in one gigantic huff
Had hidden lipstick, cold cream, powder puff.
in anguish
The fuse has blown and all is darkness now.
No . . .
                    — shaken by her rage a frightened bough
Has fallen down and snapped the electric cable.
I'm wrong . . .
She's found them on her dressing-table —
For in our bedroom, beaming with content,
I see one bulb.
holding out arms
                                O Darling, do relent.
hesitatingly approaching
She's at our window now. She must have beckoned...
But if I am mistaken . . .
indicating his heart
                                        Wait a second!
I'm right. I knew my darling would be kind.
starting back
Dear me!
                    What's that?
                                        She's banging down the blind.
considering
I must be cautious, stay awhile, then creep
Along the banisters, when she's asleep.
with sudden resolve
No, I'll endure the dawn, with tragic gloom,
Hugging the sofa in the breakfast room.
My heart is . . .

trying to remember line
           dated . . .
                    no . . . weighted . . .
                                deflated . . .
edging right, in a stage whisper   Cue.
edging nearer
    Quick, quick, the cue, please.
                VOICE OF HARLEQUIN
right, sepulchral
    Pierrot!

                PIERROT

jumping back, alarmed
        Who are you?
to audience
    A ghost as prompt!
                VOICE OF HARLEQUIN
in normal tone
               Think, Pierrot!
               PIERROT

in terror

                      Harlequin!
    What do you want with me?
            VOICE OF HARLEQUIN
                    I've come to win —
              PIERROT

realising
    To win —
            VOICE OF HARLEQUIN
        your wife.
              PIERROT

wildly
             You can't. She's too demure.
    And we are newly wedded.
            VOICE OF HARLEQUIN
             Are you sure?
             PIERROT

shrilly
    Yes, yes.
           VOICE OF HARLEQUIN
      Your tones are most heart-rending.

PIERROT

hysterically
> Go back . . . this play must have a happy ending . . .
> Back . . . peer through fanlight, dart around street
>   corner,
> Leap corridors. I'll call my wife, I'll warn her,
> Tell how you toyed with my confidence the last time
> We met, until I prattled for your pastime;
> The friend who made my difficulties clearer,
> But when they came — the self same disappearer!
> The friend, who, when I spoke of all my hope meant,
> Was fondly thinking of a new elopement:
> The friend who knew the slow words not the fast
>   stick.
> My patience stretches, paler than elastic
> At breaking point. Back, silent masquerader,
> My heart is free of you. I'm not afraid or
> Dejected now. I know what devils feel.
> I've seen at last —

VOICE OF HARLEQUIN

>   the wing upon my heel?

PIERROT

> Hint as you like. I'm strong. I can resist.

VOICE OF HARLEQUIN

> You can't decide.

PIERROT

Who then

cutely, as a sudden thought strikes him
>   — the dramatist?

VOICE OF HARLEQUIN

with assumed blandness
> Of course.

PIERROT

triumphantly producing typed play from pocket
> I have you, Harlequin. You tripped
> Into my trap —
coming nearer but still at a safe distance
>   a copy of the script.
> The carbon and the ribbon were not nearer
> In thought than you and I were, once.
>   Back, sneerer,

For I can prove by every tap and page,
You cannot come to-night upon this stage.
waits, listening, then investigates cautiously
    He's gone.
            I'm really getting very clever.
shaking himself
    But what is running down my back?
                         — a shiver!
    I dare not risk another prompt.
fingering his forehead
                  What's next?
to audience
    If you will pardon me, I'll read the text.
reading slowly
    ' Pierrot becoming sad and rather pensive ' —
indignantly
    I'm not. I'm feeling very apprehensive.
    There's some mistake . . .
turning pages feverishly
                This cannot be the play.
    The lines are different. My head's astray.
coming front, reading title page
    ' A Comedy ' . . . this light is much too dim . . .
    ' By Austin Clarke ' . . . I never heard of him.
confidently to audience
    I'll read the stage directions, scan the plot.
He reads slowly, instinctively obeying each direction
    ' First, Pierrot moves up, centre —
                   to the spot.'
The spot lights up
    ' Back curtains open ' —
As he waves his hand, reading, they do so
            ' Cyclorame — pale blue,'
He looks up, nods approvingly
    ' Sits down on grassy bank ' —
He does so
                ' Music on cue —
    He falls asleep . . . and daintily tip-toeing,
    A Columbine — from right.'
Jumping up and putting script in pocket
                I must be going.

I'm married now.
blowing a kiss

                    So, Columbine . . . goodbye.
pausing
I wonder what she's like.

                              No harm to try . . .
Precaution: just pretend to be asleep.
sternly
Now promise, Pierrot, nothing but a peep.
Sits down, closes eyes and smiles. Smile fades. Opens eyes
No Columbine! I'm much too ill-at-ease.

Ah! something I forgot —
runs to footlights, to orchestra
                    the music, please!
*Runs back and sits down as soft music starts, closes eyes,
then with a happy sigh makes himself more comfortable
and falls asleep. The music fades away and there is silence
for a few seconds. Columbine enters, right, upstage,
hesitant, and as if in fear. She is dressed exactly in the
same costume as Pierrette but wears a mask. She moves
gracefully and yet sadly to left, discovers Pierrot and
crosses to right. The audience at this time has considerable
advantage over the dreaming Pierrot and realises that
Columbine is being played by the same actress who has
already appeared as Pierrette. Slow action.*

                    COLUMBINE
gently
Pierrot!

          Pierrot!

                    PIERROT
slowly rising, rapt
          Columbine!

                    COLUMBINE
running to him
                    They kept
Me, darling, in the darkness, though I wept.

                    PIERROT
as if to himself
Imaginative darkness none can share.

                    COLUMBINE
in alarmed anguish, as he starts back
What is it Pierrot?

PIERROT

urgently
>That mask. Why do you wear
>That mask again? Why do you wear it? Tell
>Me, tell me, Columbine.

COLUMBINE

in gentle reproach
>>You know too well.

PIERROT
>Yes, yes, I know too well. Poor eyelids red
>With weeping. Shadow of tears that must be shed.

Trying to be cheerful, with a quick gesture towards her eyes
>To make those pupils dance, my Columbine,
>The poison drops of joy!
>>See how they shine!

COLUMBINE
>Only because my lashes still are wet.

PIERROT
still trying to be cheerful
>We must examine them.

He moves to unfasten mask. She stops him

COLUMBINE
>>I dare not yet.

PIERROT
>Dark domino, a thought can separate us!

going centre, right
>What have we done that mind should always hate us,
>The old conundrum need a new solution
>For every turn of brain? Is evolution
>No more — and faith the fashion for bare knees?
>Shall we unscrutinise, uphold, appease —
>With flattery, continual applause —
>Last exercise of hands and feet and jaws?
>Can we be saved, perhaps, by mathematics?
>Too hard !
>>Let's be profound.

Runs to her pretending to have a stethoscope, leaps back, pointing triumphantly to her heart
>>Why, even *that* ticks
>And proves the universe still goes by clockwork!

COLUMBINE

sadly, coming to him
    We found the dreadful door.

PIERROT

              But wiil the lock work
Or bend the hairpin that you gave me, dear,
For key?

COLUMBINE

softly
        So long ago.

PIERROT

        We reappear
With consciousness and find, for all we think,
The copybook has run off with the ink.

COLUMBINE

    Poor Pierrot !

PIERROT

puzzled
      Columbine.

COLUMBINE

obediently
        Yes, dear.

PIERROT

           What happened
The last time? Did some unexpected clap end
The comedy?

COLUMBINE

as they sit down
     Think, dear.

PIERROT

trying to remember
        A countryside
Between the towns —

COLUMBINE

       where birds had gone to hide
In little woods —

PIERROT

      no higher than your shoulder —

COLUMBINE

So many birds, the eggshell made them bolder,
Outpecked by song.

PIERROT

shuddering

But, Columbine, those cries on
The branches after dark and that horizon —
The sun, a burning mine among the trees,
Still there at night, pitfall of armouries,
Fire-washers, huge pig-iron smelting works.

COLUMBINE

Pierrot, we knew the suddenness that lurks
In air to strip the plaster from each room
And foolishly we fled into the doom
Of city after city.

PIERROT

Terrible sound
Came faster than sight, killing its own rebound —

COLUMBINE

Obeyed the needle nodding round the dial —

PIERROT

The rapid calculation —
last espial

COLUMBINE

Of expert earth.

PIERROT

Could skies be starrier?
Expanding sparks and all they carry, err
In dropping cemeteries blown to pieces?
Can passing finger know what it releases?

COLUMBINE

Flyaway bodies lighter than cubes of air
They suck as sweets; young men went up to dare
The sunny prism, gay with tab and facing,
Though future childhood died; specks that were
    chasing
A glory, frail as the uniform they donned,
Chasing it through the vacuum beyond
Our globe.

light begins to dim

PIERROT

How could poor citizens escape
When solids took again their ancient shape
Of unsubstantiality?

COLUMBINE

We fled
As ghosts when all belief in them is dead,
A glimmer of white clothes —

PIERROT

mere phosphorus —

COLUMBINE

For comedy had seen the last of us.
They are in darkness

PIERROT

rising

Where are you, Columbine? I cannot find
You anywhere.

COLUMBINE

Here, darling, close as mind.
Light rises again, gradually grows gay, with rose and amber hues

Look, Pierrot, a skylight! Laugh and learn your part
Again.

PIERROT

searching

My script?

COLUMBINE

I know our lines by heart:
They sit down

COLUMBINE

The trivial circumstances that tormented
Our waking hours, the authors who invented
Excuses when we tried to run away
Together — lest we spoil another play.

PIERROT

And all the wicked gossiping and fuss
That seemed to make our love ridiculous.
Dark gallery and pit, those hidden faces.

COLUMBINE

Appointments kept —

PIERROT

but always in wrong places.
unhappily

That park bench in the rain, the dredge of leaves,
I sat there wrapped in miserable sleeves,

All winter. Then I heard a great clock strike
The dark; and climbed the railings —
            COLUMBINE
                                    and the spike

That tore your jacket —
            PIERROT
                        bruised my arm —
            COLUMBINE

tenderly
                                    I bound it —

            PIERROT
    And left an iron kiss.
            COLUMBINE

softly
                        That night, I found it
    Above your heart — another violet.
            PIERROT
    But we were always happy when we met.
    The picnic rolls —
            COLUMBINE
                        enough for two —

He sits at her feet

            PIERROT
                                    . . . that day

    Among the mountains over Fiesole!
    The bread we carried —
            COLUMBINE
                            bigger than a baton.
            PIERROT
    The wine-fall in the flask at noon.
            COLUMBINE
                                    We sat on
    The ground among rock-roses in a pine wood.
            PIERROT
    The paper napkin that you wore — how mine would
    Keep falling down.
            COLUMBINE
                        That sausage —
            PIERROT
                                peppered!

COLUMBINE
pink!

PIERROT
A clown might envy it —

COLUMBINE
each bite —

PIERROT
a drink.

COLUMBINE
The world went wrong —

PIERROT
yet right —

COLUMBINE
because the moon
Came out to see the sun —

PIERROT
an hour too soon.

COLUMBINE
At dark we heard a serenade below,
The double parts that kept together —

PIERROT
holding her hand

slow

Upon guitar —

COLUMBINE
and fast on mandolin.

PIERROT
Those voices answering through thick and thin,
Such melody — we stopped to listen —

COLUMBINE
kissed

More often than we meant to, dear,

PIERROT
— and missed

The tram.
As a tremendous idea occurs to him, getting up
Wait, Columbine.

COLUMBINE
obediently
Yes dear.

PIERROT

                                                    I wonder
Was all that misery, each stupid blunder
Our share, because we weren't always good.

COLUMBINE

Rock-roses do not grow in every wood,
Pierrot.

PIERROT

            Suppose . . . how can I put it . . . Well
In order to become respectable,
Suppose that we . . .

                        you promise not to frown . . .

COLUMBINE

I promise, dear.

PIERROT

            . . . get married, settle down.

COLUMBINE

laughing
            The first time either of us thought of asking!

PIERROT

You will?

COLUMBINE

rising
                    Of course.
                    Now I can dare unmasking!
            Pierrot, don't look till you have counted three.
*He covers his face partly with his hands and counts slowly
with lip mime. She turns, throws away mask and turns
round again, hiding her face now with her hands as if in
playful parody of him*

PIERROT

turning
            Why do you smile yet keep your eyes from me?
            Your very hands reflect them as they shine —

COLUMBINE

And hide the blushes —
*She turns away so that her face is still hidden as she
lowers her hands*

                            of your Columbine!
She runs off right, followed by Pierrot

COLUMBINE
far away
    Pierrot!
        Pierrot!

PIERROT
off
        Columbine.
               Where are
    You, dear?
nearer again
        Where are you?
He appears at back against cyclorame, from right
            Have I gone too far?
Bewildered, he runs off, right, again
    I cannot hear you calling.
The cyclorame gradually becomes a darker blue and a low ominous drumming is heard. Pierrot is seen backing in from right, in terror, towards the stage. Drumming becomes louder, stops, as Harlequin leaps in from right. Through the eye-slits of his demi-mask appear goggles. He carries a little rod or wand

PIERROT
                  Harlequin!

HARLEQUIN
All darkens, Pierrot. Top begins to spin
And hum: the final giddiness of globe. Isle,
River and rock — geography is mobile.
Mankind arrived too late to learn the truth,
But roars each time it cuts another tooth,
Fighting to gain possession of those toys
Which end in silence, but begin with noise.
If hotheads play at giants, hit too hard,
What matter if the building blocks are charred?
I am the spirit of all new inventions
Known for their speed and excellent intentions.
My pantomime was once the sweating stoker,
A funny fellow with a red-hot poker.
I found a smaller act to save that toil
And on a billion tons of heat and oil,
I fed my new performing flea, the spark
That tickles happy travellers through the dark:

And while you fall in love, each time, more frantic,
I talk in air, I leap the great Atlantic;
So prove my right, Pierrot, to take the stage,
The spirit of the quick in every age.

PIERROT

wildly

Back, back! Your balanced couplets are a trick
To catch my Columbine.

HARLEQUIN

deprecating

The hemistich
Is far too wooden.

PIERROT

more wildly

And you substituted
That play for mine —

HARLEQUIN

and so electrocuted
Your missing heart!

PIERROT
You loathe me.

HARLEQUIN

Yes.

But true
To friendship, put the other point of view.

PIERROT

Back, Harlequin, I know your roof at last,
God's messenger — a midge upon the blast,
The devil striving to be orthodox —
The coffin-lid of hope . . . Jack-in-the-box,
Black in the face with rage that cannot hurt,
A tiny upstart waggling in a shirt
And jumping to a wire-pull, halfway in
And halfway out, the toyman, Harlequin.
All history shows the harmless and the meek win.
When gone are spangle, diamond and sequin.

The cyclorame has become bright again

HARLEQUIN

Pierrot, I think you've lost your sense of humour.
No brush above the chimney ever drew more
Than bags of soot, Fire likes a little smoke!
I meant it all, believe me, as a joke,

indicating
> A painted lath, a borrowed pair of goggles
> At which your pained imagination boggles.

PIERROT

Another trick!

HARLEQUIN
> No. No. Your love endures.
> And Columbine? She is already yours.
> And just to prove no wife could be so fond,
> Pierrot, I will pretend to have a wand.

Low drumming is heard

PIERRETTE

off, left, downstage
> Pierrot!

Harlequin smiles, vanishes in black-out, during which back curtains are drawn. Pierrette appears at a garden gate, in white silk pyjamas, carrying a Chinese lantern. She has an embroidered wrap and pretty mules

PIERRETTE

running to him
> Pierrot!

PIERROT

still dazed
> Pierrette!

PIERRETTE
> Can you forgive
> Your naughty little wife?

PIERROT

by rote
> How can I live
> Without you, dear?

PIERRETTE
> And yet I left you, all

> Alone!

anxiously
> Your sleeve is dusty.
> Did you fall?

PIERROT

nervously
> No. No.

PIERRETTE

as she brushes his coat
                   We must not quarrel any more.
                            BOTH

       We promise truly.
                            PIERRETTE
                                    And you do adore

           My shadow?
                            PIERROT
                         Even now when it has fled —

sighing
           Wish for the moon!
                            PIERRETTE

giving him lantern
                              I brought this one instead.
                            PIERROT
           You think of everything!
She looks up, alarmed

                            PIERROT
                                    But you are frightened?
                            PIERRETTE
       The clouds are strange, Pierrot,
                              Suppose it lightened!

                            PIERROT
soothing her playfully with a triplet
           Only a summer storm among the hills.
           Down comes the rain, chases the silly rills
           Into the great new reservoir and fills —
           A milli-millimetre!
                              You remember.
           The day we saw it all, the mile-long camber
           Of concrete —

                            PIERRETTE

softly
           Dear, the week of our engagement —
                            PIERROT
           The travelling crane—you asked me what the cage
              meant —
           The chain, the steam that grovelled in mud and
              marling.

PIERRETTE
Now let the clouds come down in buckets.
BOTH
Darling!
While they are clasped in a long kiss, the curtain begins to descend
PIERROT
to stage hands
One moment, please.
The kiss is renewed.
At last Pierrot picks up lantern and they turn towards the garden gate
PIERRETTE
I left the curtains undrawn.
Look, flowering trellises and half the lawn.
PIERROT
No light in any villa now but ours.
PIERRETTE
rapt
Rock-roses in the garden —
PIERROT
smiling
keep late hours.
Pierrot closes the gate and the curtain falls

THE END

THE PLOT SUCCEEDS

A POETIC PANTOMIME

CHARACTERS

Manannaun MacLir

Mongan Mor of Ulster

Manus, *his Adviser.*

Dulaca, *Wife of Mongan*

Blanaid, *Wife of Manus.*

Branduv of Leinster.

Abbot Cormac

Brother Malachi

Fergus

Grainne, *his Sister.*

Captain

Soldiers

Servants

THE PLOT SUCCEEDS

PROLOGUE

Sea Music. The Curtain rises on a dark stage and in a bluish-green spot appears Mannanaun Mac Lir in the guise of jester with comic half-mask. After a rapid dance, he disappears and the Speaker, wearing a medieval cloak and similar mask, appears. He speaks the following lyric:

Over the stony fields
That sharpen the hook in Connaught,
Alone with the drenching sky
Through cloudish grass, I ran
From every inch and inlet
Until the trees began.
I came under a wood
To water pale as rye
And heard in a place that was good for harps
The sun drip with the rain
And carpenters in a green workshop
Elbowing the plane.

I wakened a land so quiet
The glens were herded by a horn,
But I followed far into the south
The bird-lakes of the morning.
Three times I changed my shape for sport
Before the cocks were up,
Then lay awhile on an island
In a reed-tipped mile of the Shannon
And in the meadows, flat as corn,
Haymakers were rowing about
And women brought the blue-veined milk,
For they turn the butter out.

If boats, up and down from Kerry,
Go west for good fishing and oars give
Rock-hags that curl the tide-tops
New money from the netting,

I'll roll as bilge to one side
And somersaulting from the harbour,
Bow to MacCarthy himself and get
A share of the dish and the barrel
By swearing the fishermen spied,
Where the shoal of mackerel ran
With me, beyond a distant skerry,
The goldskin sails of Bran.

Last night in a house, all confusion,
I tumbled, I juggled, I danced,
To-day on a fife I was stopping the music
For women in Skye and soon after
I talked with poor men in Cantyre.
I sprawl in rags and bad shoes
By the fire of a small king in Leinster.
I will play for his ease or I won't.
I will do what I will, as my mind is pleasing,
And if I am gone, I am here.
But when tide turns, I foam upon the seas—
For I am the Son of Lir.
The figure of the Speaker disappears.

SCENE I

*A Leinster wood with bright spots. Beyond the trees can
be seen a sunny evening sky. On the right is a grassy bank.
Mongan enters rapidly from left, up stage, in a pilgrim's
cloak, followed by the supplicating Manus in similar costume. Mongan unhoods himself and flings back the robe
with an extravagant gesture, revealing his own costume
underneath.*

MONGAN
Now for the spell. I've found the very spot here!
All that it needs—a river; and the plot
Succeeds.

MANUS

Stop, stop, before it is too late.
The saints alone can interfere with nature,
Upset the Shannon, dam Liffey with their staffs.

MONGAN

Then why be so afraid of what comes after?
Can words unfable the past, mere busybody
Make water obedient—as a man of God
Changing the very weather? Fiddlesome sailors
When squall is jibbing them and fire within hail,
Blame Mannanaun, mistake foam for that jester
Tackling their ropes and putting caulk to test
Until day point again and capes are greener.

He slips off pilgrim's cloak and throws it on grassy bank.
Others believe when solids are unseen
That all has boiled away. So many stories
Have rolled the centuries upon our shores,
I'll make my choice. Without a knowing wink,
No gossip in Ireland can tell what we are thinking.

MANUS

Bad word goes round. Don't try it, I implore you,
What will they say in Ulster? Mongan Mor
Became a pagan, swore by the straws that dart
In dreams, forgot the miracles at Tara
And called back devils to the dipping font.
What of our faith, if every man who wanted
To see his wife again, had worshipped wave-top
Or flame?

MONGAN

And what should I have done then, shaved
My crown? Retired to a monastic dwelling
When Branduv, gaping from my table, fell
In love with my own wife, fled home, then raged
Across the border, hundred-hoofed, wagering
The mightiest of horns for her?

MANUS

He won

Dulaca in that game of chess.

MONGAN

My blunder.
I never should have moved against his bishop.

MANUS

I warned you at the time. You had your wish
And lost your darling for a drove of cattle.

MONGAN

I challenged him to fight me after that,
But she was braver than my word of honour.

MANUS

And left you . . .

MONGAN

took your wife to wait upon

Her.

MANUS

Did I blame you? No. Disguised as pilgrims,
We've squelched together from bog and wood to hills
    dim
With rain: your spies fall in the net and Branduv
Guesses that we are scratching at his land,
But I would risk all mortal danger to save
Your soul.

MONGAN

Dulaca said that she forgave me
And would be true to Ulster. I gambled heart
And now I'll stake what's left.

MANUS

going

Then we must part.

MONGAN

We can't.

MANUS

Why not?

MONGAN

smiling

The wood has been surrounded.
Soldiers are seen crouching behind the trees.

MANUS

May Heaven hide us now for if we're found,
They'll kill us first, then say we were escaping.

MONGAN

And yet a wish could change our very shapes.
whispers

MANUS

No, no, not that . . .

MONGAN

It's body now or soul,
Manus.

MANUS

We'll kneel and pray to all that's holy.
He clings to Mongan.
They're watching us.
raising him

And are you still afraid
To try?

MANUS

still trembling
Not now.

MONGAN

Then Mannanaun will aid us!
*Rapid whirl of blue-green lights as soldiers dash forward
with cries of "Mongan Mór." Black out. Lights up.
Soldiers are bending over captives bundled in their robes.*

CAPTAIN

What's wrong?

SOLDIERS

The moment that we grasped them, Captain,
They rounded on us.

Their nails grew long.

CAPTAIN

Unwrap
Our prize
*As the soldiers disclose them, the dishevelled captives are
seen to be Dulaca and her companion, Blanaid, for Mon-
gan and Manus have been changed into their shapes. The
parts are taken by the actresses who later appear as
Dulaca and Blanaid.*
Dulaca, wife of Mongan!

'DULACA'

Yes,
His wife—
indicating
—and her first cousin.

Gape like our dresses.
Admire upon our arms—

'BLANAID'

sotto voce   and elsewhere—

'DULACA'

                                                    bangles

In the latest black and blue . . .

'BLANAID'

sotto voce   enough to hang

The lot.

'DULACA'

If guests of Branduv venture out
Of doors, must they be seized upon by shouters?

'BLANAID'

to Dulaca   Worse might have happened us.

'DULACA'

But if we named it,
Blanaid, the day would hide again in shame.
Captain, when bugles rise, should soldiers trample
Upon mere sparks that tiddle beyond the camp?

pointing

The sun's come round again, so do not fear
What saints in heaven have kept dark. Heroes
Who make such war on women are not guilty.
Strip all before you, take Ireland for your quilt!

CAPTAIN

But, lady . . .

'DULACA'

Branduv will speak the next. Blow-hards,
Around the guest house,

leaving left, downstage, with a sarcastic bow.

                                        pipe our noble foe.

*'Blanaid' snatches the two robes from the astonished
soldiers and, with a contemptuous nod, follows 'Dulaca'.
There is now a comic mime to a flageolot. The Captain
expresses bewilderment, calls his men to attention. They
salute and goose-step towards right. Then, looking back,
suddenly take to their heels.*

MANUS

peeping in

They're gone. They're gone.

Enters, followed by Mongan.

bewildered, pointing

But I remember . . . your wife
Was standing over there.
gravely

                    Am I your life-long

Companion?

MONGAN
Of course you are, Manus.
MANUS

                    Then tell me

A secret. Was it you?
Mongan nods

                  And so the spell

Did work.
feeling himself

                Then I was . . . Blanaid.

MONGAN
coming to him

                 What have you lost now?

MANUS
My wits. Identity plays pitch and toss
With them.

MONGAN
But wife and husband are one flesh.
MANUS
sarcastically going
So there's no need for separate confession.
MONGAN
Where are you going?
MANUS

                        Home.

MONGAN

                 Are you insulted?

MANUS
When space and time become a catapult,
Good aim is all.
He halts

MONGAN
Who's there?
MANUS

                 An abbot and monk

Are climbing towards the wood.

Running round
                                        Will any trunk hide
        Our sins from them?
                        MONGAN
calmly
                        I know his holiness.
        Dulaca sent for him.   I read the message
        At noon.   Her note . . .
palming it
                        MANUS
to audience
                                Another trick of Satan.
                        MONGAN
at edge of wood
        Look how the sun is polishing their pates
        As if it knew of their important call.
        While there is time, I'll prove that nothing's solid,
        Summon a river here in deep respect
        And so delay her spiritual director
        And his companion on the brink.   Religion
        Must not be mocked at—but there'll be no bridge.
                        MANUS
        What then?
                        MONGAN
        We'll take their likeness, every hope
        Of ours come true.   Door after door will open
        And servants bow us in.   We'll kiss and fondle
        Our wives again before the pair have conned
        The last page of their breviaries.
                        MANUS
                                Stop, stop,
        Think of the cows that you have won, cropping
        Their way, as slow as moves upon the board,
        So strong that they have fought the bull and gored
                him,
        Yet best of yielders, white and curly brown.
        Think how the ancient Romans would have crowned
                them
        With flowers of May and led them to the altar.
        Grazing is sure for no man is at fault
        When opposites agree.   But pull the peg

And property will vanish, faith go begging
Once more.

MONGAN

Too true.   But were we not discussing
That distant relative of Proteus
Who saved our lives just now, and by the same token
Is elementary in every joke
He perpetrates?   Snatching the pole from raftsmen
Who dread him, when they feel too big a draught,
He gives it back a mile down-stream.   Disguise
Ill suits him, though no deacon is the wiser,
For wet or dry, he reappears on earth
That men in leaky houses may be mirthful,
Short-caped as a conjuror, offends the mighty,
Playing between the socket and the sight.
But when he makes his presence known by proxy
He gulls the air and waves submerge the rocks
Below.

Stage begins to darken and a faint drumming is heard.

    Stoop, stoop and listen to him.   Shannon
Plunges with heavier salt. The Moy, the Bann
Have heard a rumour, southward the Lee and Laune
  can
Detect that ocean-goer, Manannaun
Mac Lir.   Such waters as sink underground
To find the sources of their strength are rounding
Their caves: and now to Nore and Vartry river
More tributaries,— so diminutive
They scarcely wet their beds in summer—trip
And run between their falls.

       The air has ripples
Of mimcry as widespread in behaviour—
Touch but a ray in that crystal and the waves
Are ours. Though all despise the storyteller
For what's to be, and say the wishing-wells
Are holy now, whose bucket keeps them full?
Sometimes the contents only shake a bulrush,
Sometimes the sky.

A rumble of thunder

      But do not be uneasy,
He likes to make a noise when he is pleased.

*Black out. Loud thunder. Mannanaun appears in blue-
green spot, dances. Light gradually returns, showing that
the wood has disappeared; at back is a river flowing past
with a pleasant sound. The Abbot Cormac enters puffing
and blowing from left upstage, with Brother Malachi.
Mongan and Manus are watching them from left wing,
down stage.*

ABBOT

Now for a rest. I've found the very spot here.
Brother, sit down. The day is still too hot
Despite that spell of broken weather.

They sit on grassy bank, right.

BROTHER

We ran

As fast as tallow from a carried candle.

ABBOT

Of course, poor head is slower than my heels.

Brother jumps up, clutching himself.

Brother what's bitten you?

BROTHER

Quick, Father, feel me.

ABBOT

Where, where?

BROTHER

All over.

ABBOT

What's wrong? Why do you grab
The toppings of my sleeve?

BROTHER

Father, our habits
Are dry as bread in Lent. They should be soaked
On such a washing day. Bless, bless the oak-tree
That did not shelter us. Let every bell ring
At terce.

ABBOT

half rising, hopefully

You mean?

BROTHER

Yes, yes. A miracle

Has happened.

ABBOT

highly pleased

A miracle! I always knew
I was a saint.

BROTHER

O pardon my confusion,
Father, my thoughts are twisted as the hank
Unravelled for these woollens. I kneel and thank you
Now.

ABBOT

raising him

No, no. Thank heaven for it all

BROTHER

Look, Father, not an inch of cloud has fallen
Here.

ABBOT

tentatively

Perhaps the burst was local

BROTHER

Your Holiness
Is much too humble. Let it be a lesson
To sharpen with a quill. Our monks will write it yet,
The *Vita Cormaci.*

Abbot jumps up, clutching his habit.

What's wrong?

ABBOT

The letter
That lady sent, I put it in my pocket.

BROTHER

Father, you changed into your Sunday frock.

ABBOT

sits

Pray Heaven for it. Her scrawl was very private,
The spiritual problem of two wives
Who left their husbands.

Mongan has given note to Manus, who quickly shapes it into an arrow and casts it to middle of stage. Brother Malachi turns and sees it, run forward, picks it up and opens it.

BROTHER

Could this be her note?

ABBOT

glancing at it
> Another miracle!

BROTHER
>   It must have floated
> A mile at least.

ABBOT
>   Praise, praise to all in glory,
> For now Dulaca, wife of Mongan Mór,
> Will listen to the voice of reason, change
> Her mind and and marry Branduv, escaping danger,
> Adultery, before it is too late.

BROTHER
> Her present marriage has been consummated.

ABBOT
> But lacking true consent, is null and void.

BROTHER
> Although her husband frequently enjoyed her?

ABBOT

snapping
> Of course.

>   Our news will make her feel at home.

BROTHER
> Then shall we go?

ABBOT
> We'll linger for a moment.
> Gaze at that peaceful river, and admire
> The Second Day of the Creation.
>   Quiring
> Of angels praise it.   What can be those odours?

sniffing
> Bogmyrtle, mint and watermeadow mowed. . . . .

BROTHER

interrupting him
> Father! . . .

ABBOT
>   to bring us plenty.

BROTHER

rising
>   Father. . .

ABBOT

rapt
>   . . . swifts soaring. . .

BROTHER

loudly

I never saw that river there before.

ABBOT

sharply

What do you mean? You took me by this short-cut.
Where is the house of Branduv? Is it north
Or south? Is this the Liffey, Nore or Slaney?

BROTHER

The storm and miracles turn in my brain.
I cannot tell.

ABBOT

jumping up

This place is full of pissmires
And woodlice; we are in a fairy liss,
All stinging nettles, centipedes and midgets.
Come quickly, we must find a ford or bridge.

They leave right.

Mongan hurries centre with Manus

MONGAN

Now for a lightning change. Come closer.

*There is a blinding flash and black-out. As lights come up,
Manus, who has been transformed into the likeness of
Brother Malachi, is seen running round the stage, clutching
habit to his knees. The role is of course taken by the
actor who has been playing the part of Brother Malachi.*

'BROTHER'

Mongan,

Where have you gone? The spell is working wrong.
I'm back again in skirts.

*Mongan appears from right, now transformed into the like-
ness of the Abbot Cormac. The role is taken by the actor
who has already been playing the part of the Abbot.*

'BROTHER'

Father, excuse me.

Turns to go

'ABBOT'

sternly

Come back at once. Obey me. Do you refuse
The pleasures of this brief existence, hate
All womankind, forget the merry patron

Of those who trust to luck and sometimes strike it,
Scene-shifters, poets, gamblers and the like?
He winks

'BROTHER'

Mongan, are you the Abbot?

'ABBOT'

For the nonce.

'BROTHER'

Then swear it.

'ABBOT'

By this river—and your tonsure.

'BROTHER'

feeling the back of his head
Then I am brother—

'ABBOT'

Malachi.

'BROTHER'

skips   Let's hurry
To hug our wives.

'ABBOT'

But why the sudden stir
Of interest? Come back across the border.

'BROTHER'

I won't, for by the tightening of this cord
I know at last what celibates must suffer.
One change of scenery is quite enough.

'ABBOT'

pushing him into river
Then jump to joy.
Front lights darken and Manus is seen, in green light,
trying to swim.

'BROTHER'

Help, Mongan, help. You've drowned me.

'ABBOT'

following him
Touch bottom. What is here but sight and sound?

SCENE II

An outer room in the guest-house of Branduv. The scene is played with curtains and the back curtains are withdrawn quarter-way. There is a divan on right, a settle on left. Blanaid, who has fallen asleep, wakes up as Dulaca enters from centre, calling to her.

DULACA

Blanaid, Blanaid!

BLANAID

... Yes, dear.

DULACA

I nodded asleep
Just now as I was braiding a blue keepsake
And dreamed that both of us were carried off
By men.

BLANAID

I dreamed the same!

We'll talk more softly.
These Leinster women run to every sill
And never miss an open catch . . .
Blanaid hurries right and left to make sure no one is spying.

DULACA

pilfer

A passing word,

BLANAID

. . come closer than their hairpins,

Then flash away.

DULACA

. . . swallows that dine in air,

BLANAID

But make their homes of mud.
Sitting down on settle.
Now, dear, what happened?

DULACA

Workbasket, keepsake, were gone from my lap
And we were walking in an oak wood.

BLANAID

           Twisty

With gnarl and knobble?

                 Yes, and then our wrists
Were gripped by champions jumping from the
    bracken.

BLANAID

A captain led that hand-to-hand attack.

DULACA

You know?

BLANAID

       Of course.

DULACA

          My bruises were like bracelets

That fit too tightly—

BLANAID

               Mine were elsewhere—

DULACA

                  Lace

Unneedled—

BLANAID

       Wicked grabs beyond all mention!
But I was wily as a stable wench
Who hides her fork in hay.

DULACA

                I saw, too far
From us, a monastery, then wild parsley,
White-pointed as this lace. I woke from my nap,
Workbasket, keepsake, still upon my lap
turning
Blanaid, that dream is the smoke of crop and farm.
My husband marches southward with his army.

BLANAID

He can't.

DULACA

Too true. Mongan has calf and cow
For every hug I brought him with my dowry.

BLANAID

You made him keep his promise.

DULACA

thoughtfully

                             Every mile
Was squared upon that chessboard.
                          Why are you smiling?

BLANAID
I have our dream at last. It was the turbot
We ate to-day. .

DULACA
and means . .

BLANAID
                  . . that we must curb
Our appetite.

DULACA
               But it was so delicious.
Branduv has wooed me daily with such dishes.

BLANAID
Putting his passion in big pies and batters.

DULACA
All spoon and rolling pin.

BLANAID
             You'll grow too fat
Before the year is out.

DULACA
                  On poult and plover.

BLANAID
Was ever any man so much in love?

DULACA
considering
Blanaid!

BLANAID
Yes.

DULACA
             Would you wed a second time
If you were free to?

BLANAID
             Well, I like the climate.
And how the honey-makers here would buzz
If both of us should take another husband. . .
They converse quietly

DULACA
You make me blush.
Knocking

BLANAID

jumping up
>The Abbot by all that's humble!
>I hope that Brother Malachi has come
>With him, I need his spiritual counsel.

Branduv rushes in

BRANDUV

to Blanaid

>   Leave us.

DULACA

half rising

>   Branduv!

BRANDUV

>   Dulaca, do not frown
>Because I cannot wait a year.   Pity
>A widower, for canon law admits
>The plea, and name, O name the nuptial night.
>Quick as the pen that puts it down in writing
>We'll share that joy hearing the banns called out
>For those who marry again can never doubt, when
>Religion leaves them in the dark.   I press
>The little knuckles I dote on, kiss and question
>Them.   Ache of my knees will tell how often I pray
>Beside the bolster, what meditations delay me
>At meal time, steam of platters in every mouthful.
>Relent, Dulaca, that scholars in the south
>May praise that loving act and I will show them
>Such generosity. .

DULACA

>   Go, Branduv, go.
>The Abbot may be here at any minute.

BRANDUV

>Dulaca, I am in a state of sin.
>My very soul's on fire, though the wet blanket
>Of misery is wrapped around it.

DULACA

>   Thank
>Yourself if heaven has stirred.   Am I to blame
>If husbands take to sport and prove so gamesome
>They turn in the heat of play, and spend their wives
>On dice box, chessboard, wager them for livestock?

BRANDUV

Dear, pardon every move that brought me closer
To you that night.   Matchmakers are as gross.
Passion had taught me skill but holy candles
Chastened the row of chequers that my hand
Took silently.

DULACA

relenting

Then, if you love me, wait
In patience for the legal deed and statement.

smiling

All that you won at table is in safe keeping.

BRANDUV

greedily

I count those winnings, steal them in my sleep.

impressively

Dulaca, I had news of great importance
To-day . With runners, horsemen to escort
Her, Grainne, the youngest daughter of the Ri
Of Connaught, journeys here and all who see her
Fall instantly in love, they say. A thousand
Shorthorns and half as many dairy cows
Are hers.

DULACA

Why talk to me of cattle dealing?
Marry that beauty with such beef at heel.

BRANDUV

I won't.

DULACA

You will! Pray, when is she arriving?

BRANDUV

To-morrow with her brother.

DULACA

What a lively

Proposal you will hear.

BRANDUV

I will not listen.

DULACA

You must.

BRANDUV

Come, will you dare to bet a kiss

On it?

DULACA

smiling   Perhaps.

BRANDUV

For every cow she has?

DULACA

But there are fifteen hundred out on pasture!

BRANDUV

Are you afraid to gamble?

DULACA

laughing   No, I'll curb
Your appetite!

BRANDUV

rubbing his hands
Good!
confidentially

Now let us have more turbot
For supper,

DULACA

No, it makes me dream.

BRANDUV

My cook
Will serve a saucier dish that none dare look at,
Whitest of meat when we have snatched the cover
Off.

DULACA

Was there ever a man so much in love!
knocking
The Abbot!

BRANDUV

Send him away. We are engaged now.

DULACA

jesting
No. History will never have that page,
Record such rudeness in the Book of Leinster.
The side-door quick.
*Pushes him out right. Mongan and Manus in the forms of
Abbot Cormac and Brother Malachi come in with Blanaid.*

'ABBOT'

to Dulaca.

Daughter, the power of sin
Is everywhere and you are tempted. Frequent

Confession is necessary. May we speak
In private here?

DULACA

The pleasure will be mine.
But, Father, would you like a little wine first?

'ABBOT'

No, thank you, not yet. Brother has a scolding
To give your cousin now.

Winks at Manus.

Dulaca and Mongan leave right, centre.
Blanaid and the disguised Manus sit apart on settle, awk-
ward pause, he coughs, tries to speak, fails. Looks at her,
turns away.

BLANAID

May I make bold,

Brother. .

He looks alarmed

. . discuss the problem of my husband?

'BROTHER'

Of course. You miss him, wonder what he does
Now, fear the sportive hand that catches chub?

BLANAID

sighing

A separate woman has her troubles.
Would you consider that a second marriage. . .

'BROTHER'

He'll never marry again. No bolt or bar
Can keep him away.

BLANAID

You do not understand.

I mean to say that. .

'BROTHER'

Blanaid. you're handsome,

Bouncing with health, a comfortable armful
For the man who loves you. Do not look alarmed.
Your husband is here.

BLANAID

Where? Where?

'BROTHER'

How can I tease

You any more?

plumps down

                                   Manus is at your knees.

grabs her

BLANAID

Help . . . Help . . .
*Mongan hurries in with Dulaca. He is now in his own
shape.*

MONGAN

Brother, such conduct will unfrock you.

BLANAID

Mongan! I can't believe it—

DULACA

                                   sprung from lock

And bolt to me.

'BROTHER'

                     This mocking is disgraceful.
I want to be myself. Where are my face
And hands?

MONGAN

Poor Manus, we are all on loan,
Body and soul, and who can tell the owner?
Although we laugh, keep up a brave appearance
Or go upon our knees to bring it near,
Reality can never be in sight.
Reason and will are taken from us nightly,
And I have heard the scholars say that *quid*
Is all a *quod*. The premises are hidden:
None see them eye to eye.

DULACA

                                   Let me explain,
My dear, to Blanaid, put the matter plainer.
This is your absent husband.

BLANAID

still bewildered   But who grabbed

Me round the waist?

DULACA

Manus.

BLANAID

                     I saw the Abbot

Just now.

DULACA

No, that was Mongan.

Do you remember
The invisible mantle of Saint Brigid? The hem
Lay deep in dargle and forest, twenty miles
Beyond her cell, keeping a holy silence
For travellers lost at night, but robbers saw
Those pious men as fearful shapes, pawing
The paths with fire.

BLANAID

I understand you now.
The Abbot, by his spiritual power,
Guided our dear ones to this door.

Manus,

Forgive me.

MONGAN

Wait. The pot is not the pan,
What boils so purely may be only vapour.
Truth must restore him to his proper shape.
*He raises his hand impressively and murmurs but with-
out result.*

'BROTHER'

aside to him

I knew that this would happen.

Saint-Ready-come-at

Has gone.

MONGAN

louder   I'll try again.

BLANAID

It doesn't matter.
I'll take him as he is.

'BROTHER'

The Devil spoke,
Not my dear wife.

MONGAN

You're right. He has been smoking
Around us lately.

DULACA

How can we expel him
· Without the aid of Abbot and his bell?

MONGAN

Have you a sheet or blanket, please?
Turns and snatches the coverlet from divan
                                        No, this will do

The trick.
He places the 'Brother' near the centre exit and the two
women on each side holding the ends of the coverlet.
                    Now hold it tighter than your shoestring!
Another inch to hide the wicked glow
When Devil blushes.
He makes passes like a conjuror.
                    Ready. Steady. Let go!
The stage is darkened and a red glow shines on the group.
The two women jump back, Blanaid keeping hold of her
end of the coverlet. Manus is seen standing there in a
nightshirt. His wife hastily throws coverlet around him,
laughingly. Mongan and Dulaca run out centre.
    Black out.

SCENE III

The scene takes place immediately in a rich blue light
across the front of the stage. The real Abbot and Brother
hurry in, the Abbot making a sign of knocking, left.

VOICE

off   Who's there?

ABBOT

                    The Abbot Cormac come to see
The wife of Mongan.

VOICE

                        Are you *bona fide?*

ABBOT

Is this a monastery? Do our dunces
Speak Latin? Open that door.

BROTHER

Open at once.
VOICE

The Abbot Cormac and Malachi, his monk,
Are here already. Be off, you pair of drunkards.
ABBOT

The devil is mocking us again. I know
His voice.
BRANDUV

rushing in, right Father!
ABBOT

Branduv!
BRANDUV

Are you going
So soon?
ABBOT

Indeed I'm not. I've just arrived.
We chased the devil for almost five miles,
Thunder and hail delayed us . . .
BROTHER

Not a drop
Fell on these robes. Our holy Abbot stopped them,
Performed two miracles. Let every townland
Leap now to bell and bonfire. . . .
ABBOT

stopping him

We sat down
To rest, and saw a river flowing past,
So clear, deep-gravelled, stocked, it might have lasted
Till Doom: yet it was younger than the mayflies
That step-danced above it. Soon we were led astray
By scent of mint, bogmyrtle, meadowsweet,
But when the summer months all came to meet us,
I raised my voice, denounced the Father of Lies.
We heard strange rumbles. . .
BROTHER

of many different sizes,
ABBOT

Like. . . like . .
BROTHER

—the cracking of our larger beer-vat

Last week.

ABBOT

And so the river disappeared.

BRANDUV

interrupting

But you were in the guest-house?

ABBOT

What do you mean?

Captain rushes in from right.

CAPTAIN

Sir. . Mongan has crossed the Border. We have seen
  him.

BRANDUV

Where? Where?

CAPTAIN

At Partry oak-wood.

BRANDUV

In disguise?

CAPTAIN

That of a pilgrim.

BRANDUV

Alone?

CAPTAIN

With his adviser,
Manus. They met their wives there but escaped
Us, by a coat trick. . .

BRANDUV

left my champions gaping. . .

coming forward, to audience.

I see it now—her sudden acquiescence.
But win or lose, too quick a move at chess
Has blown the holy candles out.

turning   Mongan

Is hidden in my guest-house.

ABBOT

No, you're wrong.

The devil's at your door.

BRANDUV

to Captain   Call every man out.

ABBOT

I tell you that infernal river ran
Away.

BRANDUV
You nodded when you took a rest,
Father.
soldiers come in.
Guard every post. Surround the guest-house.
Branduv rushes off, left, with some of the soldiers, followed by Abbot and Brother Malachi.

SCENE IV

As lights come up, loud knocking on left. Dulaca hurries in with Mongan, while Blanaid and her husband spring up from the couch, the latter still wrapt in coverlet. Dulaca signs to Blanaid.

BLANAID
Who's there?

BRANDUV
Outside Branduv.

DULACA
to Mongan The side-door, quick.

BRANDUV
Open
At once.

BLANAID
Yes, coming, coming.

MONGAN
to his wife Let us elope
As if we were unmarried.

DULACA
rapt like Etáin—

MONGAN
—And Midir.

BRANDUV
Open.

DULACA

sadly, smiling
                    We can't. You pledged your honour.
          Still, all that you lost at play is in safe keeping.

MONGAN

moving right, eagerly
          I'll win all back to-night before I sleep.

BRANDUV

          Open.

BLANAID

          Armed men are everywhere.

MANUS
                                    He knows.

MONGAN
                              We'll go as we came, my dear.

MANUS

comic in his terror
          Protect us, I'll do penance—

MONGAN

*snatching the coverlet from him and hurrying him out
left, with a laugh*

                                    in this shirt
          He gave you.
*Dulaca replaces coverlet and signs to Blanaid to open door
Branduv rushes in with soldiers and servants, followed by
the Abbot Cormac and Brother Malachi*

BRANDUV

to soldiers   Hold the guest-house.

DULACA
                                    Is our virtue
          So threatened that you call an army up?
          Or have your servants run to cool a supper
          So hot the very smoke of it would daunt us,
          Spoiling the dish that every woman wants?

BRANDUV

          Your husband is here.

DULACA

          Then find him.

BLANAID
          And mine.

BRANDUV

suspiciously   The side-door,
    Quick, call the guard.

SOLDIERS

coming from inner rooms, centre.
                         Sir, nobody is hiding
   here
Captain enters right

BRANDUV

    Captain, did any strangers leave the guest-house?

CAPTAIN

   No, only the Abbot and his monk.
*Dulaca and Blanaid smile at one another until they see
the horrified expression of Captain as the Abbot and
Brother Malachi come forward.*

BRANDUV

                            Arrest

Him.
   Mount, men, gallop, search crossroad, wood, hill,
      harbour.
   Take every traveller in blessed garb
   And bring him here. Sick-calls must wait and souls
   Delay their flight though body has grown colder.
   Mount, men, and be my word and sight.
soldiers rush out.

ABBOT

                         Branduv,
   This is an outrage and I must withstand
   Your lay authority at once. Call back
   Those hasty men or you will kneel in sackcloth
   When I have spoken from the altar. Cause
   For household scandal's here already and strawsmen
   Who mum at doubtful marriages repaint
   Their features black.

BROTHER

                Our Abbot is a saint now.

ABBOT

silencing him
   The plea for nullity has been postponed
   So long, all say this lady is on loan here.
   Just now a pair of cunning devils came

Disguised as us, to tempt your guests, inflame them
With base desires.

DULACA

> Why should we not obey

Our lawful husbands?

BLANAID

> Even in the daylight?

ABBOT

I cannot stay.   This language is unfitting.

BRANDUV

You must. The doors are barred.

turning to Dulaca

> You do admit

Your husband has been here, Dulaca?

DULACA

> Yes.

BLANAID

And mine.   The Abbot gave them both his blessing.

ABBOT

I never did so.

DULACA

> Then you have betrayed them.

With pious hopes, called Heaven down to aid
The plot.

BROTHER

> She lies.

ABBOT

> The woman is distraught.

The Evil One has mingled more than water
And meadowsweet to stuff our senses.

DULACA

coming to Branduv   Branduv,
Have you not won me by your skill of hand
At play? Spare Mongan now and you may woo me
Beyond the chess board.

BRANDUV

> You have been untrue—

DULACA

How could I?—

BRANDUV
. . . blown the holy candles out
Before their flame was inched.

DULACA
Why should you doubt me?
And even if I had, we could relight them
Together, dear, upon our marriage night!

BRANDUV
wavering   This is a trick to save him.

DULACA
North and south
Must be at peace: they meet upon my mouth.

BRANDUV
How?

DULACA
In fifteen hundred kisses.

BRANDUV
wildly   I have fallen
In love once more.
He's free.
signs to servants who rush out.

DULACA
holding out arms   Then take them all!
*As they start kissing, the ecclesiastics avert their heads in
horror, while Blanaid, with a broad smile, begins to count.
Interval before next scene.*

SCENE V

*An open space in moonlight. Manus, once more in pil-
grim's garb, hurries in, beating back unseen wings, and
followed by Mongan.*

MANUS
The birds are bats. I told you what would happen.

No bush or twig is safe now. Forest, gap
And rock hide danger in a thousand shapes.
You let the pot boil over but who scrapes it?
                    MONGAN
Ask me what fire-stick taught us all to flatter
The next world, spice the offered smoke!
Far off sounds of horses and men rapidly passing.
                    MANUS

                                        What's that?

                    MONGAN
A tumble of men. All Leinster is unranked
For Mannanaun has shaken out his blanket.
Branduv is checked. Valley and ford are brimming
With flood that sends his army back to him.
                    MANUS
I'll not believe in trickery of wave
Or mist. Our wives did what they could to save us
And prayer alone has caused this miracle.
Kneel down, Mongan, kneel down for Heaven tells us
By sudden prodigy that we have erred,
Then hurry home and when our souls are cared for,
Our absent ones will strengthen us by pure
Example. Pangs may come—we can endure them;
Do not the clergy, by the large endowments
We grant them, by their discipline, their vow
Of chastity, say marriage should restrain us?
                    MONGAN
From what?   -

                    MANUS
                Too light a hand upon the reins.
You smile, but, snatch the holy pen from clerk
And what is left to scratch with in the darkness?
                    MONGAN
More thought.

                    MANUS
                No, no, our pilgrimage is booked
From birth.

                    MONGAN
                Must we not touch what we have looked at
On earth?

MANUS

The eye is lidded by obedience.

MONGAN

May we not search or find?

MANUS

Where is the need?

MONGAN

Then let us swear the summer is too rash
For us and trinkets fashioned on the ash-tree
May dangle in shame since matter is unsteady.
Forget that thistles grow so light of head—
Their seed is carried down, that every fly
Is furious and all we give the lie to
Crackles and bursts the pod. Keep house like women
Who fear a bite or sting may pink their limbs.
Hide, fancy, lest the honeysuckle catch you:
This world's extravagance must meet its match!

MANUS

Was ever bachelor so much in love?
I'll find a lesson in the nearest hovel.

*Looking round. On right is now seen the cloaked figure of
an aged woman crouching over a small fire.*

Bend at this doorway, see the soul of Ireland—
A poor old woman praying by the fire.

MONGAN

I see the very hook to hang our pot on
To-night. A bride for Branduv—and the plot
Succeeds.

MANUS

What can you mean to do?

MONGAN

Shorten

A road. With runners, horsemen, to escort
Her, Grainne, the youngest daughter of the Ri
Of Connaught, smileful as a new agreement,
Is travelling to offer hand, livestock
And wealth to Branduv.

MANUS

When does she arrive?

MONGAN

To-morrow with her brother.

But this hag
And I will take their shapes now, cheat the maggots
That wait on all. Door after door will open
Again and servants greet such haste. All hope
Of ours come true at last, we'll kiss and fondle
Our wives, when Branduv signs the marriage bond.

MANUS

Have you no sense of shame? This is outrageous.
Consider the discrepancy in age.
Dulaca prays for you. Why should she weep?

MONGAN

Ssssh!

The bride is waking from her beauty sleep.
Mongan snatches the cloak from her, and a lovely young
girl, very lightly clad in drapes, is seen.

MANUS

Can I believe my eyes?

MONGAN

They taught you prudence

At Clonmacnoise.

aside   MANUS

How old? Would it be rude

To ask.

GIRL

overhearing
Of course not, I am five-and-ninety.

MANUS

You want to marry?

GIRL

Why should I decline?
Late marriages are customary, dear,
In Ireland.

MANUS

But if you have known an era
Of war and hate, what must the years have taught
      you?
If all the soul has added comes to nought,
Then what do sorrow, penitence and grace mean?

GIRL

who has been admiring her hands, smiles
How can I tell until I see my face?

MONGAN

Wait here awhile.

Mongan cloaks the girl and they leave, left

MANUS

More druidcraft and danger.

calling out

Good heavens.

Mongan, you forgot to change

Yourself.

*Mongan and girl look in. Mongan has now been trans-
formed into the shape of Fergus, and the part is taken by
the actor who appears later as the real Fergus.*

'FERGUS'

Quite wrong again.

GIRL

My brother Fergus.

MANUS

miming—as if walking bare-foot on flints.

I'll fast, I'll pray, I'll shiver at Lough Derg.

SCENE VI

*The scene is the same as the end of Scene IV. Branduv and
Dulaca are still kissing; Blanaid is counting. As she comes
wearily to nine-hundred-and-ninety-one, the Abbot starts
forward.*

ABBOT

Stop, Branduv, stop. before you reach a thousand
For if this lady hopes to be your spouse
Such courting is no prefix to the state
Of matrimony. Monk, emaciated
By fast and vigil, hand joined to hand in struggle,
Though winter freeze him, will not even hug
Himself. I'll fetch example from the sky
To move you.

dramatically

Think of Columcille flying
Miraculously through the air in combat
With seven tempters. As the fiery scrum
Swept on, peninsulas were less than ink-blots
A scholar wipes out with sand. Soon every chink
Was cloud. Far off in Rome the Pope looked out
From his high window, heard the demons shouting.

From Alp and Apennine, a storm of snow
Came round the eight. All glaciers were flowing.
Those stays of ice on limb, the blood held fast:
Think of that mighty chill.
                                        Consider lastly,
If such predicament is not enough,
What Brother Malachi and I must suffer.
                    BROTHER
It needs a miracle and not a wish,
Father, to solve this problem of partition.
                        ABBOT
A miracle . . . I'll try. May Heaven free them.
Tubas off
'Fergus' and 'Grainne' are announced and enter, followed
by men and women of the household
                    ANNOUNCER
Grainne, the youngest daughter of the Ri
Of Connaught, and his son, Fergus.
                    ABBOT
                                        Fulfilment

Of all our prayers.
                    BROTHER
                                        Another miracle—
For who can doubt such evidence?
                    'FERGUS'
                                        Pardon
Our haste, Branduv. We galloped until hard
Was soft, high—low, the beaten track—a mist.
All Leinster was a story that my sister
And I were hearing, bit by bit,—we rode so fast.
And your renown—an army that outpassed us
Yet showed us the right o'way, making us eager
To leave our retinue as many leagues
Behind us as we could—in jest—twirling
The twigs together for our camp.
                                        Young girls
Ask if their husbands will be dark or fair
And who will blame the fancies they are sharing:
Although religion bless the loss of it,
Such curiosity may be permitted
To innocence.

BRANDUV

gazing at 'Grainne', rapt.

                      Sleep in a fairy liss
Must overcome a hundred thousand kisses
They say, and I could well believe such pagan
Survival, though the poets are so vague,
For all avoid those green rings, none dare till them.
You come from Connaught. Has a gentle hill
Opened—
coming to her

                   —and is this elder-blossom wrist
Her own or not?

                     Are you indeed his sister?
No, do not speak as yet. Withhold your voice.
My faith, returning, would keep it in that cloister,
To hear it answer in the sweet responses
That bride and bridegroom only make but once.

ALL

A noble pair!

BRANDUV

                    I ask you to perform
The solemn ceremony, Abbot Cormac.

ABBOT

Leinster rejoices, Branduv. May your union
Be blessed with issue and this house immune
From evil. When do you desire the marriage?

BRANDUV

To-night.

ABBOT

           But that would be irregular

BRANDUV

Then I shall double . . .
Abbot shakes his head.

               treble the marriage fee.
Abbot nods consent
turning to Fergus
    And hereby ratify immediate treaty
With Connaught.

'FERGUS'

              I demand a price.

BRANDUV

It's paid.

'FERGUS'

smiling   I, too, have fallen in love.

BRANDUV

With whom?

'FERGUS'

indicating Dulaca   That lady.

BRANDUV

She's yours.

DULACA

Father, is this a fairy tale
Where nothing counts, despite our human failings,
So all end happily—and by what text
Does pleasure prove this world to be the next one?
Let Branduv choose a light o' love from hillside
Or rath, must I forget that 1 am still
The wife of Mongan Mor?

BRANDUV

Did I not win you
With his own chessmen, bone by bone?

ABBOT

More sin
And scandal. Let us exercise restraint
In public affairs.

BROTHER

Our Abbot is a saint now . . .
A river has obeyed him.

ABBOT

to Brother   Who is speaking?
to Fergus   Young man, reflect, consider for a week
That law is blind when glances are too rash.
This means a plea for nullity at Cashel.

'FERGUS'

The bargain has been made—

ABBOT

not with remorse.

BRANDUV

Go quickly, Fergus, with her, take fresh horses.

ABBOT

This question of divorce must be debated.

BRANDUV
Not now, not now. Our marriage cannot wait.
A procession is formed and all leave, left, except 'Fergus',
Dulaca and Blanaid.
'FERGUS'
Blanaid will pack for you. We travel light,
All that you need, a cloak, a comb, your nightie.
He waves Blanaid off centre.
DULACA
What do you mean by this? Who are you?
'FERGUS'

                                    Mongan.
DULACA
Can it be true?
'FERGUS'
Did I delay too long?
DULACA
confused
No . . . you were just in time . . . I was distressed . .
You looked so different . . . How could I have
        guessed it?
'FERGUS'
Forgive a last deception, my Dulaca,
What was it but a plot—
DULACA

                                    To win me back?
'FERGUS'
To Ulster.
DULACA
        But that marriage . . . and the bride . . .
Who was she?
He whispers

DULACA
Ninety-five! How Branduv eyed her
Like a great house-fly!
gravely   Then it was a spell?
He smiles

DULACA
anxiously   And to-morrow?
'FERGUS'
        What can the real Fergus tell him?

DULACA

If he suspects . . .

'FERGUS'

What enemy has laughter?

DULACA

Too true. But, Mongan, it was druidcraft
And that will bring ill-luck.

'FERGUS'

with pretended gravity   I did it all
For you.

DULACA

Some evil surely will befall us.
Must we not dread what is beyond our breath?

'FERGUS'

smiling   It may have been a long-forgotten method
Of thought-suggestion.

DULACA

Should I kiss a stranger
Who takes my very sight?

'FERGUS'

You have permission.

DULACA

yielding happily
What wife would not obey her husband's wish?
They kiss.

'FERGUS'

starting back   Can absence glow like this?

DULACA

What is it, Mongan?
Why do you stop?   Have we done something wrong?

'FERGUS'

rapt
Can I blame Branduv now for all his mischief?
If in the hope of gaining such a kiss
From you, he sent his army to pursue me
To-night, what would a thousand do?

DULACA

Why, darling, bring it back to him.
*He looks surprised but she draws him back again into her
arms.   After some time she withdraws*
No . . . no . . .

My Fergus . . . I mean Mongan . . . I must go now.
Blanaid may need my help.

'FERGUS'

Are you offended?

DULACA

How could I be, but where can all this end?
Run, bring me back the likeness that you took
From me. To be yourself, dear, you must look it.
How could our days be quiet and domestic
If dreams like these disturbed our nightly rest?
*She leaves centre, he leaves right. After some time Dulaca
and Blanaid come in carrying travelling cloaks, etc.*

DULACA

turning to go back   My keepsake!

BLANAID

holding up a robe de chambre of light blue silk
   It's here.
They laugh.

DULACA

We had a happy time.

They both sigh

BLANAID

Why do we sigh, my dear?

DULACA

We liked the climate.

BLANAID

And how those women would have been a-buzz—

DULACA

If both of us—

BLANAID

—had taken another husband.

Mongan and Manus hurry in right.

MANUS

Blanaid!

BLANAID

Manus!

DULACA

My husband has come back

To me.

MONGAN

Fully restored to sight, Dulaca.

And now that our matrimonial woes are over,
What were they but a tale to tell at Shrove
When we good Christians can forget our fear
By tickling our own ribs and drawing nearer
The fire? Come, for a story's sake, assume
Despite the frown of space and time, that humour
May yet be found to give us hope, world
Beyond world, amongst the energies that hurled us
From nothingness, and let us share the joke
We fail to see—nor dread that we have broken
A new commandment, however great our fall,
Nor think the human mind is at the solstice.

MANUS

gloomily

Laugh on the way, while Branduv is in love,
But in the morning all must be discovered.

MONGAN

Why then, to prove that wonders are unceasing,
May Ireland, north—

DULACA

and south,

ALL

remain at peace.

*Mongan and his wife run left, the other pair run right to
see that all is clear; all come again to centre as curtain
falls.*

EPILOGUE

*Late next morning. The scene is outside the royal bed-
chamber and the back curtains are drawn quarter-way.
Noise off-stage. The real Fergus and his sister enter with
supplicating Abbot, men and women of household.*

FERGUS

Father, this farce must end.

ABBOT

> Be calm, I implore you.

FERGUS

But I tell you we were never here before
And none shall call us double-faced. I demand
This audience to make it clear. Does Branduv
Keep such late hours that chaplain dare not tell
When he gets up . . . and are we to be welcomed
To Leinster by a plot that hides all meaning
From eye and ear, or proves that the unseen
Must be unheard of? Are these whispers and nod-
    dings—
Back answers in obedience to the rod
That overshadows Ireland?—Disapproval
Of second marriages? Say so—and the hooves
My sister brings are gone. Should every dowry
Be stall-fed now? Are fifteen hundred cows
From Shannon grass not good enough to rub
Themselves against your scratching posts?

ABBOT

> The trouble

Is spiritual. Do not be insulted
If we consider for awhile. *Quis vult?*
Come, Brother Malachi.

going left   This, this is dreadful.
What can we say?

BROTHER

> But who is he in bed

With?

ABBOT

Malachi, I scarcely can discuss it:
Branduv is sleeping with a succubus.

BROTHER

A female devil! But you married them
Last night.

ABBOT

I was deceived by those dissemblers.
But I'll declare the marriage null and void.
Free Branduv now . . .

BROTHER

> Although he has enjoyed her?

ABBOT

snappily   Of course.

BROTHER

The lady may not recognize
Divorce.

ABBOT

She must, for I will exorcise her.

BROTHER

So great a rite may be too bold. They say
The clergy often die of it.

ABBOT

What layman
Has spread such superstition?

GRAINNE

Fergus, come home,
How could my heart be happy here?

ABBOT

coming over   One moment,
My son, I must confess with grief and shame,
There is a demon in the royal chamber.

To Grainne
Do not be frightened, child. We shall pronounce
The exorcism . . .

BROTHER

give the fiend a trouncing
In Latin . . . Wait until you hear the yelp.

CROWD

A demon, a demon bride!

*Abbot begins exorcism. A yell off stage. Branduv rushes
in centre, still in night attire, but wrapped in a voluminous
cloak*

BRANDUV

Help, Father, help me.
Ugh . . . Ugh . . . There's an oul' wan in my bed
With whiskers, gums for grinders, mumbling she's
wed now
To Branduv and her twenty nails are crooked
As harrow tops clutching the clods.

Peeping again   Look. Look.
She's sitting up and saying her prayers.

turning to crowd

                                             Who sniggered?
Was this a trick? I'll make the joker jig
Among the crows for this and soot the strawsmen
Who mock at marriages without due cause.
Where have you stuck your tongues?

ABBOT

                                        I have controlled
The spirit.

BRANDUV

seeing the real Grainne
Grainne! What gossip have they told you
That you are up and dressed? You cannot leave
Like this: if our embraces could deceive us,
What can love be? I fell asleep at the dawn hour
And dreamed an ancient tale of Mannanaun
For poets say, could we but see it rightly,
The ocean is a flowering plain of delight.
We lay in the daisies there—and yet were swimmers
Who float on foam and never stir a limb.
 Have you forgotten all our joy?

FERGUS

                                        Stop, stop,
Such pagan conversation is improper.
Is this how Leinstermen propose?

GRAINNE

                                        Take me
Away at once.

BRANDUV

seeing Fergus   Fergus! Am I awake
Yet? Where is Mongan's wife? Have you deserted
Her?

FERGUS

            Come, dear.

BRANDUV

on his knees   Grainne, stay.

FERGUS

pushing him   Let go her skirt.
There must be devils here in every bin.
They leave.

BRANDUV

Captains, unlock my stables for I will win her

Again by force of arms. She is my wife.
> ABBOT

You are mistaken.
> BRANDUV
>> Monk, you dare to trifle

With Branduv, Ri of Leinster, and deny
You married us or that the fees are higher
For late night-services.
> ABBOT
>> Let me explain

What is beyond our nature. You have lain with
A she-devil.
> BRANDUV
>> Take care . . . she is my wife.
> ABBOT
>> No, no

You do not understand. She is your foe, man.
The teachings of the wise are clear. Augustine
Maintains the husband can be free of lust
In such a case if he is ignorant
Of all collusion.
> BRANDUV
>> Am I frantic?

Father, I tell you I have never known
Such happiness, such love as she has shown me.
Why has she gone? What have you said . . . what
    packet
Of lies: . . .

Lights begin to dim
> ABBOT

Blasphemer, she is coming back.
> BRANDUV

Grainne, my wife?
> ABBOT
>> No, no, the wicked spirit

I exorcised. Your will has summoned her
To gratify you and the air has lent
Its flimsiest material.
>> Quick, repent now.
> BRANDUV

Gabble your news from heaven to our nursemaids

In nine months. If love is better, what is worse?

VOICE OF HAG

off   Duckie . . . Duckie . . .

CROWD

The hag!

They fly

BRANDUV

stepping forward   A trick.

ABBOT

Pray, pray

With me. All mortals crumble in a clay bed.

BRANDUV

scornfully

What newly married pair has feared the shovel?

ABBOT

raising his hands in despair.

Was ever any man so much in love!

Light becomes normal and 'Grainne' appears centre door-
way, lightly clad in transparent drapes as in Scene V.

BRANDUV

Grainne!

ABBOT

Hide, Brother, from unholy sight

Hastily leads the backward-glancing Brother off stage.

BRANDUV

So you are mine again.

'GRAINNE'

Had you a night-mare?

Poor darling!

BRANDUV

Yes, but dreams can peel the rind

From reality. I love you for your kindness.

You sneeze, my pet . . . you must be catching cold

sharing his cloak with her

Come, let me wrap this warmth around your
        shoulders.

Joy stirs and we must celebrate our wedding.

'GRAINNE'

What shall we do?

BRANDUV

Have breakfast now in bed.

They leave. Black out. Manannaun appears in bluish-green spot and dances as curtain falls.

THE MOMENT NEXT TO NOTHING

A PLAY IN THREE ACTS

To

JAMES WHITTAKER

CHARACTERS:

Ceasan   Eithne

The Search Party

Period and Place:

Ireland at the time of St. Patrick.

THE MOMENT NEXT TO NOTHING

ACT ONE

Scene One.

*A clearing in an oak-wood beside the River Boyne, on a
summer's evening. The stage has two levels, and the river
is at the back. On left there is a seat formed along the
ramp: near it, a small circle of stones for a fire. On
right, downstage, the sawn base of an oak can be used
as another seat. On right, back, there is a group of oaks:
behind them, unseen or off stage, we imagine a grave
with a small flat cross of stone. As the curtain rises,
Ceasan is pacing slowly around the clearing, praying, his
Psalter in hand. He is dressed in a monastic habit, grey
in colour, and conventionalised rather than strictly correct.
He is about to leave, left, when he hears a sound, stops,
listens, and moves cautiously downstage to watch. Eithne
enters, rapidly, and in distress, from left, upstage. She
is wrapped in a cloak which partly conceals her richly-
coloured dress. She sees the grave, and hesitates in
surprise and bewilderment.*

EITHNE

to herself
> What can it be?

CEASAN

approaching

> Lady, it is the grave
> Of Marravaun, a man who was reborn
> In spirit among these woods.
>
> But do not look
> Alarmed. The prayers he planted here, deeper
> Than spade, can shelter the passer-by, for they
> Have oaked and spread themselves invisibly
> Until he breathes again on the Last Day.
> Soiled as his body, thick-set with blessings above us,
> They keep, beyond our questioning, the place of
> His resurrection.

EITHNE

His resurrection?

CEASAN

Yes.

EITHNE

I do not understand.

CEASAN

Are you not one

Of us, Lady?

EITHNE

What do you mean?

CEASAN

I mean—

Are you of God's people?

EITHNE

How can I

Be certain? Are there not many gods? I lost
My way beneath these branches. Right and left
Were false and my own footsteps quick as lies . . .
And then . . .

pointing

I saw that stone there, cut so badly
I thought the ignorant blows that held it down
Must surely have shaken the socket of hammer or
  blade,
And yet it seemed to comfort me, tell me
Of something I did not know, some happiness
In pain.

CEASAN

Lady, all mortals have been lost
Before they found themselves on earth. But the way
Is straighter than this wood to those who know it
By twist and turn, though many in Ireland still
Are unconverted. That cross, rude as the haft
A stone could humble from spark to spark, can save us
From torment of mind. Has it not brought you safely
To blessed ground?

They come, centre

EITHNE

And what must we believe?

CEASAN

rapt

That finger and thumb, long after they have been
Corrupt, will run with ichor, last for ever!

turning to her

Therefore, we do not burn our dead, smoking
Them out with fearful haste as pagans did,
But lay them piously in mould, certain
That they will shape themselves again from such
Mysterious rot, when all is next to nothing,
And that the bodies of the merciful
Will, then, be glorified.

EITHNE

Your words are strange,
Secret as distance, yet I think they stir
The air that shades itself among these leaves
With solemn meaning, for I can almost see
Those wonderful bodies of which you speak, lighter
Than air, as quick and as unwoundable.

pointing, uneasily

But what is hidden from us behind the sun,
Glittering like a far-off enemy?
Tell me, tell me, if nothing can be lost
Where is the lonely spirit of Marravaun
That is so bodiless?

CEASAN

In Heaven, I trust.

EITHNE

In Heaven?

CEASAN

Mankind has found all happiness
Beyond that sky you seem to fear.

EITHNE

Truly,
It is a place or state of perfect being?

CEASAN

Though all look down on their remains,
Lady, their happiness is incomplete
Until the spirit—or soul—has been united
With body again.

EITHNE
You mean such glorious flesh
Will last forever when this life is nothing,
The merciful be young as it, moving
Finely within a finer element
That brings all things to mind?

dreamily
I seem to see
That land of happiness, where winter is
Forgotten, wishes come true and the other seasons
Are three in one—bud, blossom, fruit,
On the same branch.

CEASAN

surprised
Lady, all mortals long
For happiness and even in the folly
Of old religions, truth, though fabulous,
Can recognise its own tormented self,
Pallid in flashes of an unfixed star.
Terrible sacrifice was known in the past,
Erroneous rite of proffered food and drink.
The holy wells which heal our sick, restore
The sight or hearing, clap a sorry limb,
Were venerated. Though you speak, no doubt,
Of Tirnanogue, that legend, too, foretells
The joy to come: for when the world is gone
And Judgment given, all those who are in Heaven
Will not be more than thirty years of age.

EITHNE
How can I go to Heaven?

CEASAN
You must die
First, Lady. Life on earth is but a trial.
The beating in the body keeps us here
Until it stop, the soul unstifle the self.
We suffer into joy.

EITHNE
Surely that pain
Is worth what seems to have no end.

CEASAN
Goodness

Has brought you to this place! Believe me, I
Was lost in greater error and this world
Seemed priceless as my curiosity
Before I was converted.

EITHNE

Tell me about

Yourself.

CEASAN

My name is Ceasan . . . a humble clerk
As yet in minor orders.

EITHNE

You live alone,

Ceasan, within this wood?

CEASAN

Yes, for a year

Now, meditating in silence.

showing her, left, downstage

Beyond

Those oak-boughs you can see the simple hut
In which I sleep—

EITHNE

smiling

as bark'd and knobbly as they are.

CEASAN

—Indeed the bees, those little fellows of learning
Computed by the Brehon laws, mistake
The way at times, when they are hurrying
With honey for their waxen tablets—and buzz
Around the chinks. It sheltered Marravaun
In his old age with gnarl and knot. I want
To be as worthy of it.

EITHNE

Was he so gentle?

CEASAN

So gentle that when he prayed in this very spot,
Birdflocks were litanied about him
With tiny ejaculations. Because of that,
The superstitious, bending from their cobbles
To lift a night-line or come to set a grass-snare,
Whispered that it was Aongus Oge they saw,
Hidden in holy habit.

EITHNE

slowly

Aongus Oge
I've heard that name before . . . I cannot remember
Where.

CEASAN

Then you are a stranger to these parts,
For the sedges that rub together in the breeze
And summer bushes flowering along
The Boyne, have stories of him, so to speak.
The very trees have been his evil-spreaders
In the old days. Men say he was the god
Of kissers, known by his pure wickedness
And the birds that flew around his temples.
Pushing the leaves back, clawed by music, that love-
   catcher
Set traps for lonely thought.

bringing her upstage

He came, they say,
From that great tumulus which you can see
Across the river there. It has an entrance
Of whirlwind bronze—scroll within scroll—
To his invisible kingdom.

EITHNE

What do they call

It?

CEASAN

Bru-na-Boinne.

EITHNE

It makes me tremble.

CEASAN

I, too,
Have been afraid of it.

EITHNE

Then why do you live
So near that brazen earth?

CEASAN

with sudden vehemence

To rid myself
Of superstition. We must unfather, unmother
Ourselves to find a lodging in our veins,

muttering
  Yes . . . yes . . . a lodging.
calming himself

                    Lady, one
  I scarcely dare to name has sent me here
  To fight against my birth-wrong—Patric, son
  Of Calpurn.
                    EITHNE
          Who is he?
                    CEASAN
              A captured man—
                    EITHNE

softly
    A captured man—

                    CEASAN
              who brought the truth to us
  Across the sea.
                    EITHNE
          Where is he now?
                    CEASAN
                    Lady,
  He winters far in the north, for he is old,
  Must labour with lesser mouths. But it would take me
  Too long to tell how nature has obeyed
  This failing man, recount the wonders he
  Has worked for us. Life clings to him, jealous
  Of his eternal rest. Still, every year
  He makes a circuit of the south, with half
  His household, psalmists, reciters, catechumens,
  His candle dippers, hammerers of fine metal,
  Smiths, tonsurers and champions of the faith.
  Their strength brings back the places he has known
  And often of a summer's evening, he sits
  Outside the green branch of his tent, in peace,
  Breaking his word into such sweetness, young
  And old can share it at the one time. The day
  After to-morrow, I shall see him, God willing,
  Not far from here within that crowded camp
  And if he deem me worthy of it, leave
  This wood forever.

EITHNE
What will you do then?
CEASAN
Return.

To my studies and after ordination preach
The truth by lake and river.
EITHNE
Lake and river?
But do you worship a god of water?
CEASAN
No.

You do not understand. The element
Is necessary as an outer sign
That soul is purified. Therefore, we practise
Total immersion, dip our neophytes
And speak above their heads: this being called
The rite of baptism.
EITHNE
Instruct me, Ceasan,
That I may understand.
CEASAN
Gladly.

They sit down

EITHNE
Begin
At the very beginning.
CEASAN
Once, once in no time,
Before the world was made, there was a war
In heaven.
EITHNE
A war in heaven?
CEASAN
Yes. Great spirits,
Which we call angels, revolted in their pride.
But God defeated them, tossing their armies
Into a lower state of flame, there to
Be tortured and consumed, like shriek after shriek,
Yet unconsumed, for spirits cannot lose
Their consciousness.
excitedly

> Lady, our punishment
Can be the same as theirs because they have power
To tempt all those who live on earth.

he rises

CEITHNE

What is it?

Why do you stop?

CEASAN

Look . . . look . . . the moon
Is tapering the reeds in the pools. Night
Has spread a thousand errors through the wood.
The paths are twistier with roots, the branches
  knotted
Above them with searching blows. You cannot stay.
Return to-morrow for instruction. I
Will guide you beyond the trees. Where do you come
  from?

EITHNE

dazed

I do not know.

CEASAN

You must . . . what is your name?

EITHNE

Eithne.

CEASAN

Where are your people?

EITHNE

I cannot remember . . .
I cannot . . . I leaned to pluck a tall iris
From the Boyne and found myself alone. I must
Have fallen asleep there in the sunshine . . . I woke
And the river was so different, I thought
That I was on the other side of it.
I saw a mooring stump, grey, unroped,
Bent like a half-drowned tree—

CEASAN

I know that inlet . . .

Not far from here—

EITHNE

I was frightened and ran
Under the trees. The sorrel was so chill—

My ankles might have been bare—so pale the sun
Seemed shadowy as this moon, locking the wood
With silver wards now. Every turning was wrong
As I have told you and my footsteps lied
To me . . . and then . . . I knew no more of life
pointing
    Until I saw that grave.

CEASAN

                         Illness, bereavement,
Can close the busiest of doors. Try, try
To think.

EITHNE

        I cannot . . . Truly I cannot.

CEASAN

Do not despair. It may be God has sent
This temporary affliction as a veil
Against your past. All that we recollect
Must go to Him at last.

EITHNE

                  Affliction . . . yet
I know that I have suffered something greater
Than this, some happiness still incomplete
As if . . . as if . . .
As she sinks, he supports her.
faintly
                I were in heaven.
He lays her down, anxiously, clasps her hands, slowly
draws the cloak around her

CEASAN

                          The truth
Has been too much for her and she has died
Of it.
rising
        What can I do with this new fear
That clasps itself and runs behind the trees
In some fantastic attitude of prayer
Knowing that anguish has too many hands?
No silence now can punish my loose tongue
For telling her of fearful mysteries
Too soon . . . and yet the moment that I saw her
I thought she was a Christian. Patric, you warned

The faithful not to speak at first of hell.
The heart, you said, is an oratory bell—
We must not shake it rudely. God help me now
For what this ringing has undone.
turns, steals back

                         No. No. She breathes!
It may not be too late to save her soul
From Limbo, void no longing for the dead
Can reach, no theologian define
Exactly.
           God, look down into this wood
And if it be Your will that I should do it,
Keep her alive, until I sprinkle her head
Conditionally . . . Grant her ignorant wish
That she may go to heaven now.
He runs out left, downstage. Pause. She stirs. He runs with
a patella. As he supports her, she makes a sign toward the
water. He holds the vessel as she drinks from it.

                   CEASAN

                         I thought,
I thought . . .

                   EITHNE
recovering
               No, no, Ceasan. I only fainted—
From fatigue or lack of food.

                   CEASAN
                    And yet, you listened
So long.

                   EITHNE
           You spoke of the new faith.
                   CEASAN
                       But I
Forgot the law of hospitality,
Older than all religious differences.
I've little to offer a guest, my wants are few—
But it is yours, a round of bread, a pick
Of river-cress and goat-cheese . . . and you can stay in
My hut till morning.

                   EITHNE
               But would that be right,
Ceasan?

CEASAN

There is a shelter close to it
Where I keep spade, mattock, and firewood.
smiling
Indeed, it will be much too good for me
To-night.
                    Come, I will help you up.
                         EITHNE
                                        I feel

Much better.

                         CEASAN
                    God has given back your strength
To you.
                         EITHNE
                    Ceasan, what is that?
                         CEASAN
                                   Where?
                                        Glinting

Against that oak.
                         CEASAN
                         Only my fishing rod.
Last evening, the trout in the lower pools
Were snapping like black fingers at the air,
I never saw so many.
                         EITHNE
thoughtfully
                              Did you catch
None?

                         CEASAN
                    Every dap was greedier than they were.
I took it as a sign that I should fast.
                         EITHNE
inspired
Go quickly, Ceasan, drop another cast.
God will provide for both of us to-night.
                         CEASAN
It is too late, not even a midger would bite.
                         EITHNE
I know that He prepares a holy feast
For us, if you will hurry. Truth cannot lie
Upon the tongue when it has beaten from heart
To heart.

CEASAN

Such pagan faith makes me ashamed
Of mine—and yet we cannot ask so great
A favour.

EITHNE

Go before it is too late.
I'll find wood in the shed to make a fire
And broil the salmon you catch.

CEASAN

The salmon? I tell you
It is impossible. I have no net,
No gaff, no torch. Besides you cannot do
Such servile work. You need to rest a while.

EITHNE

I must be humble like you, learn to bend
Both back and knee.

Giving him the fishing rod

Go now.

CEASAN

But if I fail!

EITHNE

You cannot.

Hurry before it is too late.

*Hesitantly he goes. She leaves, left. Pause. She returns with
twigs, lays them down, goes off for more.*

CEASAN

off

Eithne

He hurries in with a salmon

Eithne, a salmon!

EITHNE

Was I not right?

CEASAN

God sent you
Astray to-night.

EITHNE

Quick, tell me how
It happened.

CEASAN

I went to a ledge, beyond
A may-tree where I keep a pot of bait.

I jabbed the hook, I closed my eyes, I prayed,
Then threw the line out, lightly as I could,
Watching the sinker go below the ripple.
But scarcely had it done so than my hands
Were up and I saw the salmon, moonlighting over
The flags in a thousand drops. The rod was alive
With sap, reeling out of my grip, but I swung
Beneath the butt, I leaped against the rushes,
To take what I knew was coming to me, turned
And the grass was about me, fingers full
Of escapes. Then all was different. Branches
Were under and over me, the sky was water
And the miraculous fish had tumbled out
Of it—into my lap.

> EITHNE
>> You have caught more
> Than a salmon to-night, Ceasan.

> CEASAN
>>> More
> Than a salmon?

> EITHNE
>> Me.
>> For all I do not know
> And cannot know is my belief now. I am
> Your first convert.

> CEASAN
>> May God be praised who took
> And gave to-night. Surely it is a sign
> That you will be a saint—that, in the future,
> Your name will be invoked and special prayers
> Go up to you for favours, night and day
> From Ireland.

> EITHNE
>> No, no, I am afraid, Ceasan,
> Of what I was, rejoice in what I am.
> But when my other self comes back, pray God
> I do not struggle wildly, break the rod.

CURTAIN

Scene Two

*The same, next morning. As the curtain rises, the back
of the stage is shadowy, and the figure of a hooded monk
is seen among the oaks. Ceasan enters from left, holding
a basket in his arms. He crosses the front of stage, lit by
a sunny spot, sees the stranger, and puts down his basket,
right. As he approaches, the figure turns rapidly and draws
back the hood as the stage fills with morning sunshine.
The stranger is seen to be Eithne, dressed in an old,
patched habit.*

EITHNE

Good morning, Ceasan! How do you like this frock
On me? I found it in the hut just now,
Frayed by good works, worn to a poor shade,
As if it had been fasting by itself there!
Example, surely, of all I have cast off
With faith I have forgotten.
                              But why do you look
Displeased? Have I done wrong in wearing it?

CEASAN

Not wrong . . . but . . .

EITHNE
                    Then, I have.
                              Believe me, I meant
No harm by it. When I woke and thought
Of all you told me, after the fire fell down
Last night, through ashing twigs, I hurried to see
The place where I had learned the truth. A shower
Was going lightly from wood to wood for I heard
The little sounds it left and ran by the holly
To them—and can you guess?

CEASAN

—No.—

EITHNE
                              came beyond
The trees, and, fallen all around me, saw
The starred hail of the elder-blossom . . .

CEASAN

        and then . . .

EITHNE

A pool that I could bathe in, below a spring.
I stood in wonder, for the noon seemed there
Already among ferns, and I was hidden
Closer than honeysuckle in that light
As I undressed.
        I was so happy there,
I felt like Eve, on her first day in the world,
Looking at all about her, touching one bud
And then another, searching beyond the reach
Of newest fingertip, in hope to find,
Among continual small gifts of speech
That came to her, the proper name for each.
But I was quickly ashamed, seeing my dress
Had fitted me too well for innocence.
How could I tell the cost! It was so waisted,
With not an inch to spare, so taken in
By vanity, each tuck could mock the stretch
And stint of poverty.

Dejected

        That's all.
             If I
Have erred in borrowing a habit of yours,
I wanted only to be modest, hide
In what is loose to sight.

CEASAN
        Well, I am vexed
No longer for your matins were not quite sinful.
But there is much you do not understand
As yet.

EITHNE

pleased

        Then I can be a hermit, live
On little, keep these clothes that skirt the grass
And go above the head?

CEASAN
        I will explain
Eithne, our pious practice. Come, sit down.

EITHNE

obediently
　　Yes, Ceasan.

CEASAN
　　　　　Women who consecrate themselves
To God, must live together in a great house
Apart from men, observe a rule of silence
Between the intervals of praise, for tongue
That should be held in love, too often tries
To share its littleness. In daily rounds
Of exercise, they pace the holy grounds.
Each pair—

EITHNE

interrupting
　　　　　But what religious costume do
They wear—
　　　　　What flounce to show their difference
From other women?

CEASAN
　　　　　Sensible questions! Head-wrap
And veil, several robes plain in the fold
But of the very best material,
Always so white, so newly laundered, soul
Must make a feastday of each hour. Some serve
The dioceses with downcast eyes, keep nap
Of vestments free from damp, attend the book
And cup, but when a ship comes in with wine
Long waited for, see how they run to set
The holy table! So, in many-hooded
Obedience, all ban temptation, hear
Man's voice only in the offices
And . . .

slowly
　　　　　when they are dying.
He starts up, moves upstage

EITHNE
　　　　　　What is it, Ceasan?
What can you hear or see?

CEASAN
　　　　　　　The reed-tops, far
Away, are feathering the water-breeze
Of oars.

EITHNE

What can it mean?

CEASAN

Armed men are coming,
I think, in search of you. Quick, you must change
For fear of giving scandal by that frock.

EITHNE

wildly

Save, save me from them, Ceasan. Last night you said
That you would teach me Latin, analyse
The acts and hymns in that dead language, told me
It rose from pagan tombs, made pure again
By stress.

I do not want to meet them, dreadful
As plunderers burning their way through a darkness
Where mind is waiting.

Suiting action to words

O when familiar words
Are lost to us and cannot find their equals,
Poor meaning stands—with helpless, outstretched
hands.

turning to him

I am their spoil, the swift division, for they bring
My other self, a captive in every boat;
Bound in their eyes, loosened by bearded lips
That smile too late. How can I tell what evil
Stirs in those reeds that stalk the lesser sounds,
What error was my roof-tree yesterday
Before I sheltered in this wood?

Unshame me,
Ceasan, that I may go invisible
To them, clothing my ignorance with grace
Until I am like Eve, the only woman
Who never had a past.

CEASAN

leaving, back, centre

If you would be
A Christian, Eithne, you must endure the cross-
Examination, bear in mind the pain
Of this confusion. None can harm our faith.
It walks alone among the countless stories

Of miracles performed for us by Patric
And we must follow it, knowing that kings
And their servants who have raged against the truth,
Stricken by fouler mouth, by silver skin,
Fear now the hand that has become our sky.
She leaves left, returns in her own dress, crosses the stage,
hides right

CEASAN

running in
    Eithne, Eithne.

EITHNE

coming back
        I am here.
He stares at her

                  What is it,
    Ceasan?
puzzled

            My cloak, of course! I'll get it now.
CEASAN
    You do not need it.

EITHNE
           Why not?
CEASAN

                  No one
    Is coming

EITHNE
        But you saw the spread of
    Oars.

CEASAN
      I was mistaken. Too easily
The senses learn to wait upon each other,
Avoiding true attention. I hurried beyond the wood
For more than double the length of every echo
In it, came through sword-grass to the shallows
Where lightest of ripples have their starting place—
EITHNE
    And saw and heard—
CEASAN

smiling
                  —only a water-hen
    Clapping herself across a gap of danger.

EITHNE

running to him
>Teach, teach me quickly, Ceasan. Discipline
>My mind with Latin or let me kneel, fasting
>With you in terrible thorns, while there is time
>To do it, for I begin to fear this world—
>Salvation is so difficult.

CEASAN

suddenly

The basket!

EITHNE

What basket?

CEASAN

Heaven forgive these hands, empty

>As mortal gratitude and yet so full
>Last night that I could scarcely see the catch
>Until the miracle was proved again
>In savouring fire and best of taste. This morning
>Another visible sign was shown to me
>That you are safe within this hermitage.

EITHNE

Safe?

CEASAN

>Yes, but in my folly I forgot
>To be its messenger.

EITHNE

No . . . No . . . The fault

>Was mine entirely, Ceasan, for putting on
>The wrong religious costume. Where did you leave
>The basket?

CEASAN

Somewhere near.

EITHNE

Then, we will search

Around.

>Look, there it is.

CEASAN

Be careful. The jug

In it is brimming.

EITHNE

Doe's milk.

CEASAN

Risen bread—
As white, as pure.

EITHNE

Honey that keeps itself
In small monastic cells as though it were
Made holy.

CEASAN

Apples—

EITHNE

that might have been gathered an hour
Ago.
Can these be gifts from Heaven?

CEASAN

smiling   Perhaps.

EITHNE

Do tell me, Ceasan, where they come from.

CEASAN

At times
When river and root are obstinate, hermits
Must live on charity. I leave the basket
And jug within a hollow oak-tree near
This place and our good people in need of prayer
Put little offerings in it, a round
Of cheese, new eggs, buttermilk or oatcake.
To-day I found all this.

EITHNE

What can it mean?

CEASAN

I think that a wealthy man in great distress
Of mind has sent a servant to my oak-press,
For all are weighed by what they can give. I think,
Moreover, that Providence reproves my haste.
Honey and milk, fruit and unbroken bread—
All these declare you must be brought to faith
By gentleness, though pang and midnight vigil
Confirm it.
going
Take them, for I must fast and pray
Awhile.

EITHNE
> But, Ceasan, there's enough for both
Of us.

CEASAN
> Can I forget these empty hands?

EITHNE
Can you forget what is to happen?

CEASAN
puzzled

> What is
To happen?

EITHNE
> Yes, for at this very moment
Now, Patric travels south again, with half
His household, psalmists, reciters, catechumens,
His candle-dippers, hammerers of fine metal,
Smiths, tonsurers and champions of the faith.
Will you be less than them and snatch away
To-morrow's journey on your knees, making
Yourself too weak with abstinence? Shall I
Not know his blessing, rise up from the Boyne
With spotless memory, all clad in white
When Patric has baptised me?

CEASAN
> Forgive your teacher.
Such faith makes me ashamed.

EITHNE
looking up

> Listen, the birds
Come back, for they have had their simple, far-
Fetched meals.

CEASAN
looking down

> The wood-bees comb tangles of dew—
And tinier amounts of mel are flown
By them—

EITHNE
—from stop to stop.

briskly

> Come, help me to bring
The table here.

CEASAN
The table?

EITHNE

—and the two stools
That we may breakfast in the sun, for if
I have my Latin lesson out of doors
Must I be late for it?
They do so

Ceasan, we need
A better knife to cut the bread with. Have
You got one?

CEASAN
Yes, I think so.

EITHNE

Then I'll set
The food out, while you look for it.
As he returns

See, all
Is ready.
They sit down. He murmurs a grace, she waits with bowed head

BOTH

Amen.

EITHNE
Bread?

CEASAN
Thank you.

What is
It, Ceasan?

CEASAN

Never have I tasted such food.
Last evening, broil of salmon, the good fire saucing
It. Now, all this abundance.

EITHNE

We can have
The salmon cold for our midday meal, sprig it
With cress and water-mint.

CEASAN

Truly God shows
His pleasure, favouring the earth with fare
Of every sort.

gravely
                    Because of our daily substance,
          Religion celebrates this mystery
          Of food. Under the Old Law, each altar
          Was built with fire-place, open grill, from which the
          Burnt offerings were hurried up in smoke
          And savour. Under the new dispensation,
          However . . .
surprised
                              You are inattentive!
                              EITHNE
                                        The honey . . .
          Taste it.
                              CEASAN
                    I have.
                              EITHNE
                    Taste it again.
                                        Does it
          Remind you of anything?
He shakes his head
                              I think it came
          From thickness of yellow blossoms like those I saw
          Before we met.
                              CEASAN
                    You mean the water-irises.
                              EITHNE
          I do.
                              CEASAN
alarmed
                    But, Eithne, they bloomed a month ago.
          Think, think again, perhaps your memory
          Has stirred.
                              EITHNE
rises
                    I'll try.
closes her eyes as she slowly rises
                              Yes, I can see them, at
          This very moment, fifty women or more,
          Bathing beyond the flag flowers in the Boyne.
          They laugh, pretending to be birds, and the water
          Runs off their bare backs! They chase it . . .

CEASAN

Don't look!

EITHNE

They've necklaces! Each jewel is a drop
Snatched from the river.

They're gone now . . .

slowly

But somebody is coming . . .

Aongus!

with a cry

There's too

Much light in my eyes.
Opens her eyes, dazed

Why is it so dark

Here?

Recovering

Please forgive me. I must have remembered
A foolish story set to music. That
Is why I seemed to know the name of Aongus
Last evening.

CEASAN

Patric has told us the false gods
Are fallen angels, wrongly imagining
A state they have forgotten, and scattering their
Ideas through hill, forest, head.

kindly

Sit down

Again and finish your breakfast.

EITHNE

obediently

Yes, Ceasan.

They eat in silence

CEASAN

smiling

And now to face the elements, on this
Fine day.

EITHNE

Dear Ceasan, I can hardly wait.
I'll clear the table, have our school-desk ready
While you are getting Latin book and slate.
When all is ready, she sits down beside him

CEASAN

And now to our studies.

For centuries in the schools of Europe the noun in the first declension with which all teachers begin is *mensa*

points

EITHNE

A table?

CEASAN

Yes.

writing it down

Nominative, *mensa*.

There are six cases, singular and plural.

EITHNE

Write them all down so that I may see you making the little lines and curves like those in your book

CEASAN

writing

Genitive, *mensae;* dative, *mensae;* accusative, *mensam;* vocative, *mensa*, ablative, *mensa*.

And now the plural:

Nominative, *mensae;* genitive, *mensarum;* dative, *mensis;* accusative, *mensas;* vocative, *mensae;* ablative, *mensis*.

Repeat them slowly after me.

EITHNE

But I know them.

CEASAN

Know them?

EITHNE

Yes. Singular: *mensa, mensae, mensam, mensa, mensa;* Plural: *mensae, mensarum, mensis, mensis, mensae, mensis.*

—And now the second declension, think of a holy word, Ceasan.

CEASAN

bewildered, at last points to himself

Monachus.

EITHNE

A monk?

CEASAN

Yes.

Monachus, monachi, monacho, monichum, monicho, monicho. Plural: *monachi, monachorum, monachis, monachos, monachi, monachis.*

CEASAN

EITHNE

That's simple.

Repeats them

I know them all backwards, too . . . *mensa, mensae, mensae . . .*

CEASAN

This is much too fast for me.

EITHNE

Please, Ceasan, write down the next declension.

He cleans the slate

But all the letters are gone. Is your Latin book like that?

CEASAN

You mean my Psalter?

EITHNE

Yes.

CEASAN

Of course not. For books we use ink on vellum. The ink is made from oak galls, and it lasts for hundreds of years, longer than these trees above us.

EITHNE

Let me see it.

CEASAN

searching

I must have left it in the hut. I'll run and get it. I won't be a minute.

She starts to write. He returns, stops, and watches. As she finishes, he comes forward. She hands him the slate

EITHNE

Here are the two declensions again.

CEASAN

You can write?

EITHNE

No, indeed. I watched you and remembered all the little lines that must be kept apart and the curves that clasp one another.

But is there some mistake?

CEASAN

dazed

No one could tell
Your hand from mine. It's another miracle!

C U R T A I N

Act Two.

*The scene is the same, late afternoon. Eithne is seated on
left, near river wearing her cloak. She is writing slowly on
slate, 'flumen, a river, flumenis, of a river, flume . . . '
She drowses. The voice of Ceasan is heard calling her.*

VOICE

Eithne! Eithne!

EITHNE

obediently

Yes, Ceaṣan.
I must have been asleep.
light dims as she comes forward
Where have you gone?
groping

Oak, elm are darker
Than when I came to them in ignorance
Last evening, saw before me holy sign
That humbles soul and raises body up.
I cannot find you, for every branch is knotted
With lash of leaf and my own footsteps lie
To me.
listening

Why are you silent in the wood
Now, silent as the prayers of Marravaun?
facinɔ back centre

Believe me, I have tried to keep in mind

What must be out of sight, because you told me
The truth was written down for us in twist
 And turn of clinging letters, that we must shrink
Beyond the doom of sun to our salvation,
Though ink stop, dry itself and so remain
For centuries.
hurrying left, downstage
                What is this fear that clasps
Our fallen nature, tears the very neck-ring
Of living language, runs behind the trees
 In some fantastic attitude of prayer?
Knowing that anguish has too many hands.
Where are you, Ceasan?
Runs off, right
Off stage

                     Where are you?
             VOICE

                       Eithne!
                           Eithne!

She comes back

             EITHNE
Why have you gone across the river, left
My name in air?
to herself
                I must have been mistaken—
Or caught an echo from the woods beyond
And made a nobody of it, lighter
Than air and as untouchable. Minute
By minute our senses wait on one another,
Avoiding true attention. By his absence,
Ceasan is surely teaching me a lesson:
A lesson that I must learn—but not from sight.
And yet his words are pupils that obey me.
I'll call them back, repeat what he has said
About God's people.
                Last evening, I stood here
Bewildered . . .
              No, I was over there.—
crosses
                    and he
Was near that oak, speaking of Marravaun—

> A ring-a-ring o' birds around him, whenever
> He prayed—

DREAM FIGURE OF CEASAN

right

> whenever he prayed—

EITHNE

softly

> —and because of that—

DREAM FIG.

> The superstitious, bending from their cobbles
> To lift a night-line or come to set a grass-snare,
> Whispered that it was Aongus Oge they saw,
> Hidden in holy habit.

EITHNE

Aongus Oge!

> I've heard that name before . . . I cannot remember
> Where.

DREAM FIG.

> Then you are a stranger to these parts,
> For sedges that rub together in the breeze
> And summer bushes flowering along
> The Boyne have stories of him, so to speak.
> The very trees have been his evil-spreaders
> In the old days. Men say he was the god
> Of kissers known by his pure wickedness
> And the birds that flew around his temples.
> Pushing the leaves back, clawed by music, that love-
>   catcher
> Set traps for lonely thought.

movement as in previous scene

> He came, they say,
> From that great tumulus which you can see
> Across the river there. It has an entrance
> Of whirl-winded bronze—scroll within scroll—
> To his invisible kingdom.

EITHNE

> What do they call

It?

DREAM FIG.

> Bru-na-Boinne.

EITHNE
It makes me tremble.
DREAM FIG.

I, too,
Have been afraid of it.
EITHNE
Then, why do you live
So near that brazen earth?
DREAM FIG.

wildly

To rid myself
Of superstition—
Figure disappears, left

EITHNE

running left

Ceasan, forgive me. Forgive me.
I never meant to ask that question again.
He laughs

EITHNE

off stage
Why do you laugh?
returning

Why did he laugh like that?
No, no, I am alone. Patches and strips
Of sleep, have dressed a tree-shadow up, a scare-soul.
And yet, I do not seem alone . . .
rich hues appear, back, as she moves towards river

Pool
Beyond pool is bathing in itself. The seasons
Mingle with one another. The reed-tops
Are still—and all the bushes, flowering
Along the Boyne, are heavier with may.
She waits, listening
Aongus!

So it was you who stood, just now
Behind the trees, hidden in holy habit.
Why have you come?

What do you want of me?
Pause, her face shows by its changing expression what she hears
No. No, I will not leave this wood. Folly

And legend drew me into the other world
A year ago....
dreamily

                              or was it in some century
After the people of Partholan had come
To Ireland, stemmed the nighting forests, cut
Them open?... I cannot remember.... I only know
That as I leaned to pluck a flower from the Boyne,
All swam around my sight. I heard the laughter
Of fairy-women snatching drops like jewels
To hang around their necks. I could not see them
Because my eyes had filled with human tears....
And then the river was different... and I
Was on the other side of it.

                              What does it

Mean, Aongus?
Pause, her lips move silently

                              You say that I left Tirnagogue
Two seconds ago, that every day on earth
Is less than a moment there.

                              I won't believe it.
Strange stories set to music took me by
Surprise as I lay ill, month after month,
At Tara, my life despaired of by my husband
And relatives. That's all.

                              Traditional stories
Had changed my mind in sleep—and I forgot
The hands that kept me by their warmth.
Pause

                              No. No.
I will not listen Aongus.... Take back
Memory of all I learned upon my sick-bed
Of a finer world beyond the grave,
For I must clay myself in time. Legend
And folly drew me there in vain, but I
Have never been your fosterdaughter. I know
I am a mortal, oppressed with every breath.
And I can prove it, prove it. Last night I slept
And I was next to nothing. Can
Pure spirit loose all consciousness... not know...
Not be? This horror of our human state

On earth compels the soul to sin, belittling
The body that must be corrupted, before
It can endure itself for ever.
light dims, drumming sound

Afflict
The elements around me, deceive my senses
Because I have come back to them. But I'll
Not leave this wood or go into the Boyne.
Aongus, no pagan spell can change my faith
Again.
Black out. Spot rises as Ceasan dashes in right, back

CEASAN
Stay, Fairy-woman, stay until
The air takes meaning from my words. I heard
Your voice and I know that Aongus, who sent you here
Last night, has shifted you in summer mist.
But tell him I defy him. Tell him the hazels
Have been cut down, the fountains spat upon,
The fire-rings trampled out. Religion shrines
Itself in every place where spirits, good
Or evil, have appeared. But men neglect
The circle-stone, the maybush now, unname
Their guardians.
Can you hear me?

I am Ceasan
The poor scholar.
Tell him that we who live
On earth are everlasting, made fit by dread
Of mind that models us in clay, made fit
By filth not faggot, stinkers, rotters, foul
Befallen. But our precious dust is pinched
And saved for us. Faith, faith keeps full account
And from an ounce our bodies will be weighed,
Breath trumpeted throughout the world once more,
When hope and shame are witnesses at Doom
And the great books are carried down from cloud
To cloud.
wilder

No. . . . I have lied. My tongue has found
Another roof, struggles against false teeth.

I scarcely know what I am saying.   Aongus
Has persecuted me within this wood
Of his for months. I sleep so badly. Father
Frowns at me, mother weeps beside my bed,
Because I have lost her faith. In dreams I am
A boy again, a child upon all fours.
I dwindle in the darkness, I am ungot,
Am nothing. Tell him I want to choose the right
Religion, be saved by it and live for ever,
Yes, live for ever. How can I endure
The torment of a single life, riddle
That has too many answers, guessing-game
Of ghosts not men? Implore him for a sign,
A plain sign here and now, no mocking one
That seems to bless, but substance I can lay
My hands on.

Light rises. Eithne is in his arms

                                EITHNE

withdrawing

                Ceasan, I am frightened. Have
        I fainted again? Why am I at the water's
        Edge?

*In full light we see that the scene is changed. It is the
inlet. Rocks left, down stage, right, a pool indicated by
reeds*

                Look . . . that mooring post! I seem to know it.
        This is the inlet where I found myself
        Last evening when I woke.

                                        What can it mean?

                Who brought me here?

                                CEASAN

meaningly   Your people.

                                EITHNE

                                        Where are they? Why
        Do they hide in the wood or down the river?

running to him

                                                Save

        Me, Ceasan, save me by your holy might.
        I do not want to meet them now, dreadful
        As plunderers burning their way through a darkness
        Where mind is waiting.

O when familiar words
Are lost to us and cannot find their equals,
Poor meaning stands with helpless, outstretched hands.
turning to him
I am their spoil, the swift division, for they bring
My pagan self, a captive...

CEASAN

interrupting her

Though you have learned
So quickly to repeat yourself, I know
At last that you are not a woman.

EITHNE

Why do
You speak so strangely, Ceasan? Your words fill me
With fear of hope. Why do you stare at me
As if, as if, I weren't here?

CEASAN

Pointing where she stands

Because
You cannot be all there. I know at last
That spirits suffer in this element
Of ours, oppressed like us by doubt and dread,
Fish out of water—as the poets say,
In mockery. But I have found some truth
Beneath the fire-rings that burn themselves away—
And dig it from the ashes.

Come I will show
Your real self to you, before your people
Have hidden all beneath my lashes.

EITHNE

Not yet.
I do not want to know myself until
I share your faith.

CEASAN

You must.
He looks cautiously around, bringing her forward

As I was reading
Outside the wood, the branches over my book
Became so quiet, I thought all growth had stopped
Or a summer storm was near. I ran beneath them
To call you, but the hollows were empty, the birds

Nested. I ran out of my echoes, left
Your name in air, then suddenly, beside
The river, I saw the yellow irises
You tried to reach.

EITHNE

But Ceasan. . . .

CEASAN

I tell you, they
Had bloomed again. I saw more. . . .

Pool
Beyond pool was bathing in itself. The seasons
Mingled with one another. Each reed-top
Was still and all the bushes flowering
Along the Boyne were heavier with may.
I came to a mist, I heard your voice in it, heard it
Clearly—you were not alone.

EITHNE

Not alone?

CEASAN

Aongus was with you.

EITHNE

Aongus?

CEASAN

Yes, Aongus Oge.

EITHNE

But such things cannot happen! You explained
That superstition when we met,
Said Aongus was the god of kissers, known
By his pure wickedness and the birds
That flew around his temples. The very trees
Have been his evil-spreaders, so you told me.
But what has this to do with us?

CEASAN

He sent you.

Here.

EITHNE

Sent me here?

CEASAN

To tempt me, trick me. You
Are of the Sidhe.

EITHNE
                    Ceasan, what folly is this?
Have you been wood-struck, or have evil spirits—
Tongue twisters—taken your words to shame us both,
Denying reality? Last evening when
I fainted in the oakwood, sank below
The reach of truth, did you not clasp me?

CEASAN
                                                        Yes,
God help me, I have clasped you.

EITHNE
                                            And just now,
You saved me from the river—I wakened in
Your arms.

CEASAN
          Spirits can be deceived as men are.
What I have held could never satisfy
My senses.

EITHNE
wildly
                Because you have taken leave of them!

CEASAN
angry
        But not of you, not yet.

EITHNE
                                Forgive me, Ceasan,
I scarcely know what I have said, what mouth
Unwomaned me. I see all clearly now.
Low spirits brought me to the inlet, made me
Walk in my sleep and would have drowned me, had
    not
Your presence disturbed them. Now, they are trying
Again to take your only convert, weaken
Your faith until it is as small as hers
Still struggling in the grip of ignorance.
They fear you, count in their hundreds, the souls
That you will save by lake and river, men
And women wading towards your spoken word
Until their shame is hidden—a lower Eden
Flowing around them. Think, think of what was
    shown

To us last night. Have we not gone from sign
To sign, and recognised the miracle
By holy taste? The ashes of that fire
We laid to broil the salmon on, are there
Within the wood. What will you find beneath them,
Forgetting the food we shared like thought? Come,
  take
Your fishing rod again, go to the river
And see what will be sent you.
CEASAN

                                                The water-sign,
The pagan sign—Salmon of Knowledge.
EITHNE

                                                     And do
You doubt what happened in the wood this very
Day? Providence reproved your haste
And you were shown I must be brought to faith
By gentleness, though pang and midnight vigil
Confirm it. Surely you remember how
We ran to the pathway, empty-handed, searched
And found—
CEASAN

wavering

                         the basket.
EITHNE

                                           Yes, but I implore you
See, with the eyes of faith again!
She mimes the scene, half kneeling, with him
                                —the jug—
In it is brimming—doe's milk.
CEASAN

                                        Risen bread—
As white as pure.
EITHNE

                                   Honey that keeps itself
In small monastic cells as though it were
Made holy.
CEASAN

Apples—

EITHNE

                                   —that might have been

plucked an hour
Ago.

CEASAN

starting back
Yes, plucked in Tirnagogue ... I know
It is a spell for I have tasted fairy food,
God help me, breakfasted beyond the world.
But I will prove before it is too late
That you were sent, despite yourself.
                                        Come with me.

EITHNE

Not yet.

CEASAN
        Come.

EITHNE

obediently

            Yes, Ceasan.

CEASAN

                        What do you see?

EITHNE

A pool.

CEASAN
    What else?

EITHNE

smiling

                My own reflection, wobbly,
Wavery.

CEASAN

            The only wrinkles that face
Will ever know.

                    Look closer, look.

The pool brightens

                        The pool
Is surfacing with more than moonlight.
She covers her face, and starts back, the pool dims,
stormy sunlight crosses stage

EITHNE

                                Ceasan,
It is the sun, I tell you, the sun performing
Its last wild offices. Kneel down and pray,

CEASAN

No, no. The waters do not lie. . . . You are
Too beautiful to be a woman.

                                              The pool

That you have looked in, proves it.

EITHNE

                                         Strange flattery
That takes my breath away! But, my poor Ceasan,
What women have you ever seen, behind
A handbook, in cell or oakwood? The very clothes
That I have on, will tell me to my face
Much more than you can know.

inspired

                                    Believe me, at
This moment in Ireland, the sun-rooms are so dark,
Companies of women leave them, hearing a stir
Of servants, candle-bearers, for they long
To see themselves in a false light, changing
From this dress into that, until a stitch,
Barely in time, makes up their minds for them.
All that men think of would be immaterial
Could they but watch these women shadowing,
Unshadowing themselves. As soon as not,
They will be busy with cheek and eyelid, each added
Touch, so unequalled it must seem the last.
Choose, choose among them. Are they not real?
    And I?
You say, am neither here nor there. Take vainer
Vows. Let tongue dare to share its littleness
In love, for something tells me the women of Ireland
Can charm away the very substance of breath,
Appear so frail—and when they smile at men,
Marriage itself could be accounted sinful.
But choose, choose quickly, for my vision of them
Is dim, because I am looking through the veil
I mean to wear.

CEASAN

                      Another trick of Aongus
Who sent you here. But what can handbook, oakwood
Hide, now we have come into the open? I
Have seen such women at nightfall, left my fishing

Bait, fled from the dip of oars that never drown
Their conversation, thin and reedy, as if
It ran upon the reed-tops, seen and heard them
Long after every boatload of their smiles
Was gone.

EITHNE

Then, see and listen to yourself.
All, all you told me after the fire fell down,
Last night, through ashing twigs, has forced my lips
Apart to question you. What are the pagan
Gods? Fallen angels imagining a world
They have forgotten, scattering ideas
From hill and forest—

CEASAN

interrupting

I won't listen.

No woman could be so intelligent
As you are—every word exact in use,
Yet unexpected in meaning . . . as if . . . as if . . .
How shall I say it? . . . you spoke in poetry.
No woman could be so intelligent.
All that I learned of our dead language, month
By month, with toil and grammaring, was yours
In a few minutes. There, among dragonflies,
You sat beside the river with calm temples
Taking my gerunds, datives, ablatives—
As though they were the gold cups Patric brought
From Rome.

EITHNE

You said it was a miracle.

CEASAN

No matter. It is written in the sky-book
That woman is inferior to man
And must obey him.

EITHNE

Then let me obey,
Go down upon my knees and learn from clay.
Ceasan, I see at last the plot against us,
Yes, recognise the fiery hatchers. Devils
Of pride, hedge masters of equivocation,
Deceived us pleasantly after our morning meal.

Taught me to read and write before I knew
By hook or crook the very alphabet.
Why should we be afraid of what's around us?
Surely the dread examination that all
Must pass is of another sort.   You told me
Knowledge will not be worth its students' rags
When all possess the richer gift of faith,
That pagan philosophy will be refuted
For good, in every walk of life, when all
Are trained to think and speak alike.   I want
To be the same as other women, chosen
By grace, wear the same habit, know the peace
Of those whose daily bread is shared in common.

appealing

Why should there be another scene between us—
When truth can end the mocking play of spirits?
Come, Ceasan, rid me of all Original Sin.
Dip, dip me in the river.   By your words
Wash mortal stain from soul and body.   Baptise
Me now.

CEASAN

This is blasphemy, I tell you.

EITHNE

joyfully

Then

You do believe.
She is at river's edge

CEASAN

Go back.   That river guards
The Country of the Ever Young.

EITHNE

No wave

Of superstition can prevent me.

I

Will prove I am a woman—
She is pulling off her clothes

—though I drown.

CEASAN

Eithne !
He leaps forward, catches her, she struggles, yields

EITHNE

Ceasan !
Slowly they draw closer, and suddenly break away

CEASAN

What have I done?   What has happened
To us?

EITHNE

You've found your faith again:
I felt it between your breath and mine. Yes, we
Were held by greater arms than mortal lovers
Have guessed at.

CEASAN

I see all clearly now, because
Your faith has restored my own.   But go, go quickly
Before a soul is lost.
pointing to auditorium

That path will bring you
To the good people who stock the rotten tree
I live by, putting their trust in my false prayers.
I have deceived you and that is why I am punished
Like this, my thoughts, my memory, in confusion.
Last night I crept to the hovel, crept to it,
Fearing you were unearthly.   I saw you there
Lying asleep in more than moonlight.   O then
I thought, for certain, your body was glorified
And my own flesh had risen with it, thought, for
One blessed moment, time was nothing. . . . I found
Myself in the dark again, in a wood
Of nettle-seed, tormented by the lust
That tied my beseeching fingers, bolted out
All shapes but one.

EITHNE

Poor Ceasan, why should you
Have suffered?   How can it be wrong
To want this living mould that lives forever?
Are we like bird, beast, insect, having
Their sportive season?

CEASAN

You do not understand
The meaning of chastity.   Marriage itself
Is an inferior state, and so, cannot

Continue in the next world.

                                        Go, Eithne, go
Before it is too late and both our souls
Are lost.

                              EITHNE

inspired

                                        No. I must stay. It is my duty,
Ceasan. All is plain to me.

                                        This morning
I wanted to fast and lie with you in terrible
Thorns. Now I know that I was sent to tempt you.
Yes, unbaptised, base with Original Sin,
I have been to test your faith and morals,
But it is only for a night, Ceasan.
To-morrow—

                              CEASAN
                        To-morrow?
                              EITHNE

                                        Have you forgotten
The appointment you must keep?

                              CEASAN

                                        With whom?

                              EITHNE

                                                  Patric.

                              CEASAN

softly

        A captured man—

                              EITHNE

                                        who brought the truth
To us across the sea.

                              CEASAN

                                        How can I dare
To think of him?

                              EITHNE

                                        You must. I want to be
An ordinary woman now, repeat
The news that I have heard, repeat it, because
You put such joy into my mouth.

                                                  Sit down
And I will tell you of Patric—son of Calpurn.
Listen, the wind is rising! . . .

                                    But at this moment
He travels south for the last time, with half
His household, psalmists, reciters, catechumens,
His candle-dippers, hammerers of fine metal,
Smiths, tonsurers and champions of the faith.
Their strength brings back the places he had known
And often of a summer's evening, he sits
Outside the green branch of his tent, in peace,
Breaking his word into such sweetness, young
And old can share it at the one time. Think, think—
To-morrow you will see him again, God willing,
Not far from here, within his crowded camp
And if he deem you worthy of it, leave
The wood, forever.
                         CEASAN
                         No. I am ashamed
To meet him.

                         EITHNE
                         You must.
                         CEASAN
                                    How can I leave you
In the wood?

                         EITHNE
                         Your Psalter will protect me.
                         CEASAN
rising
        I have wavered, failed in the test
        He set me.

                         EITHNE
following
                         That test has but begun.
                         CEASAN
                                    No man
Is master of me now, because I fear
Myself, bedevilled by the drop of bliss
That got me.

                         EITHNE
                                    Woman is not inferior
To man in this. Her vessels are as greedy.
As the wind and rain sweep through darkened sky

CEASAN

See how the storm breaks down the clouds, and
    raindrops
Acorn the woods. The river mounts within
Its ancient floods, marking their former levels.
Anger is over us, charged with repentance,
But I, God help me, can see nothing, nothing
But you.

EITHNE

Then, Ceasan, you shall not see me.
                                This downpour,
That uproar, are wayward signs that can be read
The better as we run.

As they go

                                Listen, they tell us
To shelter in the darkness of your hut.
Listen, they tell us by their violence
That we must learn the lesson of self-restraint.

CEASAN

My strength is less than breath.

EITHNE

                                I am as faint

As you.

CEASAN

—and yet make no complaint!

EITHNE

                                Why should

I fear the taint our bodies fear? I know
So well that you were born to be a saint.

The storm rises, stage empty.

S L O W   C U R T A I N

ACT III

SCENE ONE: *The next night. On right, part of the wood is seen dimly in moonlight. On left, the inside of the hut, formed by traverse curtains. Pallet right, doorway centre, left, table and stools. A small lamp, or patella, with a bead of light. Voice of Ceasan heard as he staggers through the wood . . . calling Eithne. He enters hut, breathless and exhausted. Eithne comes in immediately after him, puts down the basket which she is carrying, and hurries to him.*

EITHNE

Ceasan, what is it? Are you. . . .

CEASAN

It's nothing. . . . I stumbled
On a tumbled branch—all alive with leaves . . .
trying to smile

got here
Before my breath.

EITHNE

You must have run for hours.

CEASAN

I went astray. Right, left, were false and my footsteps
Lied to me.

EITHNE

recollecting

Like mine.

CEASAN

Darkness oaked, birched, hazelled—
I struggled from thick to thin. . . .

Sudden moon stemmed
A thousand pools—so still, I almost thought
They had found their way back to the sky.

EITHNE

But, Ceasan,
Why did you hurry?

CEASAN

You were alone here, in
The wood.

EITHNE
Your prayer-book has protected me.
She takes it from under cloak to give him, he shrinks back.
But it is something else. I know it is.
What terrible pens have shaken your hand? Why is
Your face so pale? Have you looked wrongly in
Those pools, seen more than moonlight in them?
  Tell me,
Tell me.

CEASAN
I have failed, Eithne, failed, failed
To pass my own examination.
EITHNE
                              And Patric?

CEASAN
I never saw him.
turning away

                    How could I see him?
EITHNE
                                        Your habit
Is clamming, might have flapped from cloud to cloud.
No, not a word. You must undress, get into
Bed. When you are safe from chills that shiver in
  grass,
Ground-sheets of water, you can tell me all
That happened.
                —Quick, quick.
CEASAN
                    No, let me.
EITHNE
                                        Must I
Not learn to serve, bend back and knee?
                                        And next,
    Your habit.
He hesitates
                    You took it off last night.
as he gets into bed
                                        I'll hang
    It out to dry
She runs out, returns
                    Now tell me. No, wait. What am

I thinking of! You must have supper.
                                        The basket!
                        CEASAN
The basket?
                        EITHNE
                Heaven forgive these hands of mine,
Empty as mortal gratitude.
                        CEASAN
                                        What do
You mean?
                        EITHNE
                Yesterday morning, you forgot
The happiness that filled your arms, because
Of me. Now I have failed, in turn, to carry
My message from another world, forgot
Gifts that outweigh the frown of Patric.
                        CEASAN
shocked, as she goes over for it
                                        Eithne,
What did you say?
                        EITHNE
                See how the oak has answered
Him.
Coming to him
                Honey,
pointing
                        milk,
                                fruit, unbroken bread.
                        CEASAN
                        The same gifts!
                        EITHNE
Are you still superstitious?
                        CEASAN
                                        The donor . . . I
Forgot to pray for him. Sin after sin
Upon my soul, omission without remission.
                        EITHNE
No. Visible signs that we are led at first
To God by gentleness. Besides you can pray
When you have had your supper. I had mine
An hour ago.

CEASAN
I cannot eat.
EITHNE
You must

Have faith as I have.
at table
When the trees had lightened
The last pockets of storm, a heavenly feeling
Came over me. I saw the basket, guessed
What I should do, ran with it to the hollow
Oak. Surely the wood was angel'd for I knew
The pathway by your prayers. Night closed the wet
buds,
I waited here until the moon held out
A pilgrim staff. I saw it beyond the sedge
And thought: 'it joins his hands and mine.'
coming back
Now drink

Up this.
These apples tempt me.
Winter could never worm its way within
Them.
She tastes an apple
Try one.
CEASAN
Truly God shows his pleasure on earth—
EITHNE
—And all good sorts are drawn from it.
A little

More?
trying to comfort him
While you are eating, I'll tell you what happened
To me this morning, after you'd gone.
I seemed
To hurry beside you in uproar, downpour. Young
branches
Struggled in vain with family trees, summer
With winter. The little reeds lay down, trying
To hide in their beds. We saw the foam and the flaw
race—
Boyne could never catch up with them.

CEASAN

That's strange.
I thought the same, thought you were with me.

EITHNE

Shall I

Go on?

CEASAN

Yes, do.

EITHNE

We left the oak-woods at last
But not that uproar. Every gust was a
Full stop, where more rain beat us back or bowed us
Eastward, drenched to the very skin. I clung
To you.

CEASAN

We linked our wetness,

EITHNE

shivered,

CEASAN

—seemed

To have lost the power of speech.

EITHNE

And the pathway!

CEASAN

Little—

EITHNE

was big.

CEASAN

And hard

EITHNE

—was soft.

CEASAN

Each pool—

EITHNE

A lake,

CEASAN

and every stream

EITHNE

—a tributary.

EITHNE

slowly
> We were alone together in that storm.
>> CEASAN
> The hills had lost their holy names.
>>> EITHNE
>>>>>>>>>>>>>>>>>> Ireland
>
> Was uninhabited once more.... And then
> The storm had hidden you from me.... I wakened
> Here
>>>> CEASAN
>>>>>>> At that very moment, Eithne, I felt
> Our thoughts were snatched from one another.
>>>> EITHNE
>>>>>>>>>>> Tell me
> Now, all that happened after that.
>>>> CEASAN
>>>>>>>>>>>>>>> I scarcely
> Know. Body plodded on, head down, for hours,
> Slaving beneath the outer walls of the wind,
> Knee-pit a lash-load of rain, rock-vein
> Of weakness. Body puddled on through scrub,
> Scrimmage of oak, turned northward, reached the
> Boyne
> Again. My soul was waiting for me, so small,
> It wriggled and squirrelled to my shoulder, sat there
> Familiarly until I thrust it back
> Into my skull. Salvation picked me up.
> I saw beyond the last scrapings of river
> Bank, misty knot of roof-trees, peak of Patric's
> Camp, ridge-pole of his travelling church:
> That simple story, readymade, reformed,
> There, by God's grace, to-day—

tragically
>>>>>>>> but gone to-morrow.

>>>> EITHNE
> And then you saw—
>>>> CEASAN
>>>>>>>> —Only the foam and the flaw race:
> Boyne could never catch up with them.

EITHNE

The ford

Was—

CEASAN

   —place of weeping, place of black drowning.
How
Had I forgotten plain fact, forgotten these flooded
Miles?

EITHNE

Ceasan, I forgot them, too!

CEASAN

I waited,

Prayed, waited, prayed, all hands and tongue, but no
   one
Came. No one left those rainy outposts of duty.
I scarcely know what creature filled the void,
Slammed on the slime, unfrocked to the fork,
    jumped up
Through rage and hermitted himself in uproar
From head to sandal. I collapsed, but demons
Supported me, pushed back that other fellow,
Pulled gently at my ears, began to foul
My wits.

EITHNE

What did they say?

CEASAN

I won't repeat it.

EITHNE

I want to share that inner conflict with you.

CEASAN

They whispered:

'Call, call on Patric to perform

Miracle like that man in Egypt, raise
The stick he got in Heaven and lay bare
The dirty bottom of the river, once
A goddess men could swear by. Call on him
To give safe passage to you. Humbleness
Is next his skin, no doubt, but flattering
 Attentions are bite and sup to him: coarse mouth
Of Ireland pressed upon his withered hand,
The relic of itself. Respect the clippers,

Bend and obey their holy order, gain
A special hair-cut into Heaven.   Are
Old men who go bald-headed for their joy
Worthier than young shaver, croppy boy?
I fled the dread temptation, daren't tell
What filth was at my heels.

EITHNE

                              Poor Ceasan, both
Of us were wrong, for how could any saint have
Expected you in a storm that has brought down
The weight of forests, tried the strength of man-made
Bolt.   Truly on such a rattling day as this,
All Ireland is at home.   No storyteller
Blows in.   No fire puts out the fawning smoke.
To-morrow will be different, the woods
Drying themselves and bringing up new flowers
That make their own small beds.   The waters will
Be good again and show their Sunday face,
God's people meet you at the next stopping-place.

CEASAN

Everything is over and done with
Now.   For a year I kept the rule of silence
And what have been the consequences?   A tongue
So furred with sickening words, I cannot stick it
Out.

EITHNE

You need rest and sleep.

CEASAN

                               How can I sleep?
Only a poet could lie contentedly
On a bed like this, no woman near,
Because his own breath is as sweet to hear—
Whenever he wakens up.

EITHNE

                               What do you want?

CEASAN

Myself. . . . The grinding poverty of speech
I'm used to, bits and scraps that save our skin
When we have grovelled for them.

EITHNE

                               We can stoop

Too low.

CEASAN

Have I not coveted your bed?
And not content with that, your very milk,
Your apples, your honey? Every morsel and drop
That passed my lips to-day and yesterday,
Hot supper the night before. were meant for you
Alone.

EITHNE

I took my share.

CEASAN

I have been punished—

EITHNE

Unfairly.

CEASAN

I had my journey for nothing.

EITHNE

Not
For nothing.

CEASAN

Then, next to nothing.

EITHNE

Why?

CEASAN

Because
I sinned last night.

EITHNE

But, Ceasan, that's not true,
We never yielded, however pressing the
Temptation.

CEASAN

I deceived you.

EITHNE

Deceived me?

CEASAN

Yes.

EITHNE

How?

CEASAN

By taking advantage of your ignorance,
And of my own.

EITHNE
Your own? What do you mean?
CEASAN
Demons informed me to-day.

                          'Ceasan', they said,
'You never learned in class that self-restraint
Is but the newest kind of pleasure brought
To Ireland, never put a doubtful hand up
At question time. But now you know it all.'
EITHNE
How could they say a thing like that? Roof shook
Above us in the storm last night, but we
Kept still, no need of mouth, because our souls
Were one. Can you forget the joy we felt
Together, hour after hour, in self-control,
The purity of spiritual love?
CEASAN
Such bliss is only known to those above
Not those below. Mortal pleasure is two-faced.
What did we learn together in the darkness?
The spiritual dangers of delay.
Retaining virtue, we acquired a vice.
EITHNE
But, Ceasan, what should we have done last night?
CEASAN
Been honest as the day—

                    EITHNE
                          and?

                    CEASAN
                              —sinned outright.

                    EITHNE
But afterwards?

                    CEASAN
                          We should have known sudden
Disgust, sudden repentance.
                    EITHNE
                          Disgust?
                    CEASAN
                                    Yes.

EITHNE

Are
You certain?

CEASAN

Certain.

EITHNE

wildly

It is not too late.
If all that has seemed pure and good is false,
Our better nature but our worst, then how
Can I repent except in shame? Are you
Afraid? Or am I still your fairywoman,
Ready to melt within your arms, become
A mist before your eyes?

You hesitate,
Half turn away.

Then know that I have been
Deceitful in my turn; yet I am ready
This night to laugh at and betray my husband,
Not twenty miles from Tara. . . .

CEASAN

alarmed

Your husband . . . Tara . .
What have you said?

EITHNE

I . . . I don't know. I wanted
To make you jealous. That's all.

CEASAN

Heaven has saved us
Both, stirred your memory in time. Think hard.

EITHNE

I cannot.

CEASAN

Try, try to concentrate your mind.
Laery, high-king of Ireland, in the last
Supper hall built by him at Tara, plots
Against our holy practices, pretends
Belief, supports the obstinacy of age
With pagan banqueting, false miracles.
Your . . .

your husband . . . may have . . .

She signs to him to be silent, moves centre, closes her eyes

CEASAN

What do you see?

EITHNE

slowly

A lintel—carven curiously against
The grain.

CEASAN

What else?

EITHNE

A bed—

covered with purple

And fine linen. . . .

Someone is lying on it.

CEASAN

Who?

EITHNE

I cannot see his face yet.

Ceasan, it's you!

opens her eyes, runs to him

Forgive me, please, forgive me. I can see
Nothing, nothing to-night, but you.
She comes back slowly to table, turns

Ceasan,

May I speak plainly?

CEASAN

Yes.

EITHNE

Will you do me
The greatest favour any man could think of,
Despite your conscience?

CEASAN

What?

CEASAN

Name me, unshame me
To-morrow in the Boyne, that, rid of all
Original self, I, too, may go to Heaven.

CEASAN

obediently

Yes. Eithne.

EITHNE

I'll leave you until morning.

CEASAN

But where can

You go?

EITHNE

To the other hut.

CEASAN

There's nothing in it

To lie on—only bracken

EITHNE

gently

—gathered by

Your hands.

CEASAN

Remain and I will go instead.

EITHNE

It is my turn. Let me repeat your words
The first time that you offered me your bed:
taking up lamp
'It will be much too good for me to-night.'
*She blows out flame, and leaves quickly, in dim moon-
light. He drowses, stirs uneasily.*

CEASAN

What have I promised? I cannot do it.

Eithne,

I love you, I love you.
Eithne hurries in

EITHNE

Ceasan!

CEASAN

What is it?

EITHNE

The roof

Of the hut has disappeared. What can it mean?

CEASAN

The storm last night!

EITHNE

at bedside, tearfully:

I do not understand
These contradictory signs. . . .

                                        I am afraid. . . .
     This mortal life is much too difficult.
Light dims as they embrace.

                        C U R T A I N

SCENE TWO: *The clearing, next morning. Eithne is running
from right, gaily waving to the trees. She is clad in white
under-dress and cloak.*

                              EITHNE
          Ceasan, you missed it.
                              CEASAN
off
                                        What?
                              EITHNE
                                        Another sign
          From Heaven.
                              CEASAN
enters, he wears the old patched habit
                                   Another sign from Heaven?
                              EITHNE
                                             Yes.
          As I stood here, waiting until you had dressed
          Yourself, a ring-o'-ring of little birds
          Came flying around my head with chirp
          And cheep.
                         See, I am blushing.
                                        I'm sure they gave me
          A hundred kisses at the very least,
          Lighter and quicker than my thoughts of them,
          Before I could escape from play.
                              CEASAN
                                             Kisses?

CEITHNE

Double ones—like those you told me, last night,
Young nuns may give their relatives, mere peck
On both cheeks.
                          They must be the great-great-grand-children
Of the well-trained flock that flew round Marravaun

CEASAN

troubled, in low voice
                          Marravaun.

EITHNE
                                                    But, look!
The morning beams are halfway up the trees
Already. The sun is patching our oaks after
The storm. It must be very late. Come, let us
Hurry.

CEASAN

suddenly
                          Eithne, I cannot do it.

EITHNE
                                                    Why not?
You promised me last night.

CEASAN
                                                    That was before
We . . . No, you wouldn't understand.

EITHNE
                                                    I do,
Because we are forgiven.

CEASAN
                                                    Not yet.

EITHNE
                                                    But the birds?
The kisses they gave me?

CEASAN
                                                    A woman, half
Converted, thinks too soon that all is for
The best. She smiles, when man is most alone,
And makes a small religion of her own.
How, how can I repent or be forgiven
When night is starring through my vows and
   changing
Them?

EITHNE

moved, coming very close
> Darling, I am in that darkness with you:
So close, my hand can copy yours too quickly.
turning away
> But every moment makes it worse. You know
I am half pagan still. I must renounce
The Devil.

CEASAN

But not Heaven.

EITHNE

All I ask

For, any layman could perform.

CEASAN

Only

In case of necessity.

EITHNE

Is this

Not one—for both of us? What can poor mortals
Do? They only want to rest in peace—
And that's not possible. Their very selves,
Body and soul, are hired to them for labour
In this mysterious world. Must they not scheme
And plot—to keep the little they have got
Of any happiness, yes, keep it safe
By sorrow and so make it ever young?

CEASAN

I am afraid of what you say.
pointing
Look how
The river runs—faster at every hand's turn.

EITHNE

We'll run with it to the inlet.

CEASAN

The inlet?

EITHNE

Yes.

Why should I dread it any longer, knowing
The water will keep quiet for us? I found
Myself behind the rushes, not far from that mooring
Post, quarrelled with you there—

and there, Ceasan,
    The two of us shall separate—
leaving, with a sob

              yet never
    Part.
*He follows her. There is a dead silence. Gradually can
be heard a few faint chirps of birds, then, faraway, the
sound of voices halloaing in the woods. Voices come
nearer, and suddenly two runners dash in, right.*

FIRST RUNNER

    We have him now.

            Look, there's his cooking ring
    And seat.

SECOND RUNNER

            I've never seen so hidden a
    Retreat.

      The Devil himself could scarcely find it.

FIRST RUNNER

    Ssssh!
*Two Monks enter; the first middle aged, kindly; the
second, a tall foreigner*
    Father, here is the place.

FIRST MONK

           Thanks be to God.
    Where is the hut?

FIRST RUNNER

           Father, I'll go and see.
He goes right, back, starts

FIRST MONK

    What is it? Have you found him? Is he ... dead?

FIRST RUNNER

    No, Father, it's a grave.

FIRST MONK

          A grave?

              Yes ... I
    Remember. Marravaun, the holiest
    Of bird-lovers, was buried here.
As they gather there, solemnly

             Behold
    His place of resurrection.

SECOND MONK

Time is short.

FIRST MONK

A wise retort.
to runners

Call him again.

RUNNERS

Ceasan!   Ceasan!

ECHO

Ceasan!

FIRST MONK
Listen!
ECHO
Ceasan!
SECOND MONK

That idler

Will never spare the heels.
FIRST MONK

You cannot blame

The echo this time.
Glance down the river. Our boatmen
Are rowing behind the sedges. Every shout
Of theirs has its own landing-place.
SECOND RUNNER

His shelter ...

The roof is gone!
FIRST MONK
It must have been the storm.

Pray Heaven he is safe.
FIRST RUNNER

downstage, left

No, here's a bigger

One.
FIRST MONK

reflectively
In a pleasant spot. It makes me think of
My own retirement.
SECOND MONK

Time is short—

FIRST MONK
Rugged with bark, a hive of prayer.

The bees attracted by its daily murmur
Might well be led astray.

SECOND MONK

Solitude has

Its dangers.

Look! What's on that bush?

FIRST MONK

to Runner

Quick, get it.

First Runner comes back with habit

FIRST MONK

His habit!

FIRST RUNNER

Feel it, Father.

FIRST MONK

Wet!

SECOND MONK

What did

I tell you!

FIRST MONK

Then we are too late. It must
Have happened yesterday.

FIRST RUNNER

Father, what are we

To do with it?

FIRST MONK

Best leave it back. Go, both
Of you, inspect the hut.

confidentially to fellow monk

Our Holy Father,
Patric the First, was deeply anxious. The truth
Is, he forgot this young probationer
In minor orders till to-day.

SECOND MONK

Forgot?

FIRST MONK

Even his very name. There are so many
Vocations nowadays—thank God—he can't
Remember every new man. But all came back
To him at matins. Another case, I fear
Of Cogitosus.

SECOND MONK
Cogitosus?
FIRST MONK
                                                            Yes.

A very thoughtful monk. But carnal restraint,
Low living in a derry, proved too much
For him.
              SECOND MONK
          What happened?
                    FIRST MONK
                              This is confidential
March twelvemonths, he was seen without a manly
Stitch, hopping along the tree-tops, trying
To feather his own nest.
              FIRST RUNNER

entering
                                        Father, the bed
Is warm. He must have only left it—
              SECOND RUNNER
                                              when
He heard our shouts.
              SECOND MONK
                        Disgraceful conduct.   At
This hour!
              FIRST MONK
          No, it is some thing worse.
                                  What's that?

          RUNNERS
A cry.
                  The boatmen may have found him.
              FIRST MONK
                                              God
Protect his soul.
                        Run, we will follow you
Without delay.
Second Monk hurries centre, back
                    FIRST MONK
                What is it? Can you see
The boatmen?
              SECOND MONK
                        They're rowing faster.

How do you say it.
They back . . .
                    They stop . . .
                              They are helping someone naked
Into the boat.
                    Buono dio! its a woman.
                    FIRST MONK

A woman!
                    SECOND MONK
                    No. I make mistake . . .
                              It must be . . .
It must be that young apostolic.
                              Plants
Have hidden them.
                              They come ashore. They put
His habit round him and now they're helping him
Along to us.
                    FIRST MONK
                    Then he is safe.
Two boatmen and the Runners carry Ceasan.   He is
wrapped loosely in his habit, but half naked. The Irish
Monk directs the men, as with low murmur, they place
the semi-conscious Ceasan on seat, and partly support
him. Slowly he comes to.
                    CEASAN
Eithne, I tried to save you, tried to believe,
When I had shut my eyes, it was a case of
Necessity. What made me lift my hand
And let you go before the words had dried
In my mouth? Why did you venture beyond your
    depth
And mine? I tried to save you, tried,
But I have failed, because I was afraid
To speak.
                    She cannot hear me. She is gone . . . gone.
I opened my eyes again and suddenly saw
The waters smiling up at me. I struck
Myself across their face, scattering all
Reflection. Soul hurled my body after hers
Into a world of darkness without end.
No breath could hold me down. No breath. How

could
I choke my way into God's pity? He must
Obey Himself. One sentence, unspoken, condemned
Her spirit to Limbo. . . .
                    Limbo. . . .
                              where nothing wakes . . .
Stirs . . . sleeps . . . forever.
                              FIRST RUNNER

aside

                    Father, we saw no woman.
                              FIRST MONK

You're certain?
                              FIRST RUNNER
                    Neither sight nor light of one.
                              FIRST MONK
I'll try to question him.

                              Ceasan, do

You know us?
                              CEASAN

without looking at them
                    Yes.

                              I know you all, good people—
                              FIRST MONK

God's people—

                              CEASAN
                    You are often in my thoughts.
And are you here to help me?
                              FIRST MONK
                              Yes—

                              CEASAN

                                        but here

Too late.
                              FIRST MONK

gently

                              Will you not tell us of this lady
Who has been drowned?
                              Where did she come from?
                              CEASAN

                                        Who

Can tell? She did not know herself. There were
So many stories about her, so much upon

Her mind, how could she bear to think of mistaken
Identity? But I instructed her:
She was my first, my only convert. Signs
And wonders happened all around her. River
Opened. Oak brought her honey, fruit, wild milk.
Yes, Nature laughed because its laws were broken
And Heaven rejoiced to see us both below.
But my poor faith was less than hers. I failed
To keep a promise, yet betrayed a vow.
Tell me, tell me, I implore you, is it true
Her own desire could save her, snatch at eager
Drops, changing water into words that wash
Spirit and sense?

First Monk consults foreign Monk

FIRST MONK

Yes, that is what
Our holy Church lays down.

CEASAN

Then she is saved,
For never have you seen by any lake
Or stream so promising a neophyte:
Half clad for Christian rite in modest white,
As if the primal sin had left her, of
Its own accord, when she cast down her pagan
Dress.

SECOND MONK
Dress?

FIRST MONK
Where is it?

CEASAN

In the hut.

*Runners shake their heads, but First Monk signs to them
to go*

But do
Not judge her by its wicked fashion, so cut
For men, so waisted, not an inch to spare,
Believe me she was—

RUNNERS

returning

Father, it isn't there.

CEASAN

Not there? Then somebody has stolen it,
Unjewelled the hems. But her cloak is still
Upon the river bank to prove I am
Awake

Boatmen whisper to Monk

FIRST MONK

Ceasan, the boatmen saw no cloak.

CEASAN

with hysterical laugh

She was a fairywoman after all
And every scrap she wore—a tissue of lies.
But I suspected it the very night
She came. I lent my bed to her. The door
Was open. I saw her garment hanging on
A peg. Moonlight was making little bits
Of it again. So how could it be real?

half raising himself up

Aongus, Aongus, our local god of love,
You've won that bet you made in Tirnanogue,
Mocked and deceived me, but I still defy you.
No. No. I have it!
                All this has been another
Trick, worthy of fallen sprite.
                        So I was right.
She was a woman after all—no need
Of mouth—she proved it in the darkness, hip
And thigh.

He sinks back weeping

SECOND MONK

           What's this? I am a foreigner.
I do not understand. Aongus ... love ...
A fairywoman. Plain fornication.

FIRST MONK

                        Patience!
There's more in this than meets the eye of any
Man.

He bends down

FIRST MONK

           Do you see me, Ceasan?

CEASAN

recovering

Only

Your shadow in the summer mist.

FIRST MONK

I tremble

Through your own tears, tears of repentance for
The sins committed in your mind.

CEASAN

The mist

Is closing all about me. I have nothing left
Now, nothing but the name I have taken
In vain.

FIRST MONK

Do not despair. It may be, God
Has sent this temporary affliction to veil
Your immediate past. All that we recollect
Must go to Him at last.

CEASAN

Affliction ... yet ...

I know that I have suffered something greater
Than this, some happiness still incomplete

faintly

As if ... as if ...

FIRST MONK

Will you not try to pray
A little? We come from one who folded the future
Upon our hills—Patric, a captured man.

CEASAN

softly

A captured man—

FIRST MONK

prompting

who brought—
What did he bring

Across the sea?

SECOND MONK

to save the Irish people

From superstition—

FIRST MONK

doubt—

SECOND MONK

and mortal woe?

CEASAN

agonised

I can't remember.... I can't remember....
I don't know!

The Curtain is drawn rapidly.

THE END

NOTES

Most of these plays have been performed by the Dublin
Verse-Speaking Society and the Lyric Theatre Company.
The Dublin Verse-Speaking Society was founded in 1938
by the poet, Robert Farren, and myself so that broad-
casters and actors might have practice in lyric, choral and
rhythmic speech. The Society has given many broadcasts
of poetry and verse drama from Radio Eireann. In the
small Peacock Theatre, Dublin, we presented verse plays
and poems for a week, twice a year, from 1941 to 1944,
and stage production was by Ria Mooney. When the
plays of Yeats disappeared from the Abbey Theatre and
it was clear that the imaginative aims of the dramatic
movement were in danger of being forgotten, the Lyric
Theatre Company was formed as an independent unit. In
June, 1944, we hired the Abbey Theatre and presented a
revival of *The Countess Cathleen*, which had not been
played for many years. The Lyric Theatre Company gave
special Sunday performances of verse drama for eleven
years in the Abbey Theatre until the building was closed
after the damage by fire. We gave the first production
of two plays by Yeats, *The Herne's Egg* and *The Death
of Cuchulain*, also *Happy as Larry* by Donagh MacDonagh.
We also gave plays by Gordon Bottomley, Laurence
Binyon, T. Sturge Moore, T. S. Eliot, Archibald MacLeish,
Alexander Blok, Mary Devenport O'Neill. We had the
pleasure of presenting for the first time, thirty years after
it had been written, *The Dandy Dolls*, a remarkable
experiment in rich rhythmic prose, by the pioneer Abbey
dramatist, George Fitzmaurice. Later we gave *The Magic
Glasses* by the same dramatist. This fantasy was originally
presented by the Abbey Theatre in 1913 but was not
revived, though highly praised by Ernest Boyd, A. B.
Walkley and other Irish and London critics.

Without funds, the Company relied entirely on the
voluntary efforts of its members, the generous help of
guest artists, the enthusiasm of its producers and its
scenic designers, and the support of its public.

The exuberance of the first play in this collection may
need a brief explanation. I had the good luck, as a student,

to catch glimpses of those semi-legendary years when a poet had his own theatre in Dublin. The Abbey actors who performed the plays of W. B. Yeats spoke the lines with great reverence. Despite my awe, I longed for more boldness on the stage and eventually I chanced upon a medieval Irish story of a poet kicking up his heels, a throng of merry events, edited and translated vigorously by Kuno Meyer.

All these plays are metrical because stage speech only resembles natural speech and goes more easily, being set to definite patterns. The accented syllables are never separated by more than three unaccented syllables, but when the rhythm takes control, the secondary stresses point the way, paragraphically, line beyond line.

Page 1, THE SON OF LEARNING. The comedy is a tribute to the medieval Irish tale, Goliardic in type, called *Aislinge Meic Conglinne* (The Vision of Mac Conglinne) and is meant to be acted in high spirits.
Anier Mac Conglinne (Aneer Makonglenna). Ligach (Leega). Aoibheal (Eeval): a fairy queen of Munster. Cliodhna (Clee-o-na). Cathal (Ka-hal). Gobaun Saor: a mythic mason.
Macgillicuddy of the Reeks, The Macgillicuddy Reeks, a mountain range in Kerry.
Page 7, The Red Lake. Lough Derg or Saint Patrick's Purgatory, to which great annual pilgrimages are still made, as in the Middle Ages. The pantomimic action here should be played slowly and should be well spaced out, that is to say, with the same elaborate preparations and approach employed by professional conjurers in all ages. Otherwise confusion results.
Page 51. If soldiers are not used, the words can be used by the monks, with the omission of the lay expletive. The student lyric in the second act, *Summer delights the Scholar*, is a free paraphrase of an anonymous poem, *An Mac Leighinn*, discovered at Maynooth Library. In assonantal pattern it is more or less equivalent with the classical metre of the original. The lyrics are meant not to be sung but to be spoken against music. This play was first performed at the Cambridge Festival Theatre in October, 1927, under the direction of Terence Gray. The

production and design were by Herbert M. Prentice. The play was repeated by the Lyric Theatre Company in June 1945, at the Abbey Theatre. The Scholar was played by Cyril Cusack and the King by Hamlyn Benson. Production was by Evelyn MacNeice, the settings were by Anne Yeats and the music by Arthur Duff.

Colours of Dress. " Mottled to fools, blue to women, crimson to all kings, green and black to noble laymen, white to pious priests."

The Book of Ballimote.

Page 55, THE FLAME. The flame of St. Brigid was tended at Kildare for many centuries but the practice was ultimately condemned as superstitious by the Norman archbishop of Dublin. His action was probably due to a new ecclesiastical policy but this little play is sufficiently casuistical to comprise his point of view. The play was first performed by members of the School of Speech Training and Drama in Edinburgh in June, 1932. It has also been performed by The Questors at the British Drama League Festival in 1936 and at the Oxford Festival of Spoken Poetry in 1938. First performed in Ireland by the Dublin Verse-Speaking Society in 1941. Later revived by the Lyric Theatre Company at the Abbey Theatre.

Page 81, SISTER EUCHARIA. First presented by the Earl of Longford at the Gate Theatre, Dublin, in July, 1939. The production was by Noel Illiff with the following cast:— Sister Eucharia: Jean Anderson; Reverend Mother: Ann Penhallow; Lay Sister: Nora O'Mahony; Father Sheridan: Blake Gifford; Nuns: Cathleen Delany, Vivion Dillon, Simona Pakenham, Doris Finn, Nancy Bechk; First Speaker: Hamlyn Benson; Second Speaker: Peter Copley.

Page 115, BLACK FAST. First presented by the Abbey Theatre Company in January, 1942. Cast:— Man Servant: Harry Webster; Steward: Denis O'Dea; Girl Servant: Maureen O'Sullivan; Connal More: Michael J. Dolan; Blanaid Fairnape: Ria Mooney; Mahan: W. O'Gorman; Cummian: Austin Meldon; Ulster Monks: Fred Johnson, Luke McLoughlin; Romanus: Michael Clarke; Munster Monks: Terry Wilson, Francis Foley; Cogitosus: Liam

Redmond. Play produced by Liam Redmond. Settings and costumes by Michael Clarke.

Page 143, THE KISS. First performed at the Peacock Theatre by the Dublin Verse-Speaking Society in May, 1942. The production was by Ria Mooney and the setting was designed by Victor Brown. The players were: Uirgeal: Maureen Kiely; Pierrot: Robert Mooney. The play was repeated by the Lyric Theatre Company in June, 1944, at the Abbey Theatre, with Cyril Cusack as Pierrot.

Page 163, AS THE CROW FLIES. Broadcast from Radio Eireann for the first time on 6th February, 1942, by the Dublin Verse-Speaking Society, under the direction of the author. The cast was as follows:— Father Virgilius: Laurence Elyan; Brother Manus: Ruaidhri Roberts; Brother Aengus: Ray Davies; The Eagle of Knock: Eve Watkinson; her Eaglets: Patricia Clancy, Maureen Kiely; The Crow of Achill: Florence Lynch; The Stag of Leiterlone: Robert Mooney; The Blackbird of Derrycairn: Patricia Clancy; The Salmon of Assaroe: Liam Redmond. Assonance, end-assonance, internal assonance and stopped rhyme are used in the fabulous scenes. Suggested by a Middle Irish Tale: See *Saints and Sinners* by Douglas Hyde.

Page 189, THE PLOT IS READY. First performed at the Peacock Theatre by the Dublin Verse-Speaking Society in October, 1943. Production was by Ria Mooney and the setting and costumes were designed by Victor Brown. The cast was as follows:— Muriadach Mac Erca: Seumas Forde; Crede: Marjorie Williams; Osna: Eve Watkinson; Murna: Patricia Clancy; Fergus: Richard O'Sullivan; Abbot Cairnech: Gerard Healy; Old Monk: Frank Prenton; Young Monk: Liam Gannon; Brother Malachi: Ruaidhri Roberts; First Narrator: George Green; Second Narrator: Frank Prenton; Monks: Daniel Connelly, J. McEntee, T. J. Nolan, Arthur Mahon; Grave-Diggers: E. Jacob, G. Sullivan. The play was repeated by the Lyric Theatre Company in December, 1944, at the Abbey Theatre.

Page 219, THE VISCOUNT OF BLARNEY. First presented by the Lyric Theatre Company in December, 1944, at the Abbey Theatre with the following cast:— Cauth: Maureen Kiely; Woman: Ita Little; Husband: Patrick Nolan; Old Man: Alex Andrews; Pooka: Robert Mooney; Foster-Mother: Florence Lynch; Jack o' Lantern: Donald Carlisle; Gallant and Viscount of Blarney: George Green. The production was by Evelyn MacNeice. Rhyme and end-assonance are used in this play. Based on a Wexford Folk Story taken down by Patrick Kennedy.

Page 247, THE SECOND KISS. First performed by the Lyric Theatre Company in June, 1946, at the Abbey Theatre. The production was by Cyril Cusack and the settings by Anne Yeats. The players were:— Pierrot: Cyril Cusack; Pierrette: Maureen Cusack; Harlequin: George Green; Columbine: Maureen Cusack.

Page 271, THE PLOT SUCCEEDS. The play, pantomimic in mood, is based on one of the medieval Gaelic tales, which deal with Mannanaun Mac Lir, the sea god. The Son of Lir was said to appear throughout Ireland in humorous disguises and sometimes to lend the power of transformation to others.

Grainne is pronounced *Grawn'ya:* Ri, *ree.*

The metre used in the play is experimental and, so, a note may not be amiss. Apart from the Prologue, it consists of modified heroic couplets: one of the rhyming words in each pair is dissyllabic and only the first syllable of it is rhymed. The suggestion comes partly from Gaelic prosody.

The Plot Succeeds was first performed at the Abbey Theatre by the Lyric Theatre Company in February, 1950. The production was by W. O'Gorman and the Author, and the costumes were designed by Victor Brown. The cast was as follows: Manannaun Mac Lir: Dancer: Maurice Selwyn; Speaker: Patrick Cowman; Mongan Mór of Ulster: Cyril Cusack; Dulaca: Eithne Dunne; Manus: Alex Andrews; Blanaid: Ita Little; Branduv of Leinster: Brian O'Higgins; Abbot Cormac: Robert Hennessy; Brother Malachi: W. O'Gorman; Fergus: Patrick Nolan; Grainne: Patricia Plunkett; Captain: Dermot MacDermott; Soldiers: Austin Byrne, Brendan Dillon, Matt Horgan, Gerard

Mangan, Michael McCabe, Michael Rayneau; Women of
the Household: Máiréad Connaughton, Doreen Fitzpatrick,
Joan McAuliffe, Joan Stynes.

Page 321, THE MOMENT NEXT TO NOTHING. This play
is based on part of a medieval Irish tale, *Altram Tige Da
Medar* (The Fosterage of the Houses of the Two Methers),
edited by Lilian Duncan in *Eriu* XI. Variants of the story
survived in oral tradition and several have been taken
down or recorded in recent years for the Irish Folklore
Commission. In a critical essay entitled *The Legends of
the False God's Daughter*, in the Journal of the Royal
Society of Antiquaries of Ireland, 1949, Máire MacNeill
surmises that the remote origin of the story may have
been a myth of the struggle of two gods for a goddess.
In a novel of the Celtic-Romanesque era, *The Sun Dances
at Easter*, which is banned in Ireland, I have retold the
story from a slightly different angle.
Ceasan is pronounced, approximately, *Kass-awn*, equal
stress on both syllables.
The Moment Next to Nothing was presented at the
Players' Theatre, Trinity College, Dublin, in January 1958.
The part of Eithne was played by Eve Watkinson; that of
Ceasan by Patrick Nolan. The production was by Evelyn
MacNeice, setting by Anne Yeats.